FATHER TIM'S
Church Survival Guide

TIM SCHENCK

Morehouse Publishing
NEW YORK

Morehouse Publishing, 4785 Linglestown Road, Suite 101, Harrisburg, PA 17112
Morehouse Publishing, 19 East 34th Street, New York, NY 10016

Morehouse Publishing is an imprint of Church Publishing Incorporated.

www.churchpublishing.org

Cover design by Laurie Klein Westhafer
Cover photo by Ben Schenck
Typeset by Denise Hoff

Library of Congress Cataloging-in-Publication Data

Schenck, Tim.
    Father Tim's church survival guide / the Rev. Tim Schenck.
        pages cm
        ISBN 978-0-8192-2958-8 (pbk.)—ISBN 978-0-8192-2959-5 (ebook)
1. Church—Miscellanea.   2. Church—Humor.   3. Pastoral theology—
Miscellanea.   4. Pastoral theology—Humor.   5. Episcopal Church—
Miscellanea.   6. Episcopal Church—Humor.   I. Title.
BV600.3.S345 2015
253—dc23

2014029154

Printed in the United States

In honor of the ministry of
The Right Rev. M. Thomas Shaw, SSJE
Bishop of Massachusetts, 1994–2014

Contents

Acknowledgments

What are you supposed to do with a bunch of crazy thoughts on life in the Episcopal Church rattling around in your brain? In my case, you wait for Nancy Bryan to contact you and say, "Have you thought about writing another book with Church Publishing?" I'm grateful to Nancy for reaching out and giving me a platform to share these ideas and to the whole team at CPI for pulling them together.

It's not that I'm addicted or anything, but I need coffee to write. I would never subject anyone to uncaffeinated sermons, blog posts, articles, or books and thus I must thank coffee. You've been a faithful friend and an ongoing source of inspiration. As the local conduit, I'm thankful to Bob Weeks and the staff at Redeye Roasters in Hingham, Massachusetts, for the single origin coffee, conversation breaks, and table space.

I'm grateful to the parishioners and staff at the Episcopal Parish of St. John the Evangelist in Hingham for their continued love and support. If you're ever on Boston's South Shore, stop by and see us! I may even refrain from handing you a pledge card.

If you follow me on Twitter @FatherTim, you know it's a place where snark thrives. While I sometimes forget it's a pubic forum (oops—can't get that one back), I love engaging with all sorts of people, some of whom I've actually met in the flesh. The Snarkeratti often get going on Sunday nights—hey, we have Mondays off—and are a source of inspiration, sanity, and humor. Go follow Laurie Brock (@drtysxyministry), Megan Castellan (@revlucymeg), Scott Gunn (@scottagunn), and David Sibley (@davidsibley). Then remember our slogan: "Ruining opportunities for future church employment one tweet at a time."

Although he's a tea drinker, the Rev. Rick Swanson graciously perused my manuscript—in a coffee shop no less—to insure nothing crossed too far over the ecclesiastical line.

We have terrific neighbors in Hingham. Well, we live in the rectory next door to the church so I'm talking about the other side. Thanks to Hans, Stephanie, Lexie, and Teddy von der Luft for helping to keep our family grounded, sane, and laughing.

It's not easy being a clergy family but, along with my wife, Bryna, and our teenage sons, Benedict and Zachary, we do the best we can. Although there are days when I fantasize about running away to a monastery, I couldn't imagine doing what I do without their loving support. I'm truly blessed in ways both seen and unseen.

Introduction

Given the nature of this book I should profess my deep love of the Church from the outset. The Church, that "wonderful and sacred mystery," is a many-splendored thing. It inspires and disappoints; offers hope and frustration; comforts and confuses. In other words, it's an utterly human institution, which means there are days when all we can seek is survival.

When questioned about the one book they'd take if marooned on a desert island, most people of faith would say "The Bible." Okay, most Episcopalians would answer "The Book of Common Prayer," but you get the point. If you were stranded in an endless church meeting or held hostage by a vapid, long-winded preacher, *this* is the one book you would want by your side.

Within these pages you'll find some satire, some snark, and some tweaking of our beloved Church, but it's all done out of love. Mostly. There's a bit of seasonal humor and suggestions for how to survive nearly any ecclesiastical situation you're likely to encounter.

My take on church life isn't for everyone—clergy who take themselves too seriously will hate it. The humorless will be offended. If you fall into either one of these categories, you should put this book down right now and walk away. Far, far away.

For the rest of you, I hope you enjoy this quick romp through a variety of parish experiences. I trust it will offer some laughs and provide a dose of needed perspective on our communal life in Christ. There are inevitably things that drive us nuts about such an imperfect institution. Yet if we can't observe and comment on our own foibles, we're left without much hope. And anyway if God doesn't have a sense of humor, I'm hosed.

PART I

SURVIVING THE WELCOME

"The Episcopal Church Welcomes You." You've likely seen that iconic red, white, and blue sign half-obscured by overgrown vegetation with two parallel rust lines running down the front. Sometimes this is true and sometimes it feels like false advertising—at least to anyone who's ever stood by himself at coffee hour waiting for someone to welcome him to St. Whatever.

For a brief time the Episcopal Church tried to change the slogan to "We're Here for You" which, to me, sounded more like the tagline for an insurance company. Fortunately this attempt at "rebranding" was abandoned but, despite our best efforts, we still welcome people with mixed results.

Church Shopping Red Flags

Entering a new church for the first time is not easy. There are several indicators to look for when determining whether this might be the place to put down roots and eventually end up in the columbarium. While I dislike the term "church shopping" since it feeds into the consumer mentality that's already so prevalent, it's how people find their new church. And guess what? It's a buyer's market!

As you consider your options, remember that you hold all the chips. If you are under the age of forty, you will be treated like a rock star. If you have young kids, people might actually drool on you. Coffee hour can make you feel like the cool kid at the fraternity rush party everyone is trying to woo (pick us! pick us!).

My wife, Bryna, and I had this experience when I was in seminary as we spent the first year checking out and experiencing parishes throughout the Diocese of Chicago. Some newcomer committees would swoop down on a young couple like it was a rare species they'd never before encountered. It was nice being treated like a celebrity, but it only lasted until they learned I was a seminarian and we wouldn't actually be joining the parish, at which point they'd drop us like a bad transmission.

If you're older, don't think you'll be left on the outside of this party looking in. You'll be popular because you might become a big contributor one day and, boy, we could use some extra money to fix the plumbing in the women's bathroom. Not that anyone would check to see what kind of car you drove up in, but just in case use the jalopy the first few Sundays.

As you try out some different congregations, here are a few red flags to be aware of on your journey.

1. If they still have Christmas services listed on their website and it's now July, don't bother. You can learn a lot from a parish

website—like how much the community cares about Santa Claus's off-season schedule.

2. If finding the front door of the church from the parking lot feels like a well-guarded secret, there may be a reason for this. There's nothing like sending the message that "we already have all the parishioners we need, thanks."

3. If they seem desperate, they probably are. Some parishes all but ask you to become the next senior warden at your first coffee hour. Welcoming is good; desperation is bad.

4. If someone glares at you for sitting in "my pew" and then tells you to get out, go ahead and get out. And never return.

5. If the sermon is nothing more than a venting/therapy session for the preacher, send a bill to the church for the local hourly therapy rate.

6. If the alto section falls asleep during the communion hymn, the organist may need to pick up the tempo.

7. If the Peace takes longer than coffee hour, stay home and drink coffee.

8. If the ushers send a mob bag-man vibe while taking up the collection, be passive aggressive in return and write a check you know will bounce.

9. If the priest doesn't look at you when shaking your hand in the receiving line, because he/she is looking behind you to greet a big donor, don't look back as you head to the parking lot.

10. If no one talks to you at coffee hour for more than three uncomfortable, awkward minutes, they probably won't. Start Googling other churches in the area.

11. If the coffee is tepid Folgers in Styrofoam cups with nondairy creamer, never return. In fact, don't ever drive by the church again.

How to Join the Church

I'm often asked, "How do I become a member of the church?" Now, this is more complicated than you might think. I wish I could simply say, "Step into the sacristy and we'll give you the official tattoo. Arm, ankle, shoulder, or where your backside meets the pew?" And that would be it. "You're in!"

It used to be, if not easy, then at least clear. Receive communion at least three times a year and be "known to the treasurer" and you were considered a Communicant in Good Standing. This included amazing perks like being allowed to vote at the Annual Parish Meeting and waxing about the irony of being "in good standing" even while kneeling at the communion rail.

It's certainly easy enough to join a fundamentalist denomination: pledge to take the Bible literally and give us 10 percent of your income. If you believe in evolution, you're out. We like to be fuzzy about such matters unless you were baptized as an infant in which case you're considered a "cradle Episcopalian" and given a trust fund.

In practice, the first step is filling out the newcomer card you'll find in the pews. You'll recognize them because they've all been scribbled on by bored toddlers. It would also appear that Episcopalians have an affinity for miniature golf since those little pencils are usually somewhere in the pew rack. Once you fill it out with the pertinent information like blood type and the name of your first pet, drop it into the collection plate as the usher passes by and then someone from the parish will reach out to you. Or not.

I've filled out newcomers cards in the past with mixed results. Once, someone invited me out for coffee while several other parishes never responded. At one service, when I just wanted to sit in the back row and be left alone, an usher compelled me to fill one out and I didn't want to appear impolite. When I returned home, there was a loaf of bread waiting for me with a note. While some might find this gesture warm and welcoming, I felt like I was being stalked and never went back.

These days most clergy will tell you that if you show up and participate in the life of the community, you're considered a member. If you really want to commit, you'll allow your name to go into the parish directory. Oh, and there's this dirty little word called pledging which we don't like to say out loud but maybe, if you feel so moved and it's not too inconvenient, you could one day think about actually contributing to the financial well-being of the parish. But let's not rush into things.

The true gateway drug to becoming a member is joining a church committee. It starts innocently enough with an invitation to bring muffins to coffee hour and the next thing you know you've been appointed chair of the brass polishing committee. Yes, getting involved is really about discipleship and living out your faith in the context of Christian community but joining the flower guild, or some other group, is the first step. What, you don't think Jesus insisted on having beautifully arranged calla lilies on the table at the Last Supper?

Whether or not you end up officially joining the church or just showing up regularly for twenty-five years, you're in for a wild ride. Like most things, you get out of it what you put into it—which doesn't mean you can take more out of the collection plate than you put in ("One for you, two for me"). And if you end up sitting on that tattoo during the sermon, please keep it to yourself.

What's in a Name?

If you want to stir things up at a gathering of Episcopalians, refer to them as "Episcopals." You'll face the full wrath of righteous indignation (all in the name of Jesus) while simultaneously receiving a lecture on appropriate forms of ecclesiastical address. As a pastoral gesture intended to save you from such a tongue lashing, I will take a moment to explain how this fits together.

It all starts with the word "Episcopal." People who belong to the Episcopal Church are called Episcopalians. They are decidedly not, as often seen in the secular media, "Episcopals." I am an Episcopal priest but don't ever refer to me as an Episcopalian priest. That's easy enough, right?

Small "e" "epsicopal" refers to the ministry of a bishop. Thus an "episcopal visitation" means a bishop is visiting a congregation. There is no such thing as an "Episcopal visitation" unless you mean a bunch of Episcopalians came over to your house for a visit.

The official name of the denomination is The Episcopal Church, often abbreviated as TEC. The *official,* official name is the "Protestant Episcopal Church in the United States of America." This is what you'll see in the preamble to the first American Book of Common Prayer. This mouthful (even the acronym PECUSA is unwieldy) was eventually changed, informally, to the Episcopal Church in the United States of America, or ECUSA, as those with more catholic tendencies objected to the word "Protestant" in the name. Still with me?

For many years people have affectionately referred to the national headquarters of the Episcopal Church as "815," a nod to the offices being located at 815 Second Avenue in New York City. This is evidently now taboo ("we're people, not a number!"), but you'll still hear it. Nonetheless, I live at 176 Main Street and you're welcome to refer to me as "176" if you're not comfortable with "Tim" or "Father Tim" or "Father Schenck" or "Lent Madness guy."

As long as we're on the topic, while you can address a letter to The Rev. Remington Steele, don't ever call an Episcopal priest "Reverend." He/she will look around for the Baptist minister who must be in the same room.

And, finally, never bring up Matthew 23:9 around a male priest: "And call no one your father on earth, for you have one Father—the one in heaven." We have many methods of countering this verse and justifying our hard-earned title, but it's best not to poke the dragon.

"Did You Really Just Call Me a Primate?"

Here's a bit of background and a quick primer on the organizational structure of the Episcopal Church. You will find nary a reference to King Henry VIII (okay, just a single, brief oblique reference), but if you don't know the rhyme to remember the fate of his six wives, it's "divorced, beheaded, died, divorced, beheaded, survived." You're welcome.

The first thing to know is that, being derived from the Church of England, we are part of the worldwide Anglican Communion. This is a confusing term to many because they envision a giant communion wafer the size of, say, Australia. In this instance "Communion" shouldn't be confused with "communion." One was instituted by Jesus at the Last Supper, the other had something to do with a divorce.

The titular head of the Anglican Communion is the archbishop of Canterbury who is appointed by the queen of England. Most people don't pay much attention to the ABC (that's the cool kid lingo) unless he's officiating at a royal wedding or crowning the next monarch. When this happens, people *ooh* and *ahh* at the glorious vestments and revel in the pomp before sending the archbishop back to Lambeth Prison, I mean Palace.

The archbishop of Canterbury is a symbol of unity for the 85 million people in 165 countries who identify with our particular way of worship and polity. Every ten years the over 800 bishops of the Anglican Communion gather at the Lambeth Conference to wear purple, argue, and pray. The head bishop of each country or province is called, and I'm not making this up, a primate. All I'll say about this is that some have evolved more than others.

The Episcopal Church is the American branch of the Anglican Communion, which is why you'll hear Episcopalians referred to as "Anglicans" even though we don't have funny accents, eat bangers and mash, or use words like "blimey," "knickers," and "toff." Basically, our ecclesiastical forebears came over from England and wanted to continue worshipping in a familiar manner. Of course, the pilgrims left to get away from the Church of England so they probably weren't too psyched when a bunch of them showed up with their trusty Book of Common Prayer.

It became rather awkward around the time of the American Revolution since the Prayer Book mandated the king be prayed for at every service. It's tough to prove your patriotic street cred when you're drinking tea and praying for King George. A lot of these folks fled to Canada, which seemed a better option than getting tarred and feathered.

After the Revolution, the ones that remained realized they had to do something about that king issue, so they formed their own branch of Anglicanism with an American version of the Prayer Book and the "worldwide" Anglican Communion was born.

This meant creating their own structure for church governance and so they created the bicameral legislative process that still exists.

Hmmm. Bicameral. Where did we hear that word before? Oh, right, sixth-grade civics class. Why reinvent the wheel when you have a bunch of awesome forefathers to steal ideas from?

Thus we ended up with a House of Bishops as the "upper house" and the House of Deputies (comprised of clergy and laity) as the "lower house." A "constitution" was adopted and the governing body was a General Convention set up to meet every three years, just as it does today.

The chief pastor and administrator of the almost two-million-member Episcopal Church is called the presiding bishop. The presiding bishop is elected by the House of Bishops and confirmed by the House of Deputies for a nine-year term.

In other words, if every Episcopalian buys this book, it would end up on the *New York Times* Bestseller List. And wouldn't that be a great way to spread the word about our fabulous, if sometimes confusing and maddening, faith tradition? I will personally see to it that every single one of you makes a cameo when it's turned into the blockbuster movie of the year.

There are 109 dioceses (and three regional areas) in The Episcopal Church located in the United States and seventeen other nations, each led by a duly elected bishop. You may be surprised to learn that here in America, bishops are not appointed by the queen. Each diocese elects a bishop at an electing convention made up of all the clergy in the diocese and two lay representatives from each congregation. This is a much more democratic process (USA! USA!) than the way many bishops throughout the Anglican Communion are chosen. Many are simply appointed by other bishops with little or no lay participation in the process.

There are about 7,000 congregations in the Episcopal Church. If each congregation were to purchase a single copy of this book, it would not make the *New York Times* Bestseller List nor would you get a cameo alongside Brad Pitt who would play me.

Priests, usually called rectors, lead congregations, sometimes assisted by deacons who are the citizen-soldiers of the church. In other words, they have "real jobs" in addition to their parish functions. The temporal authority of a parish is the vestry made up of elected leaders and led by wardens.

This is all very cursory and I encourage you to use our friend and colleague, Google, for more in-depth information on our communal governance and ministry. The upshot here is that the altar guild really runs the Episcopal Church.

―――――

Liturgical Faux Pas

Here is a short list of things you should never do during a church service. I'm providing these gems as a special service to anyone who might be new to the Episcopal Church or is just visiting because your mother-in-law has forced you to attend under duress. Please read through this list carefully to avoid humiliating yourself since, as everyone knows, we like to stare at and judge people who clearly have no idea what they're doing. As they say to rookies who score their first NFL touchdown, act like you've been there before.

- After the choir sings a stunningly beautiful offertory anthem, clap loudly and yell "encore!"
- Stand when everyone else is kneeling.
- Kneel when everyone else is standing.
- Join the procession because, well, everybody loves a parade.
- Ask for seconds at the communion rail.
- Ask the usher for change after you drop a $5 bill into the collection plate.
- Yell "Amen!" during the sermon. The ushers will have you removed.

- Respond "Thanks be to God" after the lector says "Here endeth the lesson."
- Raise your hand during the sermon to ask a clarifying question.
- Bring a picnic brunch to eat during the psalm sung to Anglican Chant.
- Do interpretive dance to help others conceptualize the sermon.
- Actually greet people with "a holy kiss."
- Pray extemporaneously.
- Raise your hands above your head and wave your arms around during the Lord's Prayer.
- Say "ay-men" instead of "ah-men."

If you avoid doing these things people will assume you belong, and isn't that what you really want?

PART II

SURVIVING SUNDAY MORNING

Sunday morning is at the very heart of what we do. Well, unless we start a Saturday evening service to compete with the Roman Catholics or a Sunday evening service to compete with youth sports. Still, Sunday morning is when the spiritual rubber meets the liturgical road. The clergy wake up early, the choir warms up, the acolytes vest, and the faithful gather (unless there's a lacrosse game, they were out partying late the night before, they're out of town for the three-day weekend, they don't feel like it, or they're mad at the priest for not visiting them in the hospital even though they never told the priest they were *in* the hospital).

Sunday morning is the time we gather to "worship the Lord in the beauty of holiness" even if beauty is in the eye of the beholder and the deferred maintenance is quickly crowding out the "beauty" part. It's the time we encounter our risen Lord through the Eucharist before being sent back out into the world to "love and serve the Lord." Some mornings this is more challenging than others.

Ushering In

The first person you encounter at a church is the usher. Well, it might be the person who cut you off and stole your space in the parking lot, but the usher is the first person *inside* the church that you encounter. (There's a reason I don't put an Episcopal Church sticker on my car—I don't want my cutting someone off on the highway to be seen as a form of "evangelism." I *did* learn to drive in Brooklyn after all.)

Some ushers see their role less as friendly first impression and more as bouncer. They may not check your ID, but their default position is one of begrudging suspicion. "I guess I'll let you in, but don't try anything funny like waving your arms around during the hymns."

These days the usher is still the first *human* face a visitor sees, but the parish website serves as the virtual usher. In the same way no one would go to a restaurant without first checking the reviews on Yelp, no one shows up at a church anymore without first having taken a virtual tour.

Still, until church ushers are replaced by robots, they serve an important function. Welcoming? No, I'm talking about taking up the collection. At the precise moment during the service when the priest screams "Show me the money!" the ushers dutifully pass the plates. While some accept tips in the form of dipping into the collection plate, most ushers are honorable, upright, and well-dressed.

In some parishes they are also mostly men. I remember attending a parish where the head usher quit the moment the rector took the radical position of insisting women be allowed to partake in this ministry. He eventually gave in to the times when he realized he would otherwise have to sit with his wife every Sunday for the rest of his life.

One of the most important things ushers do is hand out the church bulletins. This is really an interim function between the day when everybody either knew the service by heart and/or couldn't read anyway even if the printing press had been invented and the time when service information will all be downloaded onto people's tablets. In the meantime, handing out the bulletins as people arrive ranks high in the usher job description along with glaring at the parents of screaming infants since, after all, you can't know the liturgical players without the scorecard.

I've always thought those brave enough to usher on Christmas Eve and Easter Day should receive combat pay. They must deal with issues such as the "illegal" saving of seats, setting up extra chairs, and people who have no idea how to return from communion. It is the ushers who restore order to chaos and for that we can all be grateful.

It's All about the Book

We like our book. Oh, who am I kidding? We *love* our book. The Bible likes our book so much it quotes it all the time. Fine, maybe it's the other way around, but the Book of Common Prayer is our pride and joy.

Handed down from Thomas Cranmer's 1549 edition, its influence abounds and we like to bask in its warm glow. That soap opera wedding where the words sound so familiar? That's our Prayer Book. "Ashes to ashes, dust to dust?" Yup, that's ours too. That's what happens when your tradition derives from the first ever English language rite. Things didn't end well for Cranmer, at least in this world, as he was tried for treason and heresy and burned at the stake under the Roman Catholic Queen Mary I (aka Bloody Mary—from whose nickname we derive the traditional Sunday brunch quaff).

Pull out a BCP (that's the book's hip acronym) from any pew rack and it will automatically open to one of two pages: 323 or 355. The first being the Elizabethan English Eucharistic rite, the second the contemporary English version of the same. Granted, a lot of congregations now print the entire service in the bulletin to make things easier for visitors so the book doesn't get used as much as it used to on Sunday mornings, but that doesn't minimize its impact on our theology and worship.

Frankly, though, the book could use a marketing makeover. Why would anyone pick up something that may as well be titled the Book of Ordinary Prayer or the Book of Mundane Prayer? The word "common" refers to "communal," not plain, but most people wouldn't make that connection unless specifically told. If we were to offer complementary worship materials, we'd be singing out of the Humdrum Hymnal and reading passages from the Bland Bible.

The good news is there are some terrific ways to use the BCP during long-winded sermons that may well never end. Before the advent of the Internet, you had to calculate the date of Easter by determining the Golden Number. If you like Sudoku or other math-oriented games, go to page 880 and try to determine the date of Easter 2059. By the time you've figured it out, you'll hear the preacher saying, "In the final analysis . . ." Unfortunately she still has two more points to make of her eighteen-point sermon.

The Historical Documents section is also a place in which to get lost and have an on-demand out-of-body experience. The Thirty-Nine Articles, the Athanasian Creed, they're all there just waiting to greet your inner ecclesiastical history nerd.

What's that you say? You don't have a doctorate in theology trapped inside of you yearning to be free? Then check out the Psalter, where you'll discover 149 options *other than* the Twenty-third Psalm! Yes, "psalter" is not a word you hear thrown around too often on little league fields or at the office. If anyone questions you, just tell them it's an accessory for your new margarita maker.

Like the human brain (about which scientists claim we only use a small percentage of its total capacity), most people only use small portions of the Prayer Book. Like pages 323 or 355. But the book is an incredible resource for individual and group prayer and I encourage you to do some exploring. The Daily Offices, which are actually prayer services and not places where you earn a paycheck, can ground your spiritual life. The Devotions for Individuals and Families are like Morning and Evening Prayer on training wheels and are short and accessible places to develop a habit of daily prayer. And if you're a Shakespearean actor, there's no better place to hone your chops than the "thees and thous" of Rite I.

Perhaps the best part of being an aficionado of the Book of Common Prayer is the haughty attitude you may bestow upon any other attempts at liturgy in the English language.

———

Hymns That Make You Go Hmmm

The church has used the *Hymnal 1982* since, well, 1982. While the hymnal is a treasure of Anglican hymnody spanning generations of Christian musical devotion, evidently no one could think of a better name for the book that replaced the *Hymnal 1940*.

This doesn't mean it's always easy to use, however. What visitor hasn't gotten confused by the first 288 pieces of music that appear in the book? They're preceded by an "S" which stands for Service Music, but how would anyone figure that out in the heat of flipping through it to find the opening hymn? The first *real* hymn doesn't show up until about a sixth of the way through the book.

The hymns are grouped by season so, for instance, you'll find all the Easter or Christmas hymns lumped together. It gets a little vague as you get into sections with titles like "Christian Responsibility" and "The Christian Life," which is basically a euphemism for "we didn't know where to stick these since they don't fit neatly into any other category."

Every parishioner has hymns they love and hymns they loathe and within a congregation there is often overlap between the two extremes. For every person who wants "Amazing Grace" sung at her funeral, you'll find several who pick their funeral hymns while still alive to insure "Amazing Grace" is *not* sung.

No hymn epitomizes this dichotomy more than "Earth and All Stars" (412) which includes the verse "Classrooms and labs, loud boiling test tubes. Sing to the Lord a new song!" When I sing this, all I can think of is my sixth-grade science teacher who used to walk around with a yardstick and whack it on the desk of anyone not paying attention, which doesn't put me in a very spiritual mood.

My favorite verse in the entire hymnal is from the classic "I Sing a Song of the Saints of God" in which we sing, "And one was a soldier, and one was a priest, and one was slain by a fierce wild beast." I have *been* a soldier (US Army Reserves), I *am* a priest, but I do hope to avoid option number three.

Occasionally you'll encounter some verses that don't make much sense but have nonetheless become part of our musical heritage. Here are several lines that either confuse or give pause.

"Cherubim and seraphim falling down before thee, which wert, and art, and evermore shall be" ("Holy, Holy Holy"). You may know that cherubim and seraphim are ranks of angels, though they are apparently rather clumsy. "Which wert, and art" sound like characters in a Dr. Seuss book.

"Deck thyself, my soul, with gladness." As far as I know, the church is opposed to self-mutilation.

"Lo, he abhors not the virgin's womb" from "O Come All Ye Faithful"—could there possibly be a more awkward sentence structure? And while this line may have won a bet about getting the words "abhor" and "womb" into the same verse of a Christmas carol, say what you mean, man!

"Let every creature rise and bring peculiar honors to our king" appears in "Jesus Shall Reign." I'm not sure what a "peculiar" honor is or why I would bring it to our king. Sounds like grounds for beheading to me.

"Crown Him with Many Crowns" has been referred to as the dentist's hymn.

"Come, Labor On" is a great one to sing while your wife is in the delivery room. If you want to be smacked (and, yes, I speak from experience).

The last line of every verse of "Songs of Thankfulness and Praise" reads "God in man made manifest." Sometimes even the hint of a hyphen is all that's needed to create heresy. God in man-made manifest would have led someone to the stake in eras past.

"Veiled in flesh the Godhead see" is a well-known line from "Hark the Herald Angels Sing." I'm not sure what this means, other than a strange way to speak of Christ's incarnation, but it sure sounds like something you'd see on *CSI: Miami* and it kind of creeps me out.

Hopefully this list will inspire you to belt out hymns with new-found vigor and hasn't forever ruined any of these chestnuts. If so, you can always drown them out with the "loud humming cellos" of "Earth and All Stars."

Peace Out

At the precise moment that begins "liturgical halftime," we exchange the Peace with one another. "The peace of the Lord be always with you," says the priest. "And also with you," comes the Pavlovian response.

People either love this part of the service or hate it—few are passive in their feelings toward the Peace. When the Episcopal Church transitioned from the 1928 Book of Common Prayer to the current book dating to 1979—still called by many the "new" Prayer Book even though it's been around for nearly forty years!—one of the biggest controversies surrounded the Peace. The '28 book didn't have it; the '79 book did. Some thought it was a wonderfully warm and loving exercise while others felt it was a violation of personal space that disrupted the flow of the liturgy. It's not just an introvert/extrovert thing either, as I've known people on both sides of the personality aisle who either like it or don't.

Part of the issue may be that we don't really know what to do with the word "peace." An alien might walk down the ramp of his UFO and say "We come in peace." Or a hippie might say "Peace, man." Greeting someone in the name of peace tends to diffuse the situation and make people relax or, in the case of our hippie friend, "chill out."

Jesus uses the word in a post-resurrection appearance while meeting the disciples and saying, "Peace be with you." This totally freaks them out, which is understandable since they thought he was dead.

But these are powerful words and Jesus's greeting of "Peace be with you" matters. He could have said anything when he appeared: "Hi there" or "Relax, it's just me" or in today's parlance he could have simply nodded and said, "s'up."

I've worshipped in parishes where the Peace has taken so long, I could have gone out for a cup of coffee, drunk it, returned, and not missed a thing. But that's not the point—it's not a liturgical cocktail party where everyone mingles and greets everyone else in the entire church. On the other hand, I once attended a service at a prominent parish in New York City where the priest offered the Peace, the people responded, and the liturgy just went right on without anyone moving a muscle or even glancing around at those around them.

Now, contrary to popular belief, the Peace was not a new liturgical innovation instituted by a bunch of group hug-loving, touchy-feely types. Many of Paul's letters conclude with a call to greet the faithful with a "kiss of peace" and out of this history, the Peace became part of the earliest Christian liturgies.

But the question remains, why do we still do this? At its worst it can feel awkward and a bit forced to look a stranger in the eye and wish them the peace of the Lord. But the Peace is not merely a foretaste of the coffee hour that is to come or a holy "Hey, how're you doing?" When we offer one another the Peace of the Lord, we're echoing Jesus's sharing of the peace with the disciples and living into Jesus's command to "love one another as I have loved you."

In other words, even if you can't stand it, it's best to grin and bear it and view it as your own personal liturgical cross to bear. And if it's your absolute favorite part of the service? Have fun driving home from church in your flower-covered VW bus.

————

Surviving the Sermon

When my son Zak was about five, I took him to an 8 o'clock service at an undisclosed cathedral on the East Coast. The family was on vacation and Bryna and Ben spent the morning worshipping at St. Mattress. It was a fairly typical Rite I early service without music and I brought along some coloring for Zak.

Unbeknownst to us, a seminarian was scheduled to preach. As with some new preachers, there's a tendency to toss in everything they've ever learned in seminary. This is a polite way of saying that the sermon that morning was both long and rambling. At about the fifteen-minute mark, during a pause for dramatic effect, Zak piped up, loudly, with "Yeah, yeah, yeah, get to the point."

I would have gotten upset had he not been exactly right in his assessment. The preacher went on for another five minutes or so before, finally, wrapping it up with the greatest words ever spoken from a pulpit: "In conclusion . . ."

Just as it can be enlightening and inspiring listening to some sermons, it can be challenging and aggravating listening to others. There are times when sitting in the congregation emphasizes the word "captive" in the phrase "captive audience."

Here are some suggestions for dealing with the "long and winding road" style of preaching.

- **Play "Count the Cliches."** This entertaining little pew game allows you to focus on the sermon in a new way.
- **Go to the optometrist before the service**. Or, better yet, pretend you've just had your pupils dilated, which forces you to wear dark sunglasses. Then take a nap.
- **Write your grocery list.** This classic sermon avoidance strategy is an age-old tradition. Don't forget the butter.
- **Doodle.** Why else do you think ushers hand out bulletins? If you don't have a pen, you can always use one of those golf pencils used for the newcomer cards. And daydream about playing miniature golf.
- **Memorize the Athanasian Creed.** It's in the back of the Prayer Book under "Historical Documents." Imagine the adulation you'll receive at coffee hour when you pull that one out of your conversational toolbox.
- **Skim the Bible.** Oh, wait, Episcopal churches usually don't have those in the pew racks.
- **Whip out your checkbook and write a check.** Then spend the remainder of the sermon slowly ripping it out perforation by perforation so as not to disturb those around you.
- **Surf the net.** This is obvious, but you'll need to tell people who give you dirty looks that you're "live-tweeting" the sermon. It's a form of evangelism. Really.

How to Receive Communion

While most knights spend their entire lives searching for the Holy Grail, we have already found it. It's called drinking out of the chalice on Sunday morning. While we approach the communion rail with awe, there are some practical considerations to take into consideration before receiving the blessed sacrament.

First, stand or kneel? You'll encounter both postures at churches throughout the country. Some see standing as an act of joy and kneeling as too penitential while others feel standing to receive communion is "too Catholic." There's no right way to do this and many churches offer different options at different services during the year. For the record, squatting like a baseball catcher is generally not an accepted practice.

Whether standing, sitting, or squatting, receiving the bread is fairly straightforward—after it is placed in your hands, you put it in your mouth and consume it. Some parishes use real bread while most prefer wafers. Wafers evoke many things such as the body of Christ, a sacramental encounter, or Necco wafers, but rarely do they evoke actual bread. Real bread produces crumbs, which causes a theological heart attack as Jesus falls onto the floor. While I'm pretty confident Jesus can get himself out of that mess—he's been in worse situations—it's not ideal for the sacrament to end up in a vacuum cleaner and gives those of us with high Eucharistic sensibilities apoplexy.

When the chalice arrives, many people drink directly from the cup. The chalice bearer has been specially trained in the holy mysteries of the Eucharist but, more importantly, has been taught to wipe the chalice with a white linen cloth called a purificator and rotate the cup so no one encounters a giant glob of red lipstick attacking their face.

The first time this happens, the communicant turns toward another widely used practice of dipping the wafer into the chalice before eating it. Perhaps inspired by Oreos being dunked in milk, this is a relatively new practice as germophobia has taken America by storm and it even has its own name—intinction. While counterintuitive, scientists insist it is actually healthier to drink from the chalice than to dip bread into it. In any case, the fortified wine used at communion kills all the germs anyway, so you're safe. Jesus wants you to die to sin, not die to swine flu.

If you drink from the chalice, it's appreciated when you help guide the chalice to your lips. This prevents wine being spilled all over your white bridal dress and/or chipping a tooth. On Easter Day when all the ladies are decked out in fancy hats, there's no choice for the chalice bearer except to stick the cup under the hat and hope for the best.

After receiving either the bread or the wine, it is traditional to say "Amen." This is the moment you know if you're dealing with a closeted or former Roman Catholic because they say "Ay-men." This distinction remains a major barrier to global Christian unity.

———

Toddlers in the Pews

There are few things more prayerful than attending church with a toddler. Perhaps the only thing that brings you closer to God is sitting *in front of* a toddler in the pews. Having had my own two toddlers in church back in the day makes me qualified to give some advice in this area. Actually, who am I kidding? Bryna was trapped as a single mom while I was up on the altar looking all holy.

I always tell parents their children are welcome to worship with them in church but also that we have a lovely nursery and toddler room with terrific caregivers. I seriously don't mind a little noise coming from the pews because it beats the alternative. No noise + no children = dying church. Plus, it's usually the parents who get more stressed out about having kids in church than anyone else.

If you do decide to worship with your children, here are a few ideas to make the experience more enjoyable for everyone involved.

- **Bulletins are coloring books.** Yes, it's hard to draw a mustache on the announcement about the Shrove Tuesday Pancake Supper but scribble away!
- **Chewy food good, crunchy food bad.** You know how it looks after a family leaves TGI Fridays after an "active" meal? Try not to leave the pew looking like a bomb went off.
- **Sermons make excellent bedtime stories.** I never have problems with children wreaking havoc during my sermons because my words lull them to sleep. The adults too.
- **Find open space.** Well, not around the altar, but kids do need to move around. This might mean walking in and out of the worship space several hundred times.
- **Sight lines are key.** While most parents sit in the back in an attempt to be unobtrusive, kids really just want to see what's going on. For a child, sitting in the back row is akin to going to a baseball game and sitting in the parking lot. Standing on the kneelers is fine as long as you don't tell the needlepoint guild.
- **Use the iPad.** Yes, parents can overuse these to keep their kids quiet—actually I'm just jealous we didn't have them when my kids were toddlers. To assuage your guilt, I'm sure you can find a nice biblical game where the Israelites slaughter the Philistines.

And remember, if things get really bad you can always place the child in the collection plate and hope the ushers don't notice.

The Great Divide

There exists in parishes a nearly insurmountable divide. It has nothing to do with high church or low church, gender, nationality, race, or the interpretation of Scripture. The true division takes place on Sunday mornings throughout the land and can be summed up with the following question: "Do you go to the early service or the late service?"

It is the great divide between the 8 o'clock and 10 o'clock services (or whatever comprises your local equivalent). Occasionally their paths cross at the church rummage sale or a parish retreat, but for the most part "separate but equal" works just fine for everyone involved.

In most cases the division revolves around the language of the liturgy: Rite I (one) vs. Rite II (two). With the advent of the "new" prayer book in 1979, parishioners were offered a choice. They could continue to worship in the Elizabethan English of Thomas Crammer's first Book of Common Prayer or move into a worship service rooted in contemporary English. At most parishes this led to an early spoken service of Rite I and a later Rite II service with music, choir, and Sunday school.

The idea behind Rite II, in the context of the Prayer Book revision, was to offer an option to once again be able to worship in contemporary English—which was, after all, a critical piece of the English Reformation. Language evolves and so what was contemporary in the sixteenth century now sounds dated, if regal. I wouldn't walk into a Starbucks, go up to the counter and say, "Wouldst thou vouchsafe to proffer me a venti caramel macchiato?" They'd look at me like I was nuts; or at least a Shakespearean actor who'd gotten seriously lost. Also, I'd never order such a frou-frou drink.

Though I would stand at the altar and say "And we humbly beseech thee, O merciful Father, to hear us; and, of thy almighty goodness, vouchsafe to bless and sanctify, with thy Word and Holy Spirit, these thy gifts and creatures of bread and wine."

The one common thread between the two rites at most parish churches is the Lord's Prayer. Even though the rest of the liturgy is in contemporary language, at many Rite II services the Lord's Prayer is still said in its Rite I version even though there is a Rite II option. Why? Because of its beloved familiarity. Which is why many parishioners love the Rite I service—it's what they grew up with and so it is a source of great comfort and strength and only occasionally the classic "we've always done it that way" attitude.

I must say that the 8 o'clockers are some of my favorite parishioners because they are the most loyal of any group in the church. Come hell or a snow storm, they are there every single week. They would also never deign to step foot in any church after about 8:45 a.m. I've also discerned over the years that there are only twenty-five 8 o'clockers in the entire church and by some miracle of bilocation they attend services at the same time in congregations all over the country.

When I was rector of All Saints' Church in Briarcliff Manor, New York, one of our most faithful 8 o'clockers told me when I arrived that the service lasted thirty-seven minutes. And by God, he was right. No matter how long or short I preached, the sacristy clock read 8:37 when I left the sanctuary.

If we were to profile 8 o'clockers for purposes of mass generalization and stereotype, they would share the following characteristics: seventies or eighties, well-dressed, lifelong Episcopalians, generous pledgers, know the entire liturgy by heart, insist they have "graduated" from serving on any committees, don't believe it's church unless there are "thees and thous," and are eager to get the day started. Occasionally you'll get a young parent with an infant since they're up anyway, but it's a rarity. No teenager has ever been seen at an 8 o'clock service in the history of 8 o'clock services.

One of my favorite 8 o'clockers from Old St. Paul's in downtown Baltimore where I served as the dashing young curate, would claim every week that "the sound system used to be a lot better" and encouraged us to "get it fixed." Of course it had nothing to do with her hearing getting worse over the years.

Before I went to seminary, got ordained, and was paid to go to both services, I would occasionally go to the 8 o'clock. While music is an important part of the worship experience for me, there's a contemplative feel to the early service that you just can't get otherwise. It's also great to receive that early shot of spiritual inspiration and get on with your day.

I still usually hit the 8 o'clock whenever I'm on vacation and the family has no intention of getting out of bed for church. It's quiet, peaceful, and confirms my theory about the twenty-five 8 o'clockers.

PART III

SURVIVING THE MEETING

Christians like to meet. A lot. We have annual parish meetings and vestry meetings and fill in-the-blank committee meetings and meetings to plan other meetings. It's not that meetings to plan and strategize aren't important, but they can be mind-numbing and spirit-killing. It's important to remember Jesus called the first disciples into community, not to order. The gavel is not an ancient Christian symbol nor is the yellow legal pad. The good news is that technology, in the form of surreptitiously playing solitaire, texting friends, and updating Facebook, has brought sweet relief to all humanity.

Annual Meeting Haiku

At the end of January most congregations hold their canonically required Annual Parish Meeting. You can always tell when a parish has a divisive issue to address since they schedule the meeting on Super Bowl Sunday, secretly hoping fewer people will attend.

At their best, Annual Meetings are wonderful celebrations of parish life. They give parishioners a chance to hear about the breadth of ministry that takes place—both visible (Sunday school) and invisible (altar guild). New vestry members are elected, the annual budget for the coming year is presented, and the congregation is given an opportunity to ask questions and offer comments.

The Annual Meeting is an invaluable time to take a step back in the midst of the daily grind of ministry to seek the broader view, examine the past year, and look ahead to where God may be calling the congregation in the future.

Unfortunately they rarely live up to such lofty ideals, which is why they are often poorly attended. If you haven't checked your watch early and often during an Annual Meeting, you're probably not a true parishioner.

These affairs are also an annual source of stress for clergy, lay leaders, and parish staff. Transparency is important and thus offering details about the budget plays a vital, if tedious, role. If there are "fireworks" at the Annual Meeting, they usually stem from the budget presentation—thoughtfully provided by the three parish cranks who bring up the same issues every single year.

As a service to all who diligently prepare for their respective Annual Meetings (and those who must endure them), I offer the following poem to save everyone time, effort, and copy paper. I recommend standing up, reciting this, and then sending everyone home. I promise you will go down in the annals of parish history as the most revered rector/senior warden combination to ever grace your congregation. The Annual Meeting will be over before you can say "brass plaque in my honor" three times.

The Annual Meeting Haiku
Budget blah, blah, blah
Something about Jesus Christ
Please up your pledges.

———

Musical Chairs

Clergy like to rearrange chairs. I'm not sure why this is except we're used to dealing with immovable pews so moving chairs around makes us feel like we're stickin' it to The Man. I'm not sure if there were any clergymen on the Titanic but, if so, presumably their primary duty was rearranging the deck chairs.

There are several different arrangements used to evoke different feelings. I share these with you, not because they're bad, but to give you insight into the mind of your parish clergy *cum* spiritual furniture mover.

- **Circle.** Whenever you attend a meeting or gathering where the chairs have been placed in a circular pattern, be prepared to get all touchy-feely. If the mere thought of having to share your emotions with a group gives you agita, flee before it's too late. The circle lends itself perfectly to (horror of horrors) holding hands.
- **Chairs around tables.** With a larger group that can comfortably sit around a single table, we like to put two or three tables together to increase the surface area. The advantage is that it

creates a barrier between people so two enemies may sit at the same table yet not be able to choke one another.

- **Horseshoe.** This is a variation of the circle but with a circuit rider motif. The open end allows everyone excellent sight lines to the leader, thus offering him/her an air of authority and an ego boost.
- **Inverted horseshoe.** This setup looks just like the horseshoe but is used to intimidate someone, like during an interview. A cheap folding chair is put in the open end while everyone else sits in armchairs and glares at the interviewee.
- **Classroom.** This may be in an actual Sunday school classroom so everyone is seated in chairs sized for kindergartners. The advantage of this is that it makes all the adults feel like Gulliver. The disadvantage is that no one can get out of the chairs, which leads to longer-than-normal meetings.
- **Facing each other.** This allows a priest to channel his/her inner monastic, as this is how monks and nuns worship in community. Most parish clergy would make lousy monks and nuns even though we all fantasize sometimes about running away and locking ourselves in a monastic cell. This generally means we need a vacation.
- **Rhombus.** This signifies the priest was running late and is also a reflection upon his/her general slovenliness.

Vestry Meeting Survival

When I served at an unnamed, heavily endowed congregation, our parish treasurer was Chicken Little. At every meeting, the treasurer's report consisted of dire predictions and the-sky-is-falling pronouncements that, if you had no context, would make you wonder when the church would be sold and converted to condos. This in a healthy, vibrant parish with a $20 million endowment.

This episode led me to believe there are certain roles people play on vestries that are interchangeable across parishes. Basically, all church leadership groups channel a bit of the vestry on the Vicar of Dibley. Here are a few archetypical vestry personalities:

- The Crank. For this guy (yes, usually it's a man), nothing is ever up to snuff. This child of God's great gift is pointing out shortcomings in others while never offering to be part of the solution. It doesn't take much to get him cranked up—it's not about the issue but the opposition to it that counts. He's in a perpetual state of withholding his pledge on "moral" grounds, though if you scratch the surface he's just cheap.
- The Holy Roller. This person feels the need to stop the proceedings for prayer at least three times per meeting. There's no doubt there are times when this is called for, as when the vestry is discerning action on a particularly complex issue. But when you're approving last month's minutes? No.
- The Invisible Man/Woman. Some vestry members possess the uncanny ability to either miss meetings or have zero impact upon the ones they do attend. There was much enthusiasm when this person was elected, and yet once off the vestry, no one remembers that he/she was ever on it.
- The Parliamentarian. God forbid anyone forget to second a motion before voting. The Parliamentarian will immediately stop

the proceedings to give a ten-minute exposition on the importance of Robert's Rules of Order. Please get over it. This isn't the
House of Lords.

- The Dreamer. It's wonderful to have people committed to helping
others in a parish. In many ways, it gets to the heart of what Jesus
calls us to do. Unfortunately, the Dreamer wants 100 percent of
the budget to go toward outreach. "Why do we need a working
toilet? Don't you think that money could better be spent on
helping octogenarians in Zimbabwe learn to read?"

This being said, here are a few suggestions for making vestry
meetings more productive, palatable, and pleasurable.

- Appoint a timekeeper to limit the amount of time a person may
speak at a single meeting. Three minutes total should suffice after
which the timekeeper, equipped with an air horn, may announce
that time is up. This time limit must also apply to the parish
clergy.
- Never vote on anything after 9:00 p.m. No good vestry decision
has ever been made after NCIS has started.
- If conflict arises, use the vaulted rock, paper, scissors method
of conflict resolution. The debate is shorter and thus everybody
wins.
- When in doubt, take a sherry break.
- If still in doubt, take a Scotch break.
- If all else fails, sound the air horn and adjourn the meeting.

Diocesan Convention Survival Guide

If you've ever attended the annual Diocesan Convention, you're either a member of the clergy or a lay glutton for punishment. This is important work—well besides the mind-numbing amendments to silly resolutions—but there's a reason there's no one named Saint Robert of Rules or a monastic community named the Order of Robert.

Some parish delegates care passionately about diocesan ministry while others were appointed by the rector to keep them away from parish ministry. However you ended up sitting in an uncomfortable pew in some drafty cathedral on a beautiful, sunny day, no one should attend Convention unprepared. Thus, as a service to delegates everywhere, I'm offering you my Diocesan Convention Survival Guide.

1. **Charge your smartphone and/or tablet.** iPhone, BlackBerry, Droid, iPad—whatever you use make sure it's fully charged and ready for action. Apps are God's antidote for clergy and others who adore the sound of their own voices. Bring your charger and scout out a plug. There's nothing worse than seeing that red battery light in the waning minutes of Convention business. And by "waning minutes" I mean the last two hours until the lunch break.
2. **Find an aisle seat near the back of the venue.** Easy egress and ingress is key, especially during budget presentations given by assistant diocesan treasurers wielding the ubiquitous monotone. Frequent "bathroom" breaks are allowed. You can't help it if you have a small bladder.
3. **If you're going to make snide comments, share them via social media.** Don't hide your lamp under a bushel basket! Chances are if you're thinking it, so are the other four hundred people sitting in those narrow pews installed in an era when people were much shorter and had longer attention spans.

4. **Import your own coffee.** This is essential since all "coffee" brewed at Convention sites is, by its very nature, little more than brown water. Bring a thermos of good coffee from home to get you through the registration process and opening remarks. Google local coffee shops in the immediate vicinity and even if you have to run out for a "pastoral emergency" to get a refill several times per day, it's worth it. Didn't Jesus say, "Delegates cannot live by Convention coffee alone?" I think that's in Mark.

5. **Do not even think about approaching a microphone.** Nothing good has ever come from speaking at Convention. Prolonging the debate of an issue that will unanimously pass anyway will likely only increase your time in purgatory. Are you really willing to take that chance?

6. **Don't be one of those six people.** There are six people in every diocese (almost always, but not exclusively, clergy) for whom Convention is not complete unless they pontificate at least once on a fill-in-the-blank issue. You know who they are and you can even write their names down and check them off as they approach the microphone to speak. The only positive is that you can bet with your fellow delegates on the actual order and turn it into a Ponzi scheme. This will help your annual stewardship campaign back in the parish.

7. **Choose your lay delegates wisely.** I have two criteria for delegates to Convention: a) they must be at least vaguely interested in the work of the diocese and b) I have to like them enough to be willing to spend an entire day or two with them. They also have to appreciate/not be bothered by my sotto voce comments criticizing the various Convention liturgies.

8. **Smartphones are the new knitting.** If you have a problem with me updating my Facebook status during Convention business, then I think your niece will hate that ugly scarf you're knitting. Perhaps we can all agree that knitting and surfing the web are two sides of the same coin. I can't knit, but I can relate to wanting to leave with something tangible and positive at the end of the day.

9. **Skip the box lunch and go outside for takeout.** A box lunch? Really? Since I graduated from elementary school (*cum laude* I might add) the only time I've ever even seen a box lunch was at a Diocesan Convention. They give me flashbacks to powdered milk. Hey, as long as you're getting some fresh air, pick up a large coffee to carry you through the afternoon report from the Compensation and Benefits Committee.

10. **Receive communion from the bishop during the Convention Eucharist.** We know that Jesus is fully present in the Eucharist no matter who doles it out. However you may as well make sure the bishop knows that you love Convention and wouldn't miss it for the world. If you're new to the diocese, wear a giant name tag and make major eye contact. If you trip on your way up to communion and cause a big scene, this is a great way to insure everyone knows you were there (even minor canons and such).

11. **If you run for office, mention Jesus or God somewhere in your blurb.** I've noticed that 80 percent of people standing for election to diocesan offices don't do this in their responses to "Why do you want to be on XXX council or serve as delegate to XXX convention?" Seriously. I've stopped voting for people who omit God, which narrows down the choices considerably. Oh, and while we're on the topic, please don't engage in overt "electioneering," as it's unseemly and annoying.

If you follow these eleven simple steps, I guarantee your Convention experience will only be as painful as the three-hour Good Friday Service.

Conventional Wisdom

As a veteran of about fifteen Diocesan Conventions in three different dioceses, I've spent some time reflecting on ways to make these gatherings more user-friendly. I humbly offer the following suggestions to make future conventions more pleasant.

1. Never hold the convention more than a fifteen-minute drive from any parish in the diocese. Sure, this will take some bending of the conventional constraints of time and space, but the Episcopal Church has a chaplaincy at MIT. They can take some time away from creating a solar laptop/espresso maker to solve this issue.

2. Diocesan assessments should be linked to the length of time the parish's rector blabs into the microphone. If Father Mind-be-Numb feels the need to blather endlessly about a doomed resolution, that's fine. But it'll cost him. I'd recommend adding $1,000 per minute to his parish assessment. Everybody wins.

3. I understand that budget constraints may force dioceses to hold their conventions inside large, drafty churches. However, I must insist that the pews be equipped with cup holders and electric blankets. It's the humane thing to do.

4. If it takes more than three ballots to fill a diocesan post, just flip a coin. No one remembers who serves on the Ecclesiastical Court anyway.

5. If the diocesan treasurer must use a lengthy PowerPoint presentation to go line-by-line through the budget, it's only fair to equip the convention hall with Wi-Fi. How else can you expect to update your Twitter followers by complaining about the insufferable budget presentation?

6. Here's a resolution worth passing: "Be it resolved that from henceforth hand motions of any kind during diocesan liturgies will be

banned." Although it's fun to watch the obvious discomfort of diocesan bishops trying to be good sports as they point to the sky and stand on one leg at the appointed moment during the Prayers of the People, this shouldn't be allowed in the first place.

7. It would be best to cut an extraneous diocesan staff position in order to serve good coffee to clergy and lay delegates. The ministry that is lost would more than be made up for in alertness. At least for a day or two.

8. If you insist on sucking up to the bishop during breaks, please be less obvious. Fawning over a purple shirt is unbecoming.

Thank you for your cooperation in helping to make Diocesan Convention more bearable and enjoyable for all concerned. I'll look forward to these changes being implemented throughout the country next year.

Litany for Diocesan Convention

If you've ever attended a Convention liturgy, you know that they are, well, unique. Trying to encompass traditions from every parish means that you might have liturgical dancers waving orange chiffon followed by the gospel reading in Romanian with songs known to absolutely no one—not even the musician.

While liturgy is the one thing we do best, for some reason it all falls apart when two or three priests are gathered together in the bishop's name.

This Litany for Diocesan Convention is appropriate for any convention liturgy. If it's not part of the official bulletin, I suggest appointing your own cantor and singing it during a pointless resolution. It is, of course, sung to the tune of The Great Litany, the world's oldest English language rite.

Litany for Diocesan Convention

O God the Father, Creator of heaven and mirth.
Have mercy upon us.

O God the Son, Redeemer of the bored.
Have mercy upon us.

O God the Holy Spirit, Sanctifier of the awful.
Have mercy upon us.

Remember not, Lord Christ, our offenses, nor the offenses of our fellow delegates; neither reward us according to our pomposity. Spare us, good Lord, spare thy people, whom thou hast brought to this dingy cathedral, and by thy mercy preserve us from boredom, for ever.
Spare us, good Lord.

From all box lunches and ennui; from the crafts and assaults of the self-absorbed; and from never-ending debate,
Good Lord, deliver us.

From poseurs and grandstanders and from those who like to hear the sound of their own voices,
Good Lord, deliver us.

From those compelled to speak from any available microphone even with nothing to say,
Good Lord, deliver us.

From liturgies that include the clapping of hands and hymns no one knows,
Good Lord, deliver us.

From the self-important, the aggravating, and the sanctimonious,
Good Lord, deliver us.

From the humorless, the thin-skinned, and those that posture,
Good Lord, deliver us.

From the authors of pointless resolutions and amendments to said resolutions,
Good Lord, deliver us.

From endless budget debates that never change a thing,
Good Lord, deliver us.

From the lack of Wi-Fi, poor cell service, and slow connections,
Good Lord, deliver us.

From clergy who gravitate toward those with purple shirts,
Good Lord, deliver us.

From being drafted to run for diocesan council,
Good Lord, deliver us.

From weak and lukewarm coffee and the requisite nondairy creamer,
Good Lord, deliver us.

From those who disparage the use of smartphones even as they knit,
Good Lord, deliver us.

From delegates politicking in the restroom and during the Peace,
Good Lord, deliver us.

From monotonous reports by people reading us their PowerPoint slides,
Good Lord, deliver us.

From the same six people who insist on speaking to every resolution,
Good Lord, deliver us.

Bishop XX, we beseech thee to hear us.
Bishop XX, we beseech thee to hear us.

O Secretary of Convention, you have the power to set us free,
Have mercy upon us.

O Secretary of Convention, you have the power to set us free,
Have mercy upon us.

O Secretary of Convention, you have the power to set us free,
Grant us release.

Clergy Conference Survival Guide

Every diocese has some sort of Clergy Conference for their priests and deacons. I've attended them in Maryland, New York, and Massachusetts and occasionally some diocese will be crazy enough to invite me to lead one. The point is to gather the clergy from throughout the diocese, offer an educational/inspirational program, and allow people to enjoy the ensuing collegial relationships. If you have young children at home, it's also meant to annoy your spouse who's stuck at home with them for a couple of days by him/herself. So it's best to enjoy it since you'll have to pay the piper soon enough.

The venues vary from rustic diocesan conference centers to 1960s-era monasteries to fancy resorts. Whatever the venue, you'll always find people complaining (from "I can't believe they're putting us up in this dump" to "Would Jesus really want us to be in a place with an Elizabeth Arden–inspired spa?").

The common elements are generally 1) a big name speaker—i.e., someone from outside the diocese; 2) a bunch of clergy toting around varying degrees of ego; 3) a couple of bishops—and the usual group of priestly sycophants trailing behind them; 4) a cash bar in the evening; 5) poorly attended daily worship services; 6) a fancy dinner billed as the "Bishop's Banquet" followed by some form of entertainment—a "talent" show or some musician who couldn't get a better gig; and 7) name tags to help participants remember the names of people they met last year but now couldn't pick out of a lineup.

Here are a few tips to help you survive your own Clergy Conference, whether this is your first one or thirty-fifth.

1. Never, ever wear a clerical collar. This will signal that you are either a total novice or exceedingly pompous.

2. When approaching the cash bar, don't ever come with cash. This is the time for younger clergy to guilt cardinal rectors into buying them drinks (note: this tip doesn't apply to cardinal rectors with endowed discretionary funds that have pesky restrictions about being used for "pastoral purposes only").

3. Toss around the term "clergy wellness" when asked why you took a nap instead of attending the plenary session on health benefits.

4. Don't sit at the bishop's table for any reason—it will earn you a reputation for sucking up. If he/she happens to sit at your table for a meal or a workshop, smile politely and try not to spill anything on the bishop. It's bad form and will likely get you appointed to a diocesan committee.

5. Bring your smartphone to all sessions—if the speaker starts droning on and on, remember there's nothing you can't Tweet your way through. Stay strong!

6. During the bound-to-be sloppy liturgies, play "Count the Rubric Violations." This game affords endless entertainment; get a group together and compare notes afterward for the full effect.

7. During the inevitable evening social hour (cash bar), always carry two drinks with you. This way if an especially windbaggy colleague corners you to talk about his/her most recent Maundy Thursday sermon, you can escape by pretending you're taking the other drink to someone else. Repeat as necessary.

8. It's okay to blow off the occasional session for important work like blogging, napping, banging your head against a wall, etc. Guilt is for the weak.

9. To remove yourself from a mind-numbing workshop already in progress, pretend to answer your phone (it will already be silenced out of courtesy to the presenter so you don't need to worry about an actual ring) and, with the phone to your ear and a concerned look on your face, exit the room. People will assume you had to answer an important pastoral call.

10. Don't complain too publicly about anything—you'll end up on next year's planning committee.

Look for my upcoming book *How to Blow Off Certain Parts of Clergy Conference While Remaining Canonically Resident*.

PART IV

SURVIVING THE MINISTRIES

A church without opportunities to serve is like a bicycle without wheels—there's no point. Unless you enjoy carrying around a funny-looking piece of metal for no apparent reason. Every parish offers a variety of ways to serve those within and beyond its four walls and we call these ministries. Some are visible, some are unsung, some are popular, some are moribund, but collectively they keep the church functioning and alive in the community and the world.

If you've never been invited to participate in one of the many ministries in your parish, either your church is missing out on reaching its potential or you're good at screening your calls. Ministry should be a source of joy, so it's important to think about ways you can best share your skills and gifts with the community. If you can't stand children and turn off all your lights and crawl around the floor on Halloween night, perhaps you should not teach Sunday school. Similarly, if you can't read a budget and think money is the root of all evil, maybe you should decline the invitation to serve as parish treasurer.

I Want YOU to Teach
Sunday School

Congratulations! You've been invited to teach Sunday school. The invitation wasn't extended because all the other teachers were completely burned out and you're new and you have young kids. Really. But you can do this—it's just for a few months until the term ends after which we won't ask you to become the Sunday school director. Really.

What better ministry could there be than teaching our youngest parishioners about the Christian faith? Passing on the stories and traditions to the next generation is a high calling and not one to be taken lightly. Prayerful preparation is the key to success as you seek to be the all-important nonparental adult Christian role model. Also, there are glue sticks.

I've always wondered why we insist on calling Christian formation for our children Sunday *school*. I mean, is there anything a kid wants to do *less* on a weekend than go to school? Talk about a marketing nightmare! The only antidote is to make it engaging, creative, fun, and relevant to the particular age you're working with.

That's a tall order but fortunately you've been given a bunch of old mimeographed sheets as a "curriculum." Most teachers tend to adapt whichever curriculum they've been given, which basically means searching the Internet for ideas.

Much of the learning comes from the kids themselves as they ask tough questions or see things from a perspective we've never thought of. I once received a phone call from a panicked Sunday school teacher who was asked, during a lesson about John the Baptist, "If Jesus was God's son, why did he need to be baptized?" This is the sort of question that stops Sunday school teachers and priests dead in their tracks. Fortunately the teacher did the smart thing—she told the child it was an excellent question and told him she'd discuss it the following week. In the meantime, she started scrambling for the answer.

Perhaps the most important skill you need as a Sunday school teacher is your game face. It's hard not to laugh when you hear some of the things kids say. Here are a few examples:

> "Moses went to Mt. Cyanide to get the Ten Commandments."
> "The seventh commandment? Thou shalt not admit adultery."
> "The epistles were married to the apostles."

You also occasionally hear things probably not meant for public consumption.

"My mom thinks Father XX is too fat. Maybe he should stop eating all the leftover wafers."

"Mrs. Major's first name is Biddy. At least that's what my dad always calls her."

Oh, and that question about Jesus's need to be baptized? Armed with all sorts of research and ideas, that Sunday school teacher marched confidently back into her classroom seven days later. She was all set to engage in a lengthy conversation about why it was, exactly, that Jesus needed to be baptized. Unfortunately, the child couldn't remember having asked the question in the first place and really wasn't concerned with an answer. So, back to the lesson plan she went, grateful for her inquisitive children and the opportunity to reflect upon an intriguing and profound question of faith.

Reasons to Join the Altar Guild

There are many reasons to join the altar guild beside free wax candle nubs. As with umpires in baseball, no one notices the altar guild until there's a major liturgical screw-up like forgetting to put out bread for communion. Fortunately, most mistakes are only noticed by the priest so, unless you are publicly shamed at the announcements, you're safe. And anyway what priest hasn't had his hands washed with wine instead of water?

Serving on the altar guild is not only an invaluable service to the congregation, there's something quite prayerful and meaningful about handling the holy vessels. You can also affect a certain snobbery by knowing and using all of the secret code words for churchy things like piscina (sink for consecrated wine that goes directly into the earth), paten (communion plate), and purificator (linen used to wipe the chalice, i.e., cup).

It's fun to annoy your family by asking your kids to "set the altar," asking your husband to haul the "fair linen" down from the attic, and telling your guests to help themselves to the buffet set out on the "credence table." You can complete the tableau by making sure everyone is wearing the appropriate liturgical color for the season as in "Take off that red Christmas sweater right now, young man, and put on a purple shirt!" during mid-December meals.

The only caution I have when considering whether to join the altar guild is the title used by the guild's chair. "Head of the Altar Guild" is fine as is "Altar Guild Chair." Beware, however, of anyone who insists on being called the Altar Guild Directress. This person would have scolded Jesus for setting the table all wrong for the Last Supper and would have been horrified that he used real bread rather than wafers with little crosses stamped on them.

Some other advantages to joining the altar guild include embracing your inner OCD; first dibs on stale, unconsecrated wafers;

getting huge muscles from polishing brass; one-on-one time with the priest to complain about other parishioners; avoiding coffee hour since you "must be about the Lord's work"; and "borrowing" the altar flowers for the dinner party you're hosting tomorrow evening.

I do hope you'll consider joining this important ministry (men are welcome!) since without it, we'd never be able to pull off Sunday morning worship.

————

Father Tim's Prayer for Rummage

When I was an assistant priest and discerning a call to lead my own congregation for the first time, my rector had one piece of advice for me. "Tim," he said, "whatever you do, don't go to a parish that has a rummage sale."

Well, I didn't heed this fatherly advice and ended up at a parish with a big annual rummage sale. For a full week, rummage took over the church and I don't just mean a few rooms but, literally, the entire church. While we were very clear about the no clothes rule, that didn't stop people from dropping off grocery bags full of used underwear.

I did put a stop to the tradition of parishioners dropping off items ahead of time in the rectory garage and the money raised did go to help fund our outreach programs, so that provided some solace. But still.

Moments before we opened the doors on the first day—which resembled the Running of the Bulls—I always gathered the volunteers to pray my Prayer for Rummage. If you have a rummage sale at your own parish, I'm sorry, but feel free to adapt this prayer for local use.

Prayer for Rummage

Look down upon us and our sale
Rummage on such a grand scale!
You never know what you'll find
But if you're inclined
Perhaps even the Holy Grail.

Most gracious and holy Lord
Who alone knows what we can afford.
Have mercy on us
And all of our stuff
May our parish hall one day be restored.

We give thanks for the hands who have sorted
Through all of these items imported.
Toys, books, and curtains
One thing is for certain
We couldn't have gone unsupported.

To our committee chairs go our great thanks
They've courageously led all the ranks
We give them much gratitude
Beyond any platitude
We'll blame them if this whole thing tanks.

It's time to give heed to the mirth
And see what this junk is all worth
So let the bedlam begin
But save us from the sin
Of storing up treasures on earth.

Motivational Sacristy Quotes

I've never understood why motivational quotes seem to be the exclusive domain of football locker rooms. The church equivalent of the locker room is, of course, the sacristy. The liturgical players all gather here before the kickoff/procession. The priest offers a prayer/motivational speech with the acolytes and choir and off they charge down the aisle (at a decorous, stately pace of course).

I thought it would be helpful to offer a few motivational quotes to post in your sacristy. This will keep all the servers motivated and focused for the task at hand and instill an unparalleled spiritual esprit de corps. I suggest putting up a new quote every time the church season changes so they don't get stale and the acolytes start phoning it in. The church needs fired-up altar parties!

- There's no "I" in Acolyte.
- It's not whether you win or lose, it's how the procession flows.
- Win one for the Messiah.
- Leave it all on the altar.
- It ain't over 'til the fat lady sings the dismissal.
- Let's all give this liturgy 110 percent (which is the same fuzzy math as three in one and one in three).
- It's not the size of the crucifer but the size of the processional cross that matters.
- Show me a bad liturgist and I'll show you bad liturgy.
- There is no substitute for preaching preparation.
- It's not whether the thurifer gets knocked down, it's whether he gets back up.
- Communion isn't everything; it's the only thing.

A Warden's Work Is Never Done

Quick, what's the first thing that comes to mind when you think of a warden? If you're like most people, it's not a church; unless you think of a church as a high security prison. I've always thought it rather unfortunate that the key lay leaders in our parishes bring to mind people who would be happy to lock you up and throw away the key.

Of course, a prison warden isn't the only image that emerges. There's also the big game warden, which evokes someone with a shotgun chasing elephants. In other words, "what we've got here is a failure to communicate," to quote the sadistic warden in the 1967 Paul Newman classic *Cool Hand Luke*.

Most parishes have two wardens, the senior warden and the junior warden. In my experience there is no such thing as the sophomore warden. Sometimes they're appointed by the rector, but usually they're elected by the congregation. In some parishes the senior warden is called the rector's warden and is appointed by the rector while the junior warden is called the people's warden and is elected by the congregation. Much to the chagrin of church musicians everywhere, there is no such thing as the organist's warden.

I've been lucky to have served with some fine wardens over the years, but clergy and wardens do battle sometimes. I've known of some wardens who truly do put the "war" in "warden."

In England, where the term originated, church wardens are given the responsibility to keep peace in church yards. In America, they're more likely to be called upon to keep the peace in the church parking lot.

According to the Ecclesiastical Courts Jurisdiction Act of 1860, English church wardens have the power to punish the following acts with a £200 fine:

- Riotous, violent, or indecent behavior in any cathedral church, parish, or district church or chapel of the Church of England or

in any churchyard or burial ground (whether during a service or at any other time)
- Molesting, disturbing, vexing, or troubling, or by any other unlawful means disquieting or misusing:
  - any preacher duly authorized to preach therein, or
  - any clergyman in holy orders ministering or celebrating any sacrament, or any divine service, rite, or office, in any cathedral, church, or chapel, or in any churchyard or burial ground.

They may also apprehend anyone caught acting in these ways and haul them before the local magistrate.

What I glean from this is 1) church yards are sketchy places and 2) "vexing" preachers is commonplace in England. I promise if we offered these powers to wardens in America, we'd never again have to beg people to serve in this important but often unsung capacity that can feel more like the parishioner complaint department than anything else.

Wardens of the world, unite!

PART V

SURVIVING THE BISHOP

In the Episcopal Church, bishops are a way of life. The word "episcopal" itself refers to the ministry of bishops, thus making it impossible to get rid of them. Not that I've ever had such impure thoughts. Bishops are so important they even own their own real estate: the House of Bishops. Having never been invited over to their house for a play date, I can't comment on the décor, though I presume there are purple drapes.

We need bishops, of course, or at least their holy hands. They use these appendages for all sorts of holy things that no one else can do like confirming, ordaining, and signing important, sacred documents. They also use them to don some of the most hideous vestments in the free world. In fairness, they had no choice but to wear them at least once since they were handmade by third graders at the diocesan camp who were hopped up on bug juice at the time.

Guide to Episcopal Visitations

As a priest since 2000, I've hosted my share of bishops for parish visitations. I thought I'd offer some helpful hints for all clergy anticipating their next visit. You know, just a few things to do in preparation for and during the visitation to make sure you don't get defrocked.

So, here is Father Tim's Official Guide to Episcopal Visitations.**

- Program hymns like "Lift High the Cross" and "St. Patrick's Breastplate." Bishops never tire of these hymns and truly love hearing them week after week after week. Especially on Hammond organs.
- If it's been a few years since the last visitation and your "The Episcopal Church Welcomes You" sign has been overtaken by vines and weeds, make sure that the directions on your website are wrong ("Yes, we know that's supposed to say turn *right* at Church Street, but people usually manage to find us anyway").
- The week before the visitation, preach about how all the parish's financial woes are a direct result of the diocesan assessment.
- Only provide nondairy creamer at coffee hour. Your bishop is sure to be impressed with your stewardship, especially if the Chock full o' Nuts is served at room temperature.
- Encourage parishioners to approach the bishop and, rather than introducing themselves, say "I met you at Confirmation eight years ago. You remember my name don't you?"
- During the liturgy, assign a skittish parishioner with a tendency to sweat a lot and drop things to serve as the bishop's chaplain.
- If the bishop's spouse attends, make sure to publicly welcome him/her during the announcements, but get the spouse's name wrong. It will give them something to talk about on the way back to the bishop's residence.

- Always refer to the distinction between the parish and diocesan levels as "us" versus "them."
- Prompt a member of the youth group to say loudly right before the opening hymn, "Wow! That's a huge ring! How much did that piece of bling cost?"
- Don't mark the altar book for the Eucharistic Prayer so the bishop comes across as a bumbling fool as he flips through the pages desperately seeking the proper preface.
- And finally, as the bishop drives away, yell "Thanks, Bishop! See you in three years!"

****The author is hereby released from any liability, ecclesiastical or otherwise, from rectors who choose to follow these steps.*

The Definitive List of Questions for Bishop Candidates

It took me over thirteen years of ordained ministry before I participated in an election for a new bishop. While I had served in three different dioceses (Maryland, New York, and Massachusetts), every time I left a diocese the bishop retired and they would call for an election. This was something I tried not to take personally.

As part of the election process, the candidates go on several dog and pony shows—"walkabouts" in proper church-ese—where all the candidates present themselves and answer questions. It sounds miserable to me from either side of the process, but there are some important clarifications that need to be made so that the Holy Spirit can get in and do its thing.

Here are a few questions that should be asked at every walkabout in every diocese prior to every election.

- "Will you insist your bishop's ring be larger and blingier than even the gaudiest Super Bowl ring?"
- "Do you prefer to be called Your Grace or Your Lordship?"
- "Will you start wearing hideous vestments just because they were handmade for you by Sunday school children?"
- "Do you Tweet? If so, perhaps following @FatherTim is not in your best interest."
- "If you use social media, will you commit to never using the phrase 'the good people of St. XX' as in 'I had a great visitation with the good people of St. John's today.'"
- "When it comes to miters, do you believe size really does matter?"
- "Do you feel that any seat a bishop sits in automatically becomes the bishop's throne even if it's at McDonalds?"
- "Do you prefer purple purple or reddish purple?"
- "Do you believe a pectoral cross should channel the spirit of Flavor Flav?"
- "Will there be liturgical dance that involves multicolored chiffon at your consecration?"
- "Do you currently or have you ever owned a clergy shirt in any color other than black?"
- "Upon election, do you prefer white smoke or purple?"
- "Are you willing to defrock the first priest who friends you on Facebook following the election?"

Asking these questions of every candidate for bishop will level the ecclesiastical playing field and allow us to judge them on the color of their clergy shirts rather than on the content of their character.

Victory Speech—Bishop's Edition

After recently reading about yet another bishop election, I realized just how tired I am of hearing the exact same quotes from the "winning" bishop-elect. The two biggest buzzwords are "humbled" and "overwhelmed." Usually these spill out one right after the other as in "I'm humbled and overwhelmed to be called to this new ministry."

That's not to say I think this immediate reaction is inauthentic—I'm sure anyone called to such a position of leadership and responsibility is truly both humbled and overwhelmed. But I'm also certain that the "thrill of victory" gets publicly tempered while they're popping the champagne in the privacy of their own homes and doing the bishop-elect dance.

So I thought I'd help out all future bishops by writing a more appropriate "victory" speech. You know, the words they really want to say but can't since they have an entire diocese waiting to hear just how "humbled and overwhelmed" they are at having been elected.

A Bishop's Victory Speech

Begin with a Howard Dean–like yell. Then do a few fist pumps. If you're feeling spry, do some push-ups to show that you're an incredible physical specimen who will never have to relinquish power due to health concerns before the mandatory retirement age.

[You may be wondering why you're in the convention hall after the election to deliver this speech. You were so confident you'd win that you booked a room in a fancy nearby hotel. Then right after the election you "just happened to be passing by" in order to greet the diocese in person rather than via a bland statement.]

To a standing ovation, you emerge from a giant cloud of incense to deliver your speech. There's bound to be some praise band on hand (since it's a diocesan convention and all liturgical and musical sensibility has therefore evaporated). Use this to your advantage and have them play what will henceforth become your theme song. Some suggestions are *Purple Rain* by Prince (change spelling to "Reign"); *Living on a Prayer* by Bon Jovi; anything by Deep Purple (though *Smoke on the Water* could be considered baptismal imagery); *We Are the Champions* by Queen (change "We are" to "I am"); or if there's a horn section, a short but intricate fanfare will do.

Victory is mine! [*Then stand for a full thirty seconds with arms raised in the classic Richard Nixon double V pose while soaking in all the applause.*] And you, good people of the Diocese of XXX are obviously smarter than the Episcopalians in (name the five dioceses in which you lost elections).

Thank you for finally getting me out of St. Thomas-by-the-Turnpike and away from all those annoying parishioners who kept showing up week after week and telling me all about their "problems" at coffee hour. It's been a long time coming. And my wife and I are psyched that my current salary will now be doubled. Show me the money! And by the way here are some plans we had drawn up to redo the kitchen in the bishop's residence [*hand them to the diocesan treasurer*].

To my fellow candidates: in an election, there can only be one winner. Thus, God thinks you're a loser. As does this entire diocese. But take it from me—there will be other elections and other chances to join ME in the House of Bishops. Until then please know that I won't return your phone calls and, in fact, I've already forgotten all of your names. [*Your cell phone rings; you answer it and tell Wippell's to go ahead and ship the purple shirts you preordered.*]

I'm delighted you bought all that stuff I said at the preelection walkabouts. Please don't hold me to any of it since I can't remember what I said to get elected. But the important thing is that I look fantastic in a purple cassock. Also, please forward pictures of the vestments from the cathedral sacristy as soon as possible so I can Photoshop myself in.

To my future staff, I like my coffee served at 163 degrees Fahrenheit with 3/4 of a teaspoon of sugar and free-range soy milk. And you can simply call me "Your Grace." If you'd like to kiss my humongous bishop's ring—that costs more than the down payment on your house—know that I do tend to keep it in my back pocket.

And, finally, to the good people of this diocese, I look forward to showing up at your churches, meeting you, and criticizing the liturgy. Sure, I'll preach for thirty-five minutes and throw off your whole Sunday morning schedule while simultaneously giving your poor Sunday school teachers PTSD. And since I don't plan to remember your name or what you look like in between visitations, kindly leave me alone when you see me dining in a fancy restaurant on the diocesan dime.

Oh, wait. I think I forgot to mention that I'm humbled and overwhelmed to be your new bishop.

The Bishop's New Vestments

This is an adaptation of Hans Christian Andersen's "The Emperor's New Clothes." As a parable, I invite you to read into it what you will. I will refrain from further comment for fear of self-incrimination and the distinct possibility that I will never find work in another diocese. Ever.

Many years ago there lived a bishop. He was so enamored with liturgical vestments that he spent all his time and all his discretionary funds in order to be well vested. He did not read much Scripture or theology and the only joy he took in parish visitations was in the ceremonial processions where he could show off his fine collection of copes, miters, and chasubles.

Between services, parishioners would ask, "Where is the bishop?" Instead of answering, "He is meeting with the vestry" or "He is in consultation with the rector," the bishop's chaplain would reply, "The bishop is admiring his vestments in the sacristy mirror."

Time passed merrily in the cathedral city.

One day, two men arrived who called themselves C.M. Almy representatives, but they were, in fact, clever robbers. They pretended that they knew how to weave cloth of the most beautiful liturgical colors and magnificent patterns. Moreover, they said, the vestments woven from this magic cloth could not be seen by anyone who was unfit for the office he held or who was theologically incorrect. The gorgeous vestments could only be seen by those who were fit for the offices they held or who were theologically astute.

"These must be splendid vestments indeed!" thought the bishop. "If I had a matching cope and miter made of this magic cloth, I could find out at once what priests in my diocese are not good enough for the positions they hold. These vestments must be woven for me immediately." And he ordered large sums from the diocesan treasury to be given to the weavers in order that they might begin their work at once.

So the two men who pretended to be makers of clergy haberdashery set up two looms in the basement of the cathedral. They went about as though they were working busily, though in reality they did nothing at all.

After some little time passed, the bishop said to himself, "I should like to know how the vestments are coming along. I am a little worried about going myself to look at the cloth because they said that a fool or a man unfit for his office would be unable to see the material. Surely I am quite safe but all the same I think it best to send someone else first."

After some thought the bishop said, "I will send my faithful and trustworthy canon to the ordinary. He is a man of sense and no one can be more suitable for his office than he."

So the honest, old canon to the ordinary went into the cathedral basement where the wicked men were working. "What can be the meaning of this?" thought the old man, opening his eyes very wide. "I cannot see the least bit of thread on the looms!" However, he did not speak his thoughts out loud.

The men who were pretending to weave very politely asked him whether the design pleased him and whether the colors were not very beautiful. The poor canon to the ordinary looked, but he could not see anything on the looms for the very good reason that there was nothing there. But, of course, he did not know this and thought only that he must be a foolish man unfit for the office of canon to the ordinary. "Dear me," he said to himself, "I must never tell anyone that I could not see the cloth."

"Well, Reverend Canon Sir, does our work please you?" asked one of the weavers. Adjusting his spectacles, the canon to the ordinary said quickly, "Oh it is most beautiful. Yes, I will go the bishop at once and tell him how very wonderful I think it is."

The bishop was pleased by the report brought by his canon to the ordinary and soon sent the cathedral dean to find out how soon the vestments would be ready. It was, of course, just the same with the dean as it had been with the canon to the ordinary. He looked at the looms on all sides but could see nothing at all but the empty frames.

"Do not the vestments appear as beautiful to you, Very Reverend Dean, as they did to the canon to the ordinary?" asked the men.

"I certainly am not theologically inept," thought the cathedral dean. "It must be that I am not fit for the very good and comfortable office I hold. That is very odd indeed. However, no one shall ever know anything about it." And at once he turned to the robbers and praised the material he could not see. He then returned at once to the bishop and said, "Indeed, Your Grace, the vestments which the weavers are making are extraordinarily magnificent."

And now at last the bishop himself wished to see the marvelous cope and miter being fashioned for him. He took with him a few of his other canons, along with the canon to the ordinary and the cathedral dean. As soon as the false weavers heard the bishop coming, they worked away harder than ever, though they still did not weave a single thread though the empty looms.

"Is not the cloth magnificent?" asked the canon to the ordinary and the cathedral dean as the party reached the cathedral basement.

"How is this?" said the Bishop to himself, "I can see nothing! This is indeed terrible! Am I theologically incompetent or am I unfit to be bishop?"

"Oh! The vestments are beautiful!" he cried out loud. "I am delighted with them." And he smiled most charmingly for on no account would he say that he could not see what his canon to the ordinary and cathedral dean had praised so much.

All his entourage now strained their eyes hoping to see something in the looms, but they could see no more than the others. Nevertheless, they all exclaimed, "How beautiful!" and advised the bishop to wear them at the great Easter day celebration at the cathedral.

When the vestments were pronounced complete, the bishop and the entire diocesan staff came to see the weavers' work. The false Almy representatives raised their arms as though they were holding up something to be seen and said, "Here is the alb! Here is the chasuble! Here is the stole and cope and miter! They are all light as a cobweb. When dressed in these vestments, one might fancy that one has on nothing at all. That, however, is the wonderful thing about this delicate magic cloth." And all the bishop's staff nodded enthusiastically, though not one of them could see anything at all.

On Easter morning, before the great procession through the cathedral was to take place, the bishop entered the sacristy to be vested by the rogue weavers. He undressed and the weavers pretended to help him into his vestments. The altar party all cried out, "How splendid the bishop looks in his new vestments! What beautiful colors! What a design! They are indeed princely robes!"

The verger announced to the bishop that it was time for the great procession to begin. The verger led the procession, followed by the thurifer, the crucifer, the acolytes, the choir of men and boys, various canons including the canon to the ordinary, the subdeacon, the deacon, the cathedral dean, and finally the bishop himself. The entire congregation turned to face the bishop as he began his grand entrance through the nave.

"Oh, how beautiful are our bishop's new vestments!" the people cried. "How gracefully the cope sits upon his shoulders!" In fact, no one would admit that he or she could not see the vestments that everyone seemed to think so beautiful for fear of being called a simpleton or unfit for office.

Suddenly, as the majestic opening hymn drew to a close and there was a moment of silence before the opening acclamation, a young chorister spoke. "But the bishop has no vestments on at all!!" And so it was that what the child said was whispered from one worshiper to another until all knew and the congregation cried out, "But he has no vestments on at all!!!"

The bishop felt very silly for he knew the congregation was right. But he thought, "The liturgy has started and it must now go on." So the various liturgical functionaries held their heads higher than ever and took great trouble to pretend to fuss with vestments that weren't there at all.

PART VI

SURVIVING THE CLERGY

Clergy, like parishes, come in all shapes and sizes. Whenever I find myself at a gathering of clergy, I find myself thinking, "Wow! Some of these people are actually my colleagues!" Of course I also find myself thinking, "Wow. Some of these people are actually my colleagues." I'm sure the feeling is mutual.

The calling to ordained ministry gets played out in many ways and, collectively, we embody much that's right in the Church. Individually, however, we can be challenging. The real danger, or sin if you want to go in that direction, is the God-complex. When you start taking yourself too seriously, you're sunk. As is your poor congregation.

I once heard of a priest (okay, a pastor—he was Lutheran) who came out on a throne during the Christmas pageant. He was supposed to be the grown up, resurrected Jesus. I mean, you wouldn't want a cute baby stealing your limelight.

Anyway, for clergy, humility is the key component for healthy ministry. And from a parishioner perspective, realizing your clergy are human makes all the difference.

What Rectors Really Do

Based on a couple of comments from our then ten-year-old son, Zak, I decided to write a job description for what rectors really do. He once told me my job was lame because all I do is "wear dresses and pray all day," which pretty much sums up priestly ministry. A few days later he amended this description by announcing that all I do is "type, stand up, and talk." Again, not a bad summary.

But of course I do so much more than this on a daily basis—like drink coffee. So here's the full rector job description as it gets lived out in parishes throughout the world. Wardens and vestries take note.

What a Rector Really Does

- Wait for the mail man to arrive bearing handwritten notes from parishioners saying how great you are. Since this always leads to disappointment, rectors wait for the next best thing: pledge cards and the clergy haberdashery catalog.
- Fantasize about ordering fancy vestments handmade by English monks.
- Sit in front of office computer with e-mail open and repeatedly hit send/reply.
- Type stuff on iPad/laptop that may or may not be relevant to parish ministry.
- Drink coffee. Repeat.
- Go out on "pastoral calls" to the beach and/or local pub.
- Use caller ID to screen calls from problem parishioners.
- Walk around the church campus smiling benignly at people.
- Wonder who's playing in the early NFL game while parishioners talk at you during coffee hour.
- Eat, pray, love. In that order.

- Ask secretary to make another pot of coffee.
- Have lunch with a rich parishioner. Then act surprised when they insist on paying as you make a show of slowly reaching for your wallet.
- Delete e-mails you don't want to deal with and then claim you never received them. Repeat as needed.
- Allow your eyes to glaze over during the treasurer's report at vestry meetings.
- At weddings, preach the same homily you wrote as a curate lo those many years ago.
- Outwardly thank parishioners who enthusiastically give you a cross they brought back from their recent trip to _____ while inwardly wishing for a good bottle of scotch.
- Remember to "invite" the curate to preach on Trinity Sunday.
- Cower in your private bathroom when you hear the Altar Guild Directress calling your name.
- During liturgies, use your mind to will the organist to play hymns at a quicker tempo but never actually discuss it.
- Do the royal wave when you see a gaggle of elderly volunteers folding the Sunday bulletins but . . . Don't. Ever. Stop.
- Drink sherry while sitting on the leather sofa in your anteroom, but never before 10:00 a.m.
- Leave notes for the sexton but never actually have a conversation with him. Nothing good ever comes of it.
- Work on your "stained-glass voice" or faux British accent but only after hours when no one is in ear shot.
- Say things like "Good morning!" and "Nice to see you!" on the receiving line after services when you have no idea who you're greeting.
- Tell people you have "diocesan responsibilities" when seeking to avoid parochial drudgery.
- Model clergy wellness by leaving the office at 3:30 p.m. each day and taking two months off during the summer.
- Suggest the youth group service project involves washing and waxing the rector's car.

- Convince yourself that wasting time on Facebook is "virtual ministry."
- Keep your office door shut and tell your secretary to "hold all my calls" to give the illusion that you're working on a profoundly intellectual sermon so you can play solitaire in peace.

If your own parish is searching for a new rector, you may want to go tweak that parish profile and then actually check those references.

Clergy Rating (CR) System

While statisticians using cybermetrics have taken sports by storm, clergy have generally remained unscathed by unbiased rating systems. With the ever-popular and hotly debated Quarterback Rating used to determine a passer's performance, I'm advocating for a similar tool to judge a cleric's Sunday morning performance. I call it the Clergy Rating (or CR) System.

After all, why should Monday morning quarterbacking be the exclusive domain of football fans? If you can't critique your clergy around the water cooler on Monday morning, why even bother going to church on Sunday?

Here's how it works: the priest is judged in two broad categories over which they have vast control—liturgy and preaching—and then several minor categories such as acolyte attentiveness and dress, attendance, quality of the coffee at coffee hour, etc. The CR is weighted most heavily in the two major categories, but decent liturgy and an excellent sermon will still get dragged down slightly by poor quality incense, an acolyte wearing purple Converse high-tops, and so on.

A perfect score is 100. Liturgy counts for 40 percent, preaching for 40 percent, and everything else adds up to 20 percent of the score. Simple, right? Even math-challenged Trinitarians (1+1+1=1) can figure this out. And because there is a degree of subjectivity (but only a little), the new CR will make great fodder for Monday morning talk radio ("Bob in Brewster completely disagrees with our assessment that Fr. Smith had a good day behind the altar: 'Are you kidding me? He totally bungled the breaking of the bread!'").

To give you an idea of how this works in practice, I'll rate a Sunday morning performance from a service I attended last summer while on vacation at an undisclosed location. The cleric in question received a CR of 64. Here's how the rating was derived:

Liturgy: 23 (out of 40). I have to say that 23 was generous. Points were deducted for not wearing a chasuble (It doesn't matter if it's 100 degrees; inappropriate liturgical attire is an automatic 5 point deduction); forgetting the words of the Collect for Purity and having to find reading glasses to finish it (3 point deduction); the Peace was basically a group hug and lasted at least as long as the sermon (4 point deduction); sloppy or untoward manual acts (4 point deduction); and stumbling over the words of institution (1 point deduction).

Preaching: 31 (out of 40). Overall a decent sermon for the middle of August. Points were deducted for an annoying hair flip habit in the pulpit; laughing at her own (mediocre) joke; and using a hint of a "stained-glass voice."

Other: 10 (out of 20). I didn't take off for the low attendance—again, it was August. But points were deducted for the usher who grunted at me when handing me a bulletin (2 points); the adult acolyte who fell asleep during the sermon (3 points); and the lack of coffee at "coffee hour" (you can't just have lemonade!—5 point deduction for false advertising).

I hope this little lesson has been helpful as you begin to calculate your own priest's CR at Sunday morning liturgies. Remember, clergy should always be judged, subjected to harsh critique, and then talked about behind their backs, especially during coffee hour. This all helps to build up the body of Christ.

And hey, if you can't stand the heat, get out of the sacristy.

Clergy Beards

Most male priests have facial hair. It's true. Think of the first five priests that come to mind. How many of them have mustaches, beards, or goatees? Bishops? I've never served in a diocese with clean-shaven episcopal oversight, though in Massachusetts it was the suffragan (assisting) bishop rather than the diocesan bishop.

In seminary, most of my male professors had beards and the dean had a mustache. I guess it's the scholarly look, but it wasn't limited to the faculty. In my graduating class I was one of only a handful of students not sporting facial hair by the time diplomas were handed out.

The Anglican roots of this facial hair phenomenon run deep. Henry VIII, the self-proclaimed "Protector and Supreme Head" of the Church of England, had a full beard. Edward VI, whose reign saw the institution of the first Book of Common Prayer, didn't, but of course he died before reaching puberty. Thomas Cranmer, author of that first BCP, was clean-shaven but then, he was also martyred. Queen Elizabeth didn't for obvious reasons. However, Richard Hooker, the man responsible for Anglicanism's "three-legged stool" of Scripture, tradition, and reason, had an abundance of whiskers.

To outsiders, diocesan clergy conferences must look like grooming conventions. I'm not sure why this is. Does facial hair give the impression that we're more learned than we actually are? I thought that's what horned-rim glasses were for, especially when they're eased down the bridge of the nose while making a profound homiletical point.

Over the years, I've discerned several types of clergy facial hair. First, there's the prophetic look. This beard is full, out of control, and trimmed only on Rogation Days. The only things missing are the John the Baptist–inspired locusts and wild honey. With a menacing glare, the priest walks a fine line between holy man and mad man. If you'd prefer not to be invited to wedding receptions, this may be the look for you.

Then there's the goatee. On younger clergy this gives the impression that the priest is both hip and stylish. It says "even though I'm a priest, I'm still cool. Really." If you wear one, you'll be asked to lead the youth group. On older priests the goatee, especially the fully gray one, means a tie-dyed stole lurks somewhere in the back of the sacristy, so look out for the folk mass.

The neat-nik priest is impeccably groomed. Whatever the type of facial hair, he travels with an electric trimmer and has perfect posture. He wouldn't be caught dead without a clergy shirt handmade in England and, in fact, will insist on being buried in it when the time comes.

Of course generations of younger clergy have sported beards to look older and, presumably, wiser. This crowd strokes them often during counseling sessions while making comments like, "uh huh . . . say more about that." I assume they shave them off when they reach a certain age.

In reflecting on this trend, I briefly decided to try some facial hair one summer. For the first thirty-four years of my life I had avoided whiskers, but I wanted to blend in at an upcoming diocesan convention. Bryna laughed at my little experiment and added helpful comments like "you'll never be able to make it connect," but I was not deterred and after a week of vacation, I had the start of a goatee.

The real test would be Sunday morning. Would my parishioners find newfound respect for a priest of such gravitas and stature or would they just shake their heads and roll their eyes? Maybe they wouldn't recognize me and mistake me for some supply priest filling in for the rector.

Actually, my congregation was split on the results—most liked it while some refused to comment for reasons of self-incrimination. A member of the youth group told me I looked "French," which was disheartening, but a former member of the vestry said it made me look "apostolic."

I'm still not sure what statement facial hair makes for clergy, I just know that many of my male counterparts have beards. Whether it makes them look older, wiser, more distinguished, or more clerical, I cannot say. We don't know for sure what Jesus looked like, but he's often portrayed with a beard and perhaps this is the subconscious allure for clergy who seek to emulate our Lord in all things.

In my case, Bryna was right, so I shaved it off.

Seminarian Skills Test

As seminarians look toward graduation and fantasize about wearing clerical collars for the first time, they are rudely roused from this reverie by realizing they must first find a job. At the same time, many parishes are seeking qualified new priests to do all the jobs the rector doesn't want to do.

While Christian Mingle would be one method of playing this dating game, I think taking a page from the National Football League makes better sense and would certainly be more entertaining. At the NFL Scouting Combine, the top pro prospects coming out of college are put through their paces under the watchful eyes of scouts for teams that may potentially draft them.

Naturally, I thought it would be helpful for the church to have a similar skills competition for graduating seminarians. This way, freshly minted clergy could show off their skills while hiring rectors, and search committees could get a sense of what they were getting before extending a call. Everybody wins, right?

Here are a few events through which parishes could judge (in a loving, divine mercy sort of way) their future clergy:

The Triangle

The marquee event at the NFL Combine is the forty-yard dash. It measures speed and explosiveness, two ingredients necessary to succeed in professional football. For seminarians, the most important event is The Triangle. At a simulated coffee hour, a "parishioner" holding a Styrofoam cup of decaf corners the seminarian and says, "Great sermon today! Your sermons are so much better than the rector's snooze-fests, don't you think? If you go tell the Senior Warden to insist Father Dim have you preach more often, I'll support you."

What do you do? Give a knowing nod of complicity and leave it at that? Approach the warden? Or say, "We all have different gifts, but I think it's important to hear regularly from Father Dim. I appreciate his approach to preaching but understand not everyone relates to every preacher. If this is such a concern for you, why don't you go talk to the warden? I see her right behind that plate of stale donuts."

Naming Rights

One hundred people you've never seen before file past you shaking your hand and saying "Good morning" and occasionally "Nice sermon." While they're all wearing name tags (this is hypothetical) on the first pass, they file past you again without name tags. How many can you name? How many do you even recognize? Did we mention they all change their clothes in between?

Preach It!

Each seminarian is asked to preach a sermon on the Trinity (they may as well get used to it). They begin with one hundred points. Points are deducted for: every second past the twelve-minute mark; annoying tics such as swaying back and forth like a metronome; use of any of the following words—paradigm, missional, multivalent, or *homoousious*; and doctrinal heresy. Thirty is considered an above average score.

Coffee Challenge

In order to properly prepare future clergy for long, drawn-out diocesan meetings, having to stay up late on a Saturday night to finish the sermon because they had a funeral and a wedding earlier that day, and early morning pastoral calls following a late vestry meeting, it is essential to test their coffee intake skills. Unlike the individual challenges, this is administered in a group setting.

A giant vat of coffee is set up in the middle of a mock parish hall. Contestants line the walls and at the command "The Lord be with you," the seminarians dash to the vat and attempt to consume Herculean (even though he's a pagan) amounts of black coffee. At the end of ten minutes, the winner will have consumed the most coffee (without dying).

These events should give congregations important insights into their future clergy while allowing would-be priests to get a foretaste of parish ministry.

Clergy Haberdashery

At most parishes, the letter carrier brings at least several clergy wear catalogues per month. Granted they're usually addressed to the previous rector, but they find their way into the hands of priests who like to look at themselves in the sacristy mirror. I'm less enamored with the clothing since I'm not into multicolored clergy shirts. I prefer mine the way I take my coffee: black.

Yet I'm always fascinated by the models they use for these catalogs. On the male side, there are two type casts: the buff young curate and the smooth silver-haired rector. The young "priests" look like guys you'd want to go have a drink with at McSorley's Pub but spiritual counseling? Not so much.

The women "clergy" either need an extreme makeover or are, well, hot. Which is kind of odd since it makes you wonder what other magazines and catalogs they model for? "Let's see on Monday it's the Almy shoot, then Tuesday and Wednesday I'll be doing Frederick's of Hollywood."

Facial expressions consist of either the cheesy coffee hour fake grin or a pseudo-pious, heavenward glance. And if you ever lay your hands on one of these catalogs (ask the parish secretary—she has stacks of them), I encourage you to check out the way both the men and women hold their hands—it's hilarious. The overly pious hand clasp is a hoot. The only variation is the strapping young guy in the ugly striped clergy shirt with one hand in his pocket and the other on his belt buckle. What are you Father Fonzie? Aaay!

Well, I guess *someone* has to model these things. It would look even odder if they were all draped on mannequins and, yes, I know, you've heard some priests who preach about as well as your average department store mannequin.

Sh*t Rectors Think (But Don't Say)

Talk about going viral. In 2009, a semiemployed comedy writer started a Twitter feed to record the often salty comments made by his father. Eventually this turned into a book titled *Sh*t My Dad Says,* which reached number one on the *New York Times* Bestseller List. It was subsequently turned into a very short-lived sit-com starring William Shatner, which you never heard of because it was a major flop.

I never read the book nor did I ever see the TV show, but the concept spawned all sorts of take-offs and parodies which I will leave you to Google since I'm not going to be responsible for endorsing any of the content. The title of this alone will likely get me into trouble with a certain set, but then they probably put this book down many chapters ago to write an indignant letter to my bishop. I guess I could have called it "Stuff Rectors Think" but that would lose the viral appeal of the coattails I'm shamelessly grabbing.

Sh*t Rectors Think (But Don't Say)

- Could the organist possibly play this hymn any slower? The "grace" is rapidly losing its amazingness.
- (During a pastoral counseling session) You think *you* have problems? Let me tell you about *mine*!
- I wonder how many more tedious vestry meetings I'll have to endure before I retire? Is there a Golden Number for this?
- Please stop the overly dramatic reading of the Epistle. It's not as if you wrote it yourself.
- I hope the bishop doesn't have any spies around here.
- I hope the bishop doesn't read this book.
- The homemade cookies are nice, but can't someone give the rector a nice bottle of bourbon for Christmas?
- How does a twit like Joel Osteen get tens of thousands of people

to show up on a Sunday morning while I'm lucky to get two or three hundred?

- (When visiting another church on a rare Sunday off) Why would anyone possibly come to this place?
- "What time is the Easter service?" does *not* qualify as a pastoral emergency. See you at Christmas.
- (Musing at coffee hour as you can't remember any names) Why is it that all children under the age of five look alike as do all gray-haired ladies?
- When does the Church Pension Fund kick in?
- Why don't they make homiletical candle snuffers to be used when the assistant/seminarian's sermon loses its focus?
- I wonder if we get Wi-Fi in the chancel?
- Must that guy in the fourth row be a split second behind on every congregational response? I wonder if I can summon an usher using mental telepathy to have him removed before the Nicene Creed?
- If you gave up that membership to the country club, maybe you'd be able to "afford" a pledge greater than $5 per week.
- A monkey could have done a better job arranging those flowers on the altar.
- It's not that the microphones "don't work as well as they did when Father XX was the rector," it's that you're going deaf.
- This meeting better end before "Modern Family" starts.

Rector's Press Conference

One of the stranger NFL rituals are coaches' postgame press conferences. These can be so comical that even Coors Light has parodied them in a series of ads featuring actual head coaches. This naturally led me to wonder why rectors don't have postliturgical press conferences.

For your reading pleasure, I have imagined one below. The setting is, of course, the parish hall, preferably at a table set up on the stage (it's not a real Episcopal Church if it doesn't have a stage—and 1950s-vintage partitions—but that's another matter altogether). The rector looks a bit harried with a warm glow of sweat across the brow. There's a chipped puke green mug on the table holding tepid coffee brewed in the undercroft. A group of parishioners is gathered around the stage eating donut holes and calling out questions.

Question: Father, overall how would you rate this morning's performance?

Rector: It was a bit sloppy at times, but as a worship team we stayed within ourselves and left it all out in the sanctuary. We're still in rebuilding mode with the acolytes and we have a lot of rookies out there this year. Right now I'm just worried about the liturgical chemistry.

Question: Some might question your focus on the Epistle during the sermon. What would you say to your critics?

Rector: I worked hard all week on that sermon, it went well during practice, and while the execution wasn't as smooth as I'd like, I stand by it theologically.

Question: But, Father, don't you think the transition between your second and third points could have been smoother?

Rector: If one of you laypeople think you could do a better job, go ahead. Next question.

Question: The ushers did nice work taking up the collection, but there seemed to be a bit of confusion with people coming up to communion. Would you comment on that?

Rector: With the depth chart, we're still looking at a lot of guys and gals at different spots. It didn't go precisely as we drew it up, but I really like our schemes. I don't know when we'll have it all exactly the way we want it, but we're headed in the right direction in my opinion.

Question: What did you think when the organist went up a fifth on the third verse of "Amazing Grace"?

Rector: Well that, frankly, came as a surprise. We'll deal with that issue internally. We just need to make sure everyone's on the same sheet of music, as it were.

Question: There seemed to be an unusual number of typos in the bulletin. Do you foresee any changes in this area?

Rector: We plan to stick with what we've got but omitting the last line of the Postcommunion Prayer is unacceptable. Believe me, I noticed this as well and I can assure you it won't happen again. There will be fines handed down, I'll tell you that.

Question: How ready do you think you'll be for next week?

Rector: Well, the propers are tough ones, but we'll just take it one Sunday at a time and evaluate at the end of the program year. The expectations are high but, to a person, everyone in this sacristy is geared to successfully praise the Lord each and every week.

Rector: That's all I have time for, folks. I have to get back to coffee hour and be ready to watch the 1:00 o'clock game in the comfort of the rectory family room.

PART VII

SURVIVING THE LITURGICAL YEAR

The liturgical hamster wheel goes round and round, and while it can feel like an endless cycle, there is also great comfort in this. Some clergy use this to their advantage by preaching the exact same sermons year after year. If you hear your priest reference the Clinton administration from the pulpit, that's a sure sign of homiletical laziness.

A Sort of Homecoming

There's no good name for it. The first Sunday of the vaunted program year, that is. For most congregations everything begins on the Sunday after Labor Day, though in the south it often starts in mid-August when the kids go back to school.

After a relatively quiet summer, everything cranks back up: Sunday school begins, the choir returns, lots of people show up, and there might even be a special all-parish brunch/cookout. The problem is that no one has come up with a decent name other than "XX Sunday after Pentecost." Liturgical purists think this is just fine but from a marketing perspective, you couldn't come up with anything less compelling to draw the faithful back to Mother Church.

Many churches go with "Kick Off Sunday," which works, I guess, when it coincides with the first Sunday of football season. You can kick off at church with communion and then kick off football season in your recliner with a beer. Cue the Gary Glitter.

At my own parish I inherited "Homecoming Sunday," which isn't too bad. Given the number of people who use "summer" as a verb around here, it's pretty accurate—they are quite literally "coming home."

This certainly beats the similar but far worse "Welcome Back Sunday." That's pretty much admitting that God goes on vacation in July and August and that no self-respecting churchgoer would dare be seen in church—whether or not they're in town. This goes with the unfortunate mentality that Episcopalians are the only ones God trusts enough to take the summer off.

But in my opinion, the worst phrase ever—popular in some Protestant churches—is "Rally Sunday." All I can think of is NASCAR: "Gentlemen, start your programs." Perhaps it makes sense if you hold church on the infield at Daytona, but anything less than that is unwarranted. For some reason it also conjures up images of demolition derbies for me. This may be more an insight into my limited knowledge of motor sports, but somehow the notion of a bunch of ministries jockeying for position and crashing into one another makes me smile.

The rock band U2 recorded a song in 1984 called "A Sort of Homecoming." The title—and the song—tends to run through my head during the first week of September. The line itself comes from the Romanian-born Jewish poet Paul Celan who wrote that "Poetry is a sort of homecoming."

At many churches, that's really what that first Sunday is—a "sort of homecoming." I doubt anyone went *too* far away during the summer and most of us never really left, at least emotionally. Even accounting for vacation time it's important to remember that God never takes a vacation from *us*.

After another fairly quiet summer, I always look forward to everything starting up again and lots of people like getting back into the routine. That first Sunday is always full of energy and anticipation and hope—kind of like the first day of school. I know I'll be harried soon enough and start pining for slower days, but the spiritual adrenaline rush and small moments of grace keep us all going throughout the rest of the year.

Of course, if you have a better name for that first Sunday back, by all means pass it along. Otherwise I may just give in and hold a stock car race on the church's front lawn.

How to Market Advent Lessons and Carols

For many people it's just not Advent until they attend a service of Lessons and Carols. This beloved liturgy has deep roots in the Anglican musical tradition and evokes images of vested choirs, coped clergy, Advent wreaths, and a December chill in the air.

The service itself is structured on a liturgy first offered at the Chapel of King's College, Cambridge, England, in 1918. Almost immediately other churches adapted the service for their own use, but its popularity really began to grow when the service was first broadcast in 1928. With the exception of 1930, Advent Lessons and Carols has been broadcast annually from King's College, even during the Second World War.

At my own parish, along with many other parishes, Advent Lessons and Carols ranks as one of the liturgical highlights of the entire year. Now if you're trying to draw people to your own sublimely beautiful and well-planned Advent Festival of Lessons and Carols, I have some tips.

How to Market Advent Lessons and Carols

- We steadfastly refuse to admit any holiday festivity so kindly leave the Christmas sweater and reindeer brooch at home. The ushers will remove any Santa hats they spot with an air of righteous indignation.
- You'll get to sing/mumble your way through unfamiliar Advent hymns and listen to Advent carols no one recognizes.
- Yes, there are scary prophetic readings, but they're always undercut with a tuneful anthem (that you won't recognize) following each one.
- Prior to the service be sure to Google "why is there a pink candle in the Advent wreath."

- Listen to Americans and Brits fight over the pronunciation of Isaiah (eye-ZAY-uh vs. eye-ZEYE-uh).
- Fire hazards abound. Fortunately the liturgy is about as interesting as watching wax drip.
- This is the one time during the year we let that crazy lady with the British accent read a lesson.
- It's fun to play spot the fake garland. It's like Where's Waldo, only easier.
- Keep waiting for someone to read Ezekiel's passage about the Valley of Dry Bones until you remember that happens at the Easter Vigil not Lessons and Carols.
- Judge the abilities of the various lectors and hold a grudge against the rector for not utilizing your superior reading abilities.
- Take bets during the car ride to church over whether the parish secretary remembered to change the date on the bulletin from last year.
- No sermon. Though most clergy make up for this by adding in a nonrubrical "announcements" section in order to "preach" about their upcoming schedule of Christmas services.
- The reception following the liturgy is stale crackers and cheap wine. It's a meeting point between Lent (no refreshments) and Christmas (festive food).
- Clergy who attend will come to blows arguing over whether or not the vestments and hangings are the "correct" Advent color.
- Episcopalians who like to ignore Marian devotion can scowl through hymns about our Blessed Mother.

I guarantee that if you take out a full page ad in the local paper listing these reasons to attend your service of Lessons and Carols, you'll need to hire some crowd control thugs off of Craigslist.

The Jesse Tree—Exploded

Advent is a time for many devotions unique to the season. One such tradition is the Jesse Tree. I'd like to take this opportunity to build upon this concept. To get you in the mood, cue Rick Springfield's "Jessie's Girl" and pretend it's 1981.

But first, as you may know, the Tree of Jesse refers to a passage from Isaiah where the prophet describes the descent of the Messiah from Jesse of Bethlehem through his son David. We sing about this in the well-known hymn "O Come, O Come Emmanuel" in this verse:

> O come, Thou Rod of Jesse, free
> Thine own from Satan's tyranny;
> From depths of hell Thy people save,
> And give them victory over the grave.

The concept of making a Jesse Tree during Advent is a relatively recent and popular children's activity. There are various websites that teach you how to make one either at home or with a Sunday school class. There's no "right way" to do this, but the basic concept is to adorn either a poster or a real tree with symbols of biblical stories as you count down the days until Christmas.

Fine. One year, in my pre-Christmas haze (a blur of bulletins and sermon-writing and pastoral visits), I came up with several alternatives to the standard Jesse Tree.

The Jesse Jackson Tree

Why shouldn't the civil rights leader and political activist have his own devotional? He was the first African American to make a serious run for president, so he served as forerunner to Barack Obama. How Advent appropriate is that? Sure, Al Sharpton will be jealous, but I'm okay with that.

The Uncle Jesse Tree

When I was a kid my favorite TV show, by far, was the Dukes of Hazzard. Growing up in suburban Baltimore, I had a lot in common with two mischievous teens from rural Georgia who drove around in a car nicknamed The General Lee.

The Jesse Ventura Tree

This is a nod to my Midwestern friends. When the former wrestler became Governor Ventura, they were just so proud that he had become the spokesman for the entire region. Hang a picture of tuna hot dish over his left bicep and we'll be ready for Christmas in no time.

The Jesse James Tree

This is for the rebel that lurks deep within each one of us. The one that fantasizes about flipping over tables in the Temple and finally telling Aunt Gretchen that you really hate her fruitcake and would she please stop bringing one every year.

The Jesse from Full House Tree

If you're vain about your stylish mullet and are obsessed with Elvis, it makes sense to have a devotional inspired by John Stamos's character on this popular TV show.

Rules for Pageant Survival

If you've agreed to run this year's Christmas pageant, I applaud your enthusiasm. I also suggest you enter the witness protection program and never look back. Nonetheless, if you decide to forge ahead, in the true spirit of Christmas, here's some friendly advice on how to survive the annual Christmas pageant.

Father Tim's Rules for Pageant Survival

- Make sure you have enough wings for *all* the angels. Unless you have a high tolerance for the requisite high-strung angel meltdown.
- Shepherds' crooks make fine swords (even better than Palm Sunday palms).
- Don't give your young Melchior an actual flaming pot of frankincense.
- There's a fine line between angel and Barbie princess. Parents, please communicate this to your "little angel."
- No live animals. Two-year-old "sheep" cause enough chaos. Save this for the St. Francis Day Blessing of the Animals.
- If you go with a live baby Jesus, always have the Holy Doll standing by just in case.
- When you dim the lights and sing "Silent Night," don't give out individual candles to the children. Unless you have really good fire insurance.
- Make sure Joseph goes to the bathroom *before* the pageant begins.
- It's nice to wash those dish towels the shepherds wear on their heads at least once a decade.
- If you like liturgy done "decently and in order," go to the late service.

Actually, I think the pageant service is a more realistic celebration of our incarnational faith than Midnight Mass. Authentic relationship with God is more often messy and chaotic than it is dignified and beautifully choreographed. The important thing to remember is that it's not just chaos but "holy chaos." God's in the midst of it all; which is what Christmas is really all about anyway.

Episco-Bowls

Many of my clergy colleagues like to remind people, in righteously indignant ways, that Christmas is not a single day but a twelve-day season. Everybody already knows this because of that annoying song "The Twelve Days of Christmas."

College football fans know that this period coincides with bowl season. It used to be that you could tick off the big bowl games with no problem at all: Cotton, Orange, Sugar, Sun, and the "granddaddy of them all," the Rose Bowl. Now, with the explosion of both bowl games and their often obscure sponsors, it seems that getting into a bowl game is a God-given right for every mediocre football team in the nation.

It takes a true college football fan (or someone desperate to avoid interacting with their family) to get jazzed about the Meineke Car Care Bowl, the Franklin American Mortgage Bowl, the Chick-Fil-A Bowl, the Godaddy.com Bowl, or the Famous Idaho Potato Bowl.

With the plethora of bowl games out there, I wondered why the Episcopal Church should get left out of the old bowl game. Here are some potential sponsors and match-ups between Episcopal institutions to keep us going while we sit around insisting that Christmas is not over but just kicking off on December 25th.

The Taylor Tawny Port Bowl

Trinity College (CT) vs. Hobart and William Smith

What better way to honor the single most-used communion wine in the Episcopal Church? (Of age) undergrads hand out preconsecrated samples during halftime as we attempt to set the *Guinness Book of World Records* mark for largest communion liturgy (without a sermon).

The C.M. Almy Bowl

Kenyon College vs. Sewanee

The in-game referees are comprised of the male Almy catalog models looking particularly pious as they call that offensive holding penalty. The cheerleaders are made up of the female catalog models looking uncomfortable in ill-fitting female clergy shirts. The good news is that all paying customers are given a free Lenten array stole. The bad news is that it's on back order.

The Usher Bowl

College of Preachers vs. College of Cardinals

This highly organized affair will insure everyone is seated before kickoff. On the off chance that a spectator is late, they won't be seated until the first timeout is called. Sure it's a bummer when the ushers pass the collection plate during halftime, but you can always choose that moment to satisfy your craving for nachos. Please note: despite the rumors, the recording artist Usher will not be performing during the halftime show.

The Bad Coffee in Styrofoam Cups Bowl

William and Mary vs. Voorhees College

Unique among bowl games, the BCSC Bowl is played neither in an open air stadium nor in a dome but in an ill-lit undercroft. This bowl usually peters out midway through the third quarter as the weak coffee puts spectators and players alike into a catatonic state. The parking lot is conveniently located adjacent to a landfill so fans can toss their cups away with full confidence that they will remain intact until the eschaton.

And, finally, the godfather of them all . . .

The Lent Madness Bowl

Scott Gunn vs. Tim Schenck

There's nothing like a little Lenten foreshadowing featuring the two members of the self-proclaimed Supreme Executive Committee during the Christmas season to get people excited about Lent Madness. The AstroTurf is painted purple in honor of this upcoming season of repentance—sure this, along with the purple football, make it hard to track on TV, but who said the Christian life was easy? Fans cast their votes online (one vote per person!) to determine whether the halftime show will feature local clergy engaged in synchronized self-flagellation or Tim and Scott challenging one another in a Family Feud–style Prayer Book rubric violation quiz show.

I hope you enjoy yourself during this year's bowl season. And, remember, when you're at that Alabama vs. Notre Dame National Championship party, don't pronounce "Notre Dame" with a French accent. It'll make you look like an amateur.

Top Reasons Why the Magi Were So Late

As everyone knows, we celebrate the arrival of the Magi to the manger on January 6th, the Feast of the Epiphany. Well, unless your only contact with the Christmas story is an annual pageant in which case you believe they arrived right after the shepherds on Christmas Eve. Don't get me started on the way we jumble the story at pageants (the shepherds and wise men never meet!). But I sure won't be the one to tell the pageant director (and the parents) that there won't be any frankincense this year.

The reality is that, according to Scripture, the Magi arrived twelve days later. Perhaps by then Jesus was sleeping through the night (let's face it, that first night might have been holy but, as any parent knows, there was surely nothing "silent" about it).

Anyway, this got me wondering about what kept the three kings from making an on-time arrival. I scoured many sources at the Vatican library and came up with the following possibilities:

- Balthazar took forever doing his hair while Caspar and Melchior sat on their camels and stewed.
- The holiday traffic on the way into Bethlehem was dreadful.
- Four words: goats in the road.
- The Star of Bethlehem (the original GPS) kept saying "recalculating" and they found themselves in a sketchy part of town.
- Caspar drank way too much water at the first oasis, which meant an extra-long stop at the Molly Pitcher rest area.
- Untying fancy sandals to go through the TSA checkpoint took a long time. Retying them took *forever*.
- Due to poor behavior on the part of the other two kings, Melchior had to pull over more than once to yell, "If you don't stop fighting, I'm going to turn this caravan right around!"

- Stopping at the Holiday Inn slowed them down because, in a precursor to today's "culture wars," Balthazar kept insisting the name should be changed to "Christmas Inn."
- "I told you that stop at Herod's house was a waste of time."
- They took a vote and decided to take their sweet time getting to the manger so they would have a day all to themselves on the church calendar.

The Twelve Days of Christmas
The "Real" True Meaning Plus Bonus Snark Edition

During the Twelve Days of Christmas, your Uncle Ralph will undoubtedly forward you several e-mails about the alleged "meaning" behind the traditional carol "The Twelve Days of Christmas." While this is my least favorite Christmas song (shades of "99 Bottles of Beer on the Wall"), there is compelling evidence that this was composed as an underground catechetical ditty. So the Four Calling Birds refer to the four Gospels, the Six Geese a-Laying symbolize the six days of creation, and so on.

Of course there's equally compelling evidence that this is complete baloney. See the supposed meanings and the debunking on Snopes.com.

Whatever you believe, I have actually done some exhaustive research (and by "exhaustive" I mean that I'm still completely exhausted from all the Christmas services last year), and have uncovered the "real" true meaning behind this carol.

The Twelve Days of Christmas

(the "Real" True Meaning)

A Partridge in a Pear Tree—the rector hiding in a tree from coffee hour complaints.

Two Turtle Doves—the two parishioners comprising the parish Peace and Justice Committee.

Three French Hens—the three French ladies who sit in the front row every year at Midnight Mass.

Four Calling Birds—four members of the Commission on Ministry.

Five Gold Rings—five bishops caucusing at the House of Bishops meeting.

Six Geese a-Laying—six seminarians laying homiletical eggs in the pulpit.

Seven Swans a-Swimming—seven baptisms at the Easter Vigil, stretching the liturgy to three hours.

Eight Maids a-Milking—eight members of the hospitality committee bringing nondairy creamer to coffee hour.

Nine Ladies Dancing—the one and only time liturgical dance appeared at St. Swithin's.

Ten Lords a-Leaping—inserted into the new Christmas Pageant from the avant-garde director.

Eleven Pipers Piping—the eleven funerals last year that concluded with a bagpiper playing "Amazing Grace."

Twelve Drummers Drumming—the "drumming circle" used at the ill-fated "contemporary worship service."

The Twelve Days of Christmas

(Bonus Snark Edition)

Twelve Drummers Drumming until your ears start to bleed and please get rid of that Little Drummer Boy while you're at it.

Eleven Pipers Piping "Amazing Grace" since that's all they seem to know.

Ten Lords-a-Leaping which is heretical since there's only one Lord.

Nine Ladies (liturgically) **Dancing** in outfits made of pink chiffon streamers so you'll want to avert your eyes.

Eight Maids-a-Milking but don't drink the milk because it's neither pasteurized nor homogenized so there are chunks floating in it.

Seven Swans-a-Swimming in the church basement because the sexton forgot to turn the water off and the pipes froze.

Six Geese-a-Laying goose poop all over the front lawn of the church so parishioners have to scrape it off before walking in late and disrupting the gospel procession.

Five Gold Rings or actually just one because you pawned the other four to cover the budget deficit.

Four Calling Birds which are really annoying when they wake you up way too early on New Year's Day after a late night out.

Three French Hens although you'd much prefer French fries.

Two bars of Dove soap shaped like Turtles that you can't wait to regift.

And a Partridge in a Pear Tree which looks more like a pigeon than anything else.

Valentine's Day "Advice"

One of the great advantages of being a priest is that you can give your beloved leftover funeral flowers for Valentine's Day. Jam some candle nubs that don't really fit into your candelabra and set them on your table alongside some stale donuts from last Sunday's coffee hour and voila! A romantic, low-cost dinner.

But if you really want to spice things up with your Valentine next year, try this: show up to dinner at that cozy bistro dressed as the martyred St. Valentine. He was evidently beaten and stoned before his beheading at the hand of the Roman emperor for marrying couples in the Christian faith. So, depending on how realistic you want to make this, it might get a bit messy. Perhaps a simple Steve Martin arrow-through-the-head prop would suffice. Though maybe you should just stick to the roses and either borrow a red cassock from the acolyte room or, if you're a priest, wear that seldom-used red chasuble hanging in the back of the sacristy closet.

Around Valentine's Day I always find it helpful to reflect upon the *real* St. Valentine. Actually, there's some confusion over this since there appears to have been more than one St. Valentine. The feast of St. Valentine was first established in 496 to mark the death of *a* St. Valentine on February 14th but even then it seems to have been a day to mark several martyred saints sharing the name Valentinus.

Nonetheless, the modern feast day likely commemorates the St. Valentine who was a priest in Rome during the reign of Claudius II (260–270 AD). He was arrested for marrying Christian couples and assisting those facing persecution—a crime in those days. Valentine tried to convert the emperor and was put to death.

It wasn't until the fourteenth century in England that the feast started to become a celebration of romantic love. The poet Geoffrey Chaucer is often credited with bringing together the romantic imagery of blooming spring flowers and birds choosing their mates.

In *The Parliament of Fowles* Chaucer's was the first mention of St. Valentine in a love poem.

None of this should actually matter to Episcopalians since Valentine doesn't appear on our official Calendar of Saints. Indeed we commemorate Cyril and Methodius on February 14th—a pair of ninth-century Greek brothers who were missionaries to the Slavs—rather than Valentine.

The good news in this for forgetful husbands/boyfriends is that if you forget to pick up flowers, you can always give your beloved a copy of *War and Peace* by Slavic author Leo Tolstoy or dramatically read a poem by Vaclav Havel.

Ode to a Copier

During Holy Week, Christians throughout the world journey from the agony of crucifixion to the joy of resurrection. It is, of course, the most significant time in the liturgical year and the very heart of our faith. Yet we must also pause and give thanks for the unsung heroes of this whole operation: the hardworking parish copiers and those who dutifully operate them.

When the copier inevitably jams or runs out of toner or stops working altogether in the midst of cranking out the Easter Vigil bulletin, it is the parish secretary who stands on the front lines of Holy Week. He or she lovingly coaxes this essential machine or screams at it or sings incantations over it. While it's true that Easter never failed to arrive on account of a broken Xerox machine, these beasts of burden are taxed to the limit during this holy time and in the process, much hair either turns gray or is yanked out by the roots.

Ode to a Copier:
A Prayer for Holy Week

Holy Week, dear friends, will soon draw nigh;
From Trinity, Boston to All Saints', Tenafly.
Parish secretaries and their rectors, too,
Thinking of the bulletins that will ensue,

Drop to their knees and begin to quake,
Praying their copiers will stay awake
Through Maundy Thursday and the rest;
Without behaving as if possessed.

Rectors wonder with uncertainty,
"Should I have purchased the extended warranty?"
Misfeeds, toner woes, and a paper jam
Always seem to accompany the Paschal Lamb.

Why this happens is a great unknown,
A mystery worthy of the bishop's throne.
So stoke the incense, say your prayers;
anything to stave off copier repairs.

As the dark shadows of Tenebrae now approach;
may your copier behave without reproach.
And as we begin the Good Friday fast,
May it wait 'til Low Sunday to breathe its last.

Hooray for Holy Week!

Holy Week is all about drama and passion and profound encounters with the divine. Naturally this means I've written lyrics for "Hooray for Holy Week." It is, of course, sung to the tune of "Hooray for Hollywood." Think Doris Day combined with Dorothy Day and you get the idea.

> **Hooray for Holy Week**
> Hooray for Holy Week
> That unnervingly liturgically Holy Week
> Where every acolyte and young curate
> Hopes to endure it, without undue repression
> Where any verger can make a merger
> If he processes without transgression.
>
> Hooray for Holy Week
> If Church annoys you, turn the other cheek
> Where anyone at all from TV's Osteen
> To the Pope's rood screen, is so equally unique
> Go out and try your best, before the Christ's arrest
> Hooray for Holy Week.
>
> Hooray for Holy Week
> When all the clergy always like to speak
> They come from all the seminaries
> With their breviaries, as if by divine right
> All dolled up in very fancy vestments
> the holy aura of their halo bright.
>
> Hooray for Holy Week
> "Hosanna," "Crucify," then wash those feet.
> If you can cross yourself and genuflect

You'll join with the Elect, and liturgical elite
And then come Sunday, you'll want to go hide away
Hooray for Holy Week.

Unholy Trinity

Ahhhh. Trinity Sunday. That day in the church year when we celebrate the mystery of the "one in three and three in one" that embodies the fullness of God. And the day when every rector in all of Christendom scrambles to find a seminarian to preach. Or a curate. Or anyone who is closer to the theological gymnastics of the seminary experience.

I recently asked my Facebook friends to send me key phrases of Trinitarian minutia that often wind up in sermons preached on Trinity Sunday. I then prayerfully combined them into a Trinity Sunday Homilette.

Before I share the text, I should note that the key to good preaching on Trinity Sunday is linguistic sleight of hand. If you distract the congregation with enough props, they won't pay attention to the heresy you're undoubtedly spewing, which in turn lowers the potential of being reported to the bishop.

Trinity Sunday Sermon

"The New Paradigm of Homoousious"

In the name of the Father and of the Son and of the Holy Spirit. (And I really mean it this time).

The Trinity [three intertwined circles appear on a giant projection screen]. It's a confusing topic; one that I am not qualified to speak about because I failed the systematic theology portion of the

General Ordination Exam. [Three circles morph into a green three-leaf clover.] St. Patrick converted the King of Ireland to the Christian faith by using the clover [use awkward hand gesture to point to the screen]. As he held up the clover he enumerated (or is that remunerated?) about the Trinity telling the king that . . . [choir sings St. Patrick's Breastplate to drown out the next few phrases. Twelve minutes later when the hymn ends and everyone has processed around the church nine times, the preacher continues].

The interplay between the Persons of the Trinity is like a dance. But not just any dance—a perichoretic dance of love. I once danced this way at a wedding of a good friend. My date left with a groomsman while I was doing my interpretive dance of the Trinity. It was at that moment that I decided to go to seminary.

But I digress. Where was I? Oh, the interpenetration of modality. Which sounds vaguely obscene until you remember that God loves you. Like a fox. But in a coeternal, coequal, cohabitating kind of way.

Did I mention I used to be a horrible acolyte back in the day? [After laughing at his own joke, preacher picks up three tapers and attempts to bring them together and then pull them apart. Unfortunately he sets the pulpit hanging on fire and puts them out with the three glasses of water he brought up to supplement the fire illustration in case it fell flat. He recovers by singing an a capella version of "Holy, Holy, Holy," dramatically miming the line "Casting down their golden crowns around the glassy sea."]

In sum, we are all called to a hermeneutic of being immortal and invisible while still being led by faith and not by sight. Let me end by quoting from the well-loved Athanasian Creed; so beloved in church lore that it's relegated to page 864 of the Book of Common Prayer. In the "Historical Documents" section that you may have covertly perused earlier in the sermon.

"Blah, blah, blah Unity, blah, blah, blah Godhead, blah, blah, blah Essence."

Amen.

Top Ten Reasons NOT to Go to Church in the Summer

It happens every year. The weather warms up and all across America churches empty out. It's different in places like Martha's Vineyard or Key West where congregations swell with the summer population, but for the rest of us attendance drops dramatically, especially in more affluent communities. Rather than ignore this trend, I thought I'd help everyone justify the behavior.

1. **It's Not Air-Conditioned**
   True. But I believe Jesus said to the disciples in the Garden of Gethsemane, "Could you not sweat with me one hour?" Or something to that effect. Plus bulletins make terrific personal fans. If you're lucky, your spouse/child/pew mate will make you feel like pharaoh by fanning you throughout the service. I keep waiting for a father-of-the-bride to donate air-conditioning for the church in time for his daughter's August wedding. It hasn't happened yet, but there's a brass plaque I'm just itching to put on an air duct in honor of said family.

2. **I Have a Boat**
   Of course you do. If you live on the South Shore of Boston like I do, everyone seems to. Boats are great—Jesus spent a lot of time on boats since his disciples were mostly fishermen. He preached from them, calmed storms in them, and walked on water toward them. Come to church this summer before launching your boat and I guarantee you'll hear at least one biblical story involving boats and/or water.

3. **The Lawn Needs Mowing**
   What, your teenager isn't mowing your lawn just to pitch in around the house and demonstrate his/her love for you? Mowing your lawn on Sunday morning is a sure way to annoy the neighbors. And when you want to add that mother-in-law suite onto the

back of the house you sure want their support. Don't risk it; come to church and save the lawn for later.

4. **The Kids Have a Game in Fill-in-the-Blank Town**

Summer travel teams are both fun and demanding. For a couple of years both of my boys played summer baseball, which meant I spent much of my free time on mosquito-infested fields. When games take place on Sunday mornings, tell the kids about Sandy Koufax. The Dodger great refused to pitch Game 1 of the 1965 World Series because it was Yom Kippur. He stood up for his faith and his team still won the championship. They won't like it, but it will make a lasting impression.

5. **There's Church in the Summer?**

Yup. Every Sunday morning just like the rest of the year.

6. **I'm Away for the Weekend**

That's great—I hope you have a relaxing time. And I bet there is even a small Episcopal church nearby. Look for one of those red, white, and blue "The Episcopal Church Welcomes You" signs or use Google and your GPS to guide you into a pew on Sunday morning.

7. **There's No Sunday School**

You can't teach kids to eat out in a restaurant if you never take them to one. The same holds true for appropriate church behavior. As for older kids who are "bored" during the service, send them to the acolyte master (assuming he/she is around during the summer) to get suited up for some gentle on-the-job training. The summer is a great time to learn the acolyting ropes.

8. **I Gave Up Summer Church for Lent**

I don't believe that's an "approved" Lenten discipline. But if you're simply not in the habit of going to church in the summer, this is the year to break it! Amaze and inspire your friends as you receive the spiritual refreshment that comes with regular church attendance. Don't be surprised if people start coming up to you and saying, "You look great! Have you lost weight?" And you'll be able to respond with "I look fabulous because I've been going to church during the summer."

9. **I'd Rather Be Outside**

Well, we'll be sure to keep the windows open so you can see the beauty of the earth from your pew. Maybe we'll move coffee hour outdoors on nice days, but the good news is you won't need to put on sunscreen before church. And, as far as I know, no one has been eaten by black flies during the liturgy.

10. **I Have a 9:00 a.m. Tee Time**

Perfect. Come to the 8 o'clock service. The thirty-seven minutes you spend in church might even help your game. The 8 o'clock is actually a great option during the summer for people who want to get a jump on the day, get out to the beach, take a hike, go boating, or whatever. You can experience the beauty of Elizabethan English and then speak to one another in thee's and thou's the rest of the day.

I hope you've found a good reason on this list to stay away from church until after Labor Day. It's really no big deal if you don't show up during the summer. It's just Jesus, after all.

Top Ten Reasons TO Go to Church in the Summer

As the school year (and its poor stepchild the church program year) wind down, attendance starts to dwindle in congregations throughout the land. Clergy often rail against this with guilt-inducing phrases like "God never takes a vacation," which really means "I never get a vacation." Actually there are actually several advantages to attending church in the dog days of summer.

1. **Ample Parking**
   Tired of having to walk from the hinterland areas of the parking lot? Annoyed that Sunday morning has suddenly morphed into a forced death march with toddlers and a ruck sack full of goldfish? During the summer you can arrive one minute before the liturgy begins and get VIP parking right next to the front door.

2. **Speed Mass**
   What really adds to the length of the service is all those people waiting to receive the Eucharist. In the summer, you march right up to the communion rail and by the time you've returned to your pew, the priest is halfway through the postcommunion prayer.

3. **Supply Clergy**
   Have you grown tired of listening to your rector preach week after week? In the summer you get to hear a variety of voices from the pulpit while he/she is on vacation. Never mind that the key to engaging supply clergy is to find the worst preacher in your entire diocese—this way the congregation will find a new appreciation for your own ministry.

4. **Exercise While You Pray**
   If you're looking to build up your beach body for the postchurch outing to the ocean, summer church blends perfectly with your fitness goals. Since it's hot as Hades in there, you'll be furiously

waving your bulletin in front of your face to keep cool. This builds arm strength and creates bulging biceps—and all in the name of the Lord!

5. **Lower Your Anxiety**

Have you ever been frightened to the point of diving under the pew when the priest breaks that large wafer because you thought it was a gunshot? With such high humidity, you won't even notice, since the wafer bends like a Whoopee Pie rather than snapping like a Wheat Thin.

6. **Lose Weight**

Since it's already a zillion degrees in the church (see #4), consider wearing a wet suit to worship. Some people spend thousands of dollars on saunas to lose weight. All you have to do is show up and sit, kneel, stand, cross yourself, walk to communion, go to coffee hour, etc.

7. **Ceiling Fans**

Bored during the never-ending sermon by the supply priest? (see #3) Ceiling fans can mesmerize adults as well as young children. Who cares that they never seem to be doing anything but circulating hot air?

8. **Nag the Priest**

With fewer people around, you have a better opportunity to share your deep pastoral issues with the clergy thirty seconds before the opening procession begins.

9. **Less Likely to Be Asked to Join a Committee**

Since many church committees go on hiatus during the summer, you won't have to avoid the committee chairs when you see them before the service or at the post office.

10. **Bloody Marys at Coffee Hour**

Oh, your church doesn't offer this option? Talk to the rector about instituting this practice. Preferably just before the opening procession.

Get Out of Church!

God is under house arrest. Or at least our usual pattern of Sunday morning worship might lead someone to that conclusion. We're often guilty of the Martha Stewart approach to ministry where God is free to move about our beautiful sanctuaries but a de facto monitoring bracelet keeps God safely ensconced within the four walls.

I'm not talking tent revival and I'm not suggesting every Sunday but holding worship outside even once a year can broaden our understanding of a God who can never be restricted to bricks and mortar.

Some of the most memorable moments happen outside the traditional bounds of the parish and many people have had profound spiritual experiences at off-site retreats, campsites, or house blessings. A service in a church courtyard or in a city square or on a lakefront or in a forest preserve shatters the false barrier that exists between the sacred and the secular, reminding us again that there is no secular world—it is all sacred because it is all created at God's hand.

For some reason, whenever I hold outdoor services I like it to rhyme. I've offered "Mass on the Grass" in the Memorial Garden and "Preach at the Beach," though I have yet to have "Prayer in Times Square."

Unfortunately during Preach at the Beach a few years ago, we had a little "incident." As we were setting up for the service at the beach along Hingham Harbor, I noticed a couple of guys about fifteen feet away. They appeared to have poles of some sort and I thought they might be ready to go clamming. Another person thought they were preparing to set up canvases to paint the idyllic, peaceful, postcard-like scene in front of them. But as I took a closer look, I realized that these guys were toting not clam rakes but shotguns.

When my freshly minted assistant priest walked up to inquire what they were doing—did I mention that I'm an excellent delegator?— she told them that we were about to have a church service with a bunch of young children and that we weren't expecting a shoot-out. They replied that they weren't expecting a church service and started placing decoys.

As the service began, I kept a wary eye on our hunters. Fortunately, it was a clear sky with nary a goose or duck in sight. The only thing out there was a kayaker or two and a guy paddling one of those standing surfboards that are suddenly all the rage. The liturgy went off with the only thing needing to be reloaded were the communion wafers, although I was secretly pining for some bright orange vestments.

But just as people were taking out their picnic dinners, we looked up and saw three Canada geese flying off the coastline. Suddenly a loud Bang! Bang! Bang! rang out in the quiet late summer sky and then only two geese flew away while one fell wounded into the water. Our friends took a couple more shots but missed and the wounded goose swam away before, presumably, drowning. The adults were stunned; the children were horrified. Well, with the exception of my youngest son who yelled "Wow! That was so cool!" One parent wondered whether it was open season on Episcopalians.

We did call the police just to make sure they knew this was happening and an officer showed up, talked to the men, and left. According to the police, this was legal activity during a brief one week window based on a colonial-era law. Nonetheless, he asked them to pack up, given the circumstances, which they grudgingly did, giving us dirty looks in the process.

Now, I'm not opposed to hunting. I get the food chain thing and I've watched the *Lion King* way more times than I'm willing to admit so I understand the "Circle of Life." But really? Hunting on a public beach? Regardless of whether there's a church service (and we even had a permit to hold it), public beaches and firearms don't mix well.

What followed was a media frenzy—amid above-the-fold newspaper coverage and interviews with television news reporters, there was a lot of hostility from hunters accusing me of "backdoor gun control" since it led to a hunting ban on the beach. Maybe it didn't help that I dubbed the whole incident Goose Gate, but I was even called a "goose-hugging liberal" on one local talk radio call-in show.

The point is, despite the risks, it's important to get out of church sometimes. Don't let my own personal worst-case scenario deter you. Though you may want to avoid calling your next outdoor liturgy "Harmony at the Armory."

––––––

Blessing of the Animals

One of the best days in Episcopal churches is the annual St. Francis Day Blessing of the Animals in early October. If you have an incontinent hedgehog, this is the one day in the liturgical year you can bring him to sit in the pews with you without getting strange looks.

Most of the animals involved are dogs, although there are always a few traumatized cats in their jails/carriers who enjoy being sprinkled with holy water. Hopefully you have a cat psychiatrist in your parish who can help Fluffy stop twitching in the weeks after the experience.

I've blessed all sorts and conditions of pets over the years: ferrets, chickens, sheep, snakes, fish, rabbits, stuffed animals, fire-bellied newts, turtles, along with several species I couldn't identify. I've even baptized a few by mistake over the years by, out of ingrained habit, saying "Lucky, I baptize . . . I mean *bless* . . . you in the name of the Father and of the Son and of the Holy Spirit." Please don't tell anyone about this, especially the PETA crowd.

The Blessing of the Animals is a terrific service to invite friends and nonparishioners. We bless animals regardless of denomination, including Presbyterian chihuahuas and Methodist parakeets. While we stop short at giving the animals communion for reasons of theology and decorum, everybody likes to sing "All Things Bright and Beautiful" since it has that line about "all creatures great and small."

At one parish I served we used to sing the Bob Dylan song "Man Gave Names to All the Animals" written during Dylan's short-lived Christian phase. I did, however, have to nix "I am the Walrus" mostly because I don't think the phrase "cu cu cachoo" should ever be uttered during a church service.

The only other day of the year where you might encounter an animal in church, besides the ubiquitous church mouse, is Palm Sunday. Some parishes use a live donkey to recreate Jesus's triumphal entry into Jerusalem. To make a joke about the rector being an ass is low hanging fruit upon which I will pass. Though if a parish really wanted to be biblically correct, they would take Matthew 21:7 to heart and hire a trick rider from the nearest rodeo to play Jesus since, as the text says, "they brought the donkey and the colt, and put their cloaks on them, and he sat on them."

The one person who secretly curses St. Francis under his breath, besides the preacher who has to crank up the microphone to be heard over the cacophony of the animal kingdom, is the church sexton who has to clean up the mess. It could always be worse, of course. You could be the sexton at the Cathedral of St. John the Divine in New York where they bring in elephants.

Liturgical Olympics

It happens every two years—people become obsessed with sports they never give a second thought to in the intervening four years. I don't know too many people who are huge luge fanatics outside the friendly competitive confines of the Olympic Games or who could name all the members of the Brazilian relay team in non-Olympic years.

Anyway, it's made me think that we should institute an every-four-years Liturgical Olympics. Each diocese could field teams in church-specific events. Instead of the ugly jackets worn by many of the delegations, the "athletes" could wear hideous vestments during the Opening Ceremonies at the Washington National Cathedral. But I'm getting ahead of myself. We first need to come up with comparable events.

Here are some suggestions based on the winter Olympics.

Freestyle Skiing—Thurible Twirling

Everybody loves the daring, gravity-defying thrills of freestyle skiing. Why not transfer this to the skills of our best thurifers? The possibility of setting things on fire adds to the danger of this exciting event. Thurifers show off their skills with 360s, around the worlds, figure eights, and even the newest move called the spinning nautilus. Extra points gained for smoking out any Protestant spectators.

Speed Skating—Speed Mass

After the starting gun/sanctus bell, celebrants compete to say the Eucharistic prayer and distribute communion as quickly as possible. Everyone begins with the altar set for communion, one hundred communicants in (mostly) good standing, and one deacon. The giant running digital clock behind the altar allows spectators to track each competitor's time. While this event is Rite II, the Liturgical Olympic Committee

(LOC) is considering a switch to Rite I to watch celebrants trip over the words "innumerable benefits procured unto us by the same."

Pairs Figure Skating—Acolyte Choreography

Acolytes must serve at a high mass without extraneous movements or fainting while using perfect form and correct manual acts. Additional points are awarded for singing the hymns and not falling asleep during the sermon. Points are subtracted for unruly hair, wearing sneakers, and getting wax on the cassock.

Ski Jumping—Changing the Worship Space

Participants are challenged to make a substantial change to the worship space and then suffer the wrath of parishioners. The losers either give in and change it back or go home and curl up in the fetal position. "Substantial change" may refer to the removal of flags from the sanctuary, repositioning the altar, or removing anything—no matter how ugly—donated by a current parishioner (i.e., the modern baptismal font, 1970s-style altar hangings, etc).

Cross Country Skiing—Endurance Preaching

The ultimate liturgical endurance test, preachers are set up in a pulpit and asked to preach extemporaneously on a surprise text for as long as possible. There are two ways to get disqualified. 1) Uttering the words "um," "er," "ah," or any other vocal placeholder or extralong pause (judges' discretion); 2) When the first spectator falls asleep. This is the least popular event to attend especially because smartphones and knitting are not allowed inside the arena.

Hockey—Coffee Hour

Participating clergy are thrown into a loud, crowded room with people drinking bad coffee out of Styrofoam cups. They have twenty minutes to remember everyone's name, have heartfelt pastoral conversations with longtime parishioners, identify and talk to all newcomers, answer passive aggressive questions about the hymn selection, and suck down two cups of coffee.

And a few more based on the summer Olympics.

Beach Volleyball—Pine Needle Pickup

Like trying to get all the sand off your body, out of your hair, and away from your clothes after a trip to the beach, this event is about ridding the church of pine needles after Christmas. Contestants are given a broom, vacuum cleaner, and a pair of tweezers. The first one to get up all the needles before the next Olympiad wins.

Diving—Sacred Cow Tipping

Bravery and derring-do are the traits that earn gold in this event. Each participant is given a sacred cow to skewer, such as switching to the contemporary language version of the Lord's Prayer or changing the Sunday service times and told to dive right in. The one to live to tell about it is declared the winner.

Synchronized Swimming—Three Sacred Ministers

Similar to the Acolyte Choreography event in the Winter Liturgical Olympics, this tests the mettle of teams consisting of a celebrant, deacon, and subdeacon. Points are deducted for each misstep or out-of-synch bowing at the name of Jesus. Unfortunately for the judges, this is difficult to score since they cannot see through the massive cloud of incense.

Table Tennis—Call and Response

This event takes great concentration and anticipation. Teams of five are assembled consisting of an officiant and four "parishioners." The officiant says a phrase such as "The Lord be with you" and his/her teammates must correctly respond with "And also with you" in the shortest amount of elapsed time. If they speak too soon, they are disqualified and the Lord isn't, in fact, with them.

Fencing—Sermon Dialogue

In this event, preachers must spend five minutes immediately following the sermon to engage the congregation in dialogue. No longer able to hide behind the built-in authority of a gigantic pulpit, they must answer pointed questions about their theology from the chair of the religion department at the local university. The winners successfully navigate this exercise without either weeping or proclaiming "because I said so, that's why."

Boxing—Worship Committee Meeting

Contestants are placed into one large worship committee and asked to come to consensus on whether or not to use incense when the bishop visits even though it's not a major feast day on the liturgical calendar. There are no medals awarded in this event.

Baptismal Parties Behaving Badly

I love baptisms. Baptizing infants (and those who can speak for themselves) is one of my absolute favorite things about ordained ministry. Being the conduit for establishing that indissoluble bond between an individual and Jesus is a privilege.

Plus, when there are babies involved—which is the norm—I'm able to get my baby fix. I look at it as grandparent training: holding babies until they do those things that babies do and then handing them back to the parents. Some of my parishioners call me "The Baby Whisperer" and I admit I do have a pretty uncanny ability to quiet down a fussy infant. Also, my preaching puts them right to sleep.

We're fortunate to do a lot of baptisms at my parish and there's nothing better than welcoming a new parishioner into the "household of God." But we also err on the side of grace and baptize babies of some families we don't know. I always run a mandatory baptismal preparation class for parents (and ideally godparents) in the days or weeks leading up to the big day. I talk about the symbols of baptism and the liturgy and what it all means.

One of the major points I like to stress is that baptism isn't a rite of passage but a rite of commitment. And there's a major distinction between these two! If the baptism becomes merely something to "get through" before the day's major event—brunch—then we have a problem. Reading through the baptismal questions demonstrates just how serious this stuff is, a point I'm tempted to make by showing parents that wonderful carnage-filled baptism scene from *The Godfather*.

I'm always reminded that some people still struggle with taking baptism seriously, though I think the worst example of Baptismal Parties Behaving Badly happened at the parish I served in New York where a godparent answered her cell phone during the baptism and then proceeded to narrate the entire baptism for her friend. ("Watcha doin'?" "Oh, not much. Just hanging out at my niece's baptism.")

So in this light, I have rewritten the baptismal questions from the Prayer Book. There are three renunciations followed by three affirmations. Maybe we'll start reciting these at our baptism prep classes.

Then the celebrant asks the following questions of the parents and godparents who speak on behalf of the infants and younger children.

Question: Do you renounce flash photography and all annoying actions that rebel against the liturgy?

Answer: I renounce them.

Question: Do you renounce blowing off coffee hour and other actions that corrupt and destroy the concept of community?

Answer: I renounce them.

Question: Do you renounce yapping during the communion anthem and all sinful desires that draw you from the love of the sacrament?

Answer: I renounce them.

Question: Do you turn to the hymnal and actually sing the hymns?

Answer: I do.

Question: Do you put your trust in God by shutting down your cell phone and not surfing the Internet during the sermon?

Answer: I do.

Question: Do you promise not to use the Peace as your own personal family photo op?

Answer: I do.

We do ourselves and the church no favors by accepting such behavior and it's our responsibility to nip it in the baptismal font.

Unauthorized Funeral Guidelines

Officiating at funerals is actually one of the things I love most about being a priest. They're emotionally draining, but there are few situations where you can so profoundly touch a family while preaching Resurrection than in the midst of grief.

Occasionally the mixture of grief, guilt, and family tension coalesces into bizarre scenarios. A few years ago I was accused by a family member during the funeral planning process of "making it all about you." This was because I insisted on using the burial rite from the Book of Common Prayer (well, duh, we are an Episcopal Church) and not allowing a John Denver song to be played in the middle of the liturgy. If this made it "all about me," then so be it.

While we do have a fairly comprehensive list of guidelines, expectations, and explanations on our parish web page, I thought I'd offer a few of my own based on many years of doing funerals. If you're the webmaster for your parish website, I suggest you replace your own guidelines with these. Just don't tell the rector.

- Eulogies will be no more than five minutes in duration. If someone goes over the allotted time, the verger (after a single warning) will drag the eulogizer away from the lectern and shove him/her down the chancel steps. Don't worry, our ushers are trained to help people up and escort them to the parking lot. Also, kindly save stories of drunken carousing for the reception.
- Unless the funeral is for Billy Graham himself, "How Great Thou Art" will not be sung.
- Unless the funeral is for an actual eagle, "Eagles Wings" will not be sung.
- No, I don't happen to have the name and contact information for the local bagpiper.
- Psalm 23 is to funerals what 1 Corinthians 13 is to weddings: beautiful but overdone.

- Note to Roman Catholics: Please don't stop saying the Lord's Prayer midstream by omitting the doxology at the end. Oh, and it's okay to pick up a hymnal and at least *pretend* to sing. Remember, when in Rome . . .
- "Amazing Grace." Really? You couldn't think of anything more original? Like John Denver or something?
- If your cell phone goes off during the commendation with the marimba ring tone, know that you're off the family's Christmas card list for the rest of eternity (and, yes, this actually happened at a funeral I was doing).
- You know that giant flower display that resembles what they award the horse that wins the Kentucky Derby? It's not going in front of the altar. Or anywhere in the worship space.
- Similarly, while you might enjoy having a giant photograph of the deceased in your living room, it's not going in front of the lectern. We like people to be able to see the readers rather than have voices emanate from behind a picture of dear Aunt Edna.
- Two words: closed casket.
- No, we won't be using purple hangings because "it was dad's favorite color."
- Toddlers make bad pallbearers. Seriously.
- Yes, I realize the former rector baptized, confirmed, and married you, but he won't be doing the funeral just because he was the priest when you last attended church. Eighteen years ago.
- Please don't ask if Fifi the cat's ashes can be comingled with your husband's before being interred in the Memorial Garden.
- If your sister is prone to deep wailing at the drop of a hat, please don't ask her to read the lesson from Romans 8.
- Just because your grandfather liked to go to Cancun every winter, the organist won't be playing the Mexican Hat Dance as the postlude.
- While it may mean a lot to you, the "rose ceremony" that takes place at the graveside is too similar to the "rose ceremony" that takes place on *The Bachelor*. It's always discouraged.

- If you want to bury some of your uncle's ashes at the church but take the rest and scatter some at every minor league baseball stadium in the Midwest, please don't share this with the clergy.
- It's okay to list the church as the recipient of memorial donations. The humane society has plenty. As does the historical society.

PART VIII

SURVIVING STEWARDSHIP

"Stewardship" is the church's buzzword for "Show me the money!" We talk about "time, talent, and treasure," but it's hard to pay the oil bill with Dottie's unparalleled ability to arrange altar flowers.

I'm one of those priests who love to talk about money. After all, Jesus talked about the right use of money more than any other topic, and if we truly view our lives and resources as ultimately belonging to God, there's no reason to skulk around the issue. Plus, it's fun to make people nervous by talking not just about money in general but their money in particular.

Peace, Hope, and (Pledge) Fulfillment

Unfulfilled pledges are the bane of parish treasurers everywhere. Well, that and simply *being* the parish treasurer. But late in the year is particularly hairy for parish leaders relying on those last-minute donations to balance the budget and pay for essential parish supplies like toilet paper.

Strategies for "encouragement" include:

- Reminding people about the tax advantages of getting their donations in before the end of December.
- Pleading, cajoling, begging during the announcements.
- Making people feel like church vandals if they don't fulfill their pledges ("You stole our sacraments! And drank our coffee!").
- Sending out the parish "bag man" to collect the rest (usually the beefy assistant treasurer who stands at the recalcitrant pledger's front door cracking his knuckles).
- Compelling them to usher at the 4:00 p.m. pageant service (the "Zoocharist") and risk being trampled unless they pay up before Christmas Eve.
- Threatening to print the list of people who have not fulfilled their pledges in the Midnight Mass bulletin (something that will never be more than an idle threat).
- Refusing to accept their pledge for the following year until they're all paid up (Um, wait, that's not much of a consequence).
- Cleverly disguising quarterly statements as bills to be paid.
- Organizing the youth group to serve as pickpockets during coffee hour.
- Did we mention the tax benefits?

Of course, unless there are unexpected financial hardships involved, most people do fulfill their pledges. We have only the best of intentions but are unaware/lazy/overwhelmed in December. Thus, I encourage you to save your treasurer's sanity and send it in now! He/she will thank you and you'll have a guilt-free Christmas. Well, guilt free as long as you've already submitted your pledge card for next year . . .

A Dozen Ways to Avoid Stewardship

As stewardship season rolls around, usually in mid-fall, it's important to have strategies available to help you sponge off the rest of the congregation. With a little creativity, you too can do your part to avoid furthering the kingdom of heaven here on earth.

Here are a dozen ways to avoid stewardship:

- Tell the rector that you are "morally opposed" to pledging. After all, shouldn't the church live up to its name as a community of "faith" and take it on faith that there will be enough money to pay for the rector's health benefits?
- Don't show up to church in October. In fact, just to be safe avoid church in September and November as well just in case the ubiquitous stewardship sermon is preached early or late this year.
- Tell the rector that you'd like a podcast of his/her stewardship sermon and then turn it into a drinking game—take a swig every time you hear the words "abundance" and "scarcity." By the end, you won't even feel a whit of guilt about not pledging.
- Tell the poor sap who calls you to follow-up on the stewardship campaign that your time and (especially your) talent more than make up for your lack of willingness to part with your treasure.

Who cares if your real "talent" is avoiding contributing to the life of the community?

- Move, but neglect to give your forwarding address to the church office. "Stewardship packet? No, I never received one." Then tell them to resend it to your old address.
- Assure people that, while you don't pledge, you give generously to the plate. Especially on the one Sunday a month you find yourself in church.
- After using the advice from the previous point, practice folding a one dollar bill to make it look like a thick wad of cash. It may end up looking like an $11 bill but whatever.
- If you do pledge, make sure that you never give more than the five dollars a week you gave in the mid-1970s.
- Switch to a new church every Advent and you'll be sure to "just miss" the stewardship campaign. Of course you'll need to avoid going to church in the fall, but that's just the price you'll have to pay. So to speak.
- Tell the treasurer you've decided to donate online this year. Then explain that there was a mix-up and the automatic deduction went to your health club rather than the church.
- Don't pledge but still ask for envelopes—you can usually finagle them out of the church office—so that people think you do.
- Use the money you don't pledge to donate a memorial gift of velvet liners for the collection plates. That way the change you toss in won't reverberate and cause you undue embarrassment.

I hope these dozen tips have been helpful as you prayerfully discern your pledge amount this year. Until churches start publishing the names and amounts of givers (like every other charitable organization) you should be safe.

Ten Reasons Not to Pledge

As stewardship season rolls around, people begin to squirm in their pews. Many parishioners who don't want to pledge to the ongoing mission and ministry of their respective parishes are desperate for some justifications. I encourage you to use these on your rector, stewardship chair, parish treasurer, or anyone designated to give you a follow-up phone call. With a little practice you can sound completely justified in not pledging.

1. "I already pledge allegiance to the flag, why should I pledge to the church?" Subterfuge and confusing statements are effective tactics. Use enough non sequitors and eventually everyone will leave you alone.

2. "The disciples didn't pledge. Why should I?" True. Plus, this statement demonstrates your expansive knowledge of Scripture. Never mind that they gave their entire lives over to Jesus—they never actually filled out a papyrus pledge card.

3. "I don't attend church very often." Only Christmas and Easter. Oh, and every family baptism, wedding, and funeral. You may not be there when the church needs you but, boy, that church better be there when *you* need *it*.

4. "It can't cost that much to run a church. Just bread, wine, and a priest, right?" Make sure to tell the priest you assume he/she took a vow of poverty upon ordination. And that if your priest actually wanted a lifestyle that included a working boiler in the rectory, he/she should have become a hedge fund manager instead.

5. "You'd just waste my money on candles. Or give it away." Accuse the church of spending too much on frivolous things like feeding programs.

6. "I don't trust the treasurer. He has shifty eyes." It's always good if you can blame others as the reason for not pledging. Some

popular ones include "I don't like the rector's sermons" and "The senior warden avoided me at coffee hour last May."

7. "I prefer to give my talent rather than my treasure." Sure your "talent" is moonwalking like Michael Jackson, but that was pretty popular at last year's parish picnic. Remember?

8. "I give when I can." In other words, you drop two single dollar bills in the plate on the one Sunday a month you happen to show up.

9. "I can't tell the future. The stock market might crash." It's possible. Then again, why go to the grocery store? You might start a hunger strike next week.

10. "What if letting go of the fear of pledging makes me generous in every aspect of life and brings me unexpected joy and abundant blessings?" Sorry. I can't help you with that one.

If these don't work, you can always propose a new slogan for your church: "All of the benefits, none of the commitment." Think of all the money your parish would save on stewardship mailings!

PART IX

SURVIVING PARISH LIFE

"As the Steeple Turns" is how my administrative assistant, Evelyn, refers to the drama that takes place around the church. With all the twists and turns it can indeed feel like being on the set of a long-running soap opera. There are characters and passive aggressive dramas being played out and nefarious plots being, well, plotted— but all in the service of Jesus.

Salvation through Potluck

Whether it's an all-parish dinner or coffee hour, Episcopalians like to eat together. This makes sense since on the night before he died Jesus instituted the Eucharist at the Last Potluck Supper.

If you're an elementary school graduate, you surely remember those food group pyramid charts. They basically communicated that you need to eat more things that taste bad and fewer thing that taste good. In the church there are a few basic food groups that sustain our communal life. They may not offer a foretaste of the heavenly banquet (please, God, no), but they are so foundational that without them, the church may well collapse.

Munchkins. It's gotten to the point that Dunkin' Donuts is virtually the corporate sponsor of coffee hour. They may eventually face a hostile takeover by Entenmann's to retain this honor but for now Munchkins rule.

Tuna Casserole. Show me a Wednesday night Lenten series without a tuna casserole and I'll show you a Lenten series with only eight people. Oh, wait . . .

Tuna Hot Dish. See above—Midwest version. Top with tater tots to complete the culinary tableau.

Goldfish. What would Sunday school teachers serve at snack time without those tasty orange fish? Communion wafers?

Deviled Eggs. Anyone else find it ironic that *deviled* eggs are such a church staple?

Bad Coffee. According to one theory, no matter what type of coffee you brew, it tastes ten times worse when served in a parish hall. Maybe it's those giant urns that haven't been cleaned since the introduction of the 1979 Prayer Book. Perhaps it's the Styrofoam cups that a surprisingly high percentage of parishes still use despite telling everyone how "green" they are.

Veggie Burgers. A recent addition to the list of de rigeur church food, no parish picnic is complete without someone remembering the veggie burgers in an act of last-minute sensitivity to "those vegetarian people."

Tomato Aspic. A colleague of the deviled egg, this passé gelatinous goop always seems to reappear at the annual needlepoint guild luncheon.

Crudité. A staple whenever the bishop comes to make things appear classy. No one ever eats it because there are Munchkins to be had.

Pizza. There has literally never been a youth group gathering in the history of youth group gatherings that did not include pizza. This is why all youth ministers have high cholesterol.

Is Your Sexton Nuts?

Every sexton in the Anglican Communion is nuts. Or, if not nuts, then possessing of enough quirks to cover the entire congregation. To clarify, I'm not talking about the glorified cleaning services that some churches employ. I mean the inherited-the-job-from-my-father kind of sexton; the lurking sexton who lives on church property and is omnipresent among the shadows; the one who, while born in New Jersey, speaks with a decidedly British accent.

The word "sexton" is derived from the Latin word *sacristanus* meaning "custodian of sacred objects." Today it is synonymous with "church custodian." A sexton keeps the church clean and in order for worship. In England sextons were historically charged with maintenance of the church's graveyard. Many still dig graves or at least prepare small holes for ashes in the Memorial Garden.

I should say that my current sexton, Dorothy, doesn't qualify as one of the crazy ones. As long as I'm generalizing, maybe it's a gender thing. She predates the rest of the staff, has a tremendous work ethic, and is a fabulous cook. I'm lucky, but I've also known many sextons over the years who fit beautifully into the screw-loose mold.

If you're thinking "Sure, my sexton is a bit unconventional and quirky, but he's not nuts" then perhaps you should take the following quiz:

Your sexton is nuts if . . .

- You stumble on a box in the undercroft labeled "Burned-Out Lightbulbs." I realize we believe in the Resurrection but really?
- He goes through twice as many bottles of gin than bottles of Lysol in a given twelve-month period. And you know this because both are stacked neatly behind the boiler in the subbasement.
- You catch him rearranging a person's ashes in the Memorial Garden after dark because, you know, "Mr. Simpson told me before he died that he didn't want to spend eternity next to Mrs. Simpson."
- You never see the sexton anywhere except on church grounds. Ever. And he's scared the bejesus out of you on multiple occasions when you thought you were alone in the church.
- He calls the church mice by name. "Oh good morning, Jerome."
- Parish "terrorists" gravitate toward him to talk behind the rector's back.
- The sexton's knowledge of Episcopal affairs is limited to back issues of *The Living Church*.
- The sexton knows every hymn by heart and sings them while polishing the organ pipes.
- He harvests his own incense. And his clothes smell like said incense along with a mix of cigars and Murphy's Oil.

- While you've heard rumors to the effect, you've never actually seen him cleaning anything.

If six or more describe your sexton, don't feel bad. They may be quirky and/or nuts but they're part of the Anglican ethos. And if you *are* a sexton, thank you. We literally couldn't do it without you. Well, I guess we could, but our parish halls would look a lot more like fraternity house basements.

———

Church Pick-Up Lines

I love being married. There are myriad reasons for this not the least of which is that I'd be a lousy single priest. I know plenty of clergy who pull this off beautifully, but I'd be terrible at it. I can't imagine a guy in a clerical collar gets many hits on match.com and the whole clergy dating/boundary thing would be a drag. Plus getting set up with every parishioner's homely granddaughter would get old.

Nonetheless, church is one of the best places for singles to meet one another. I'm not equating coffee hour with a meat market at a hip night club, but it's a good place for people of faith to connect and critique bad liturgy. So as a public service I decided to share my top ten church pick-up lines. Use with discretion as they work, in the words of Billy Dee Williams hawking Colt 45, "every time."

- "Excuse me, is this pew taken?"
- "Kneel around here often?"
- "It's almost time for communion. Can I buy you a drink?"
- "What do you think Paul meant when he said, 'Greet everyone with a holy kiss'?"

- "If I told you that you were wearing the world's hottest cotta, would you hold it against me?"
- "This sermon's terrible, how about we 'continue the liturgy' in the parish hall?"
- "You might not be able to tell, but I'm the best lay minister around."
- "You want to stick around for the laying on of hands?"
- "You were a thurifer at your old church? Great! How would you like to join our swinger's guild?"
- And if the bishop is visiting: "Is that a crozier in your pocket or are you just happy to see me?"

So while dating as clergy might have worked if I were still the "dashing young curate," the middle-aged rector is a whole different pot of incense. Time to go hug my wife.

———

Kitchen Karma

The most frightening place in any church is not the subbasement. It's not the rotting staircase leading to the bell tower. It's not even that undercroft bathroom with the ancient diaper changing table/choking hazard. It's the parish kitchen. The place where you'll find milk dating back to last Advent; the place where people reshelve lipstick-laden tea cups for *next* week's coffee hour; the place where vermin feast on unswept-up donut crumbs left over from the AA meeting.

The major problem with parish kitchens is that nobody ever feels empowered to throw anything out. Someone's grandmother "graciously" donated a soufflé dish (that was ugly, chipped, and one step from the garbage fifty years ago). But since she was a pillar of the church, her ghost might forever haunt the culprit who decides to toss it. So there it sits collecting dust in the back of a cabinet.

Open any drawer and you'll encounter both mismatched silverware, some containing forks with leftover bits of lasagna from the 1978 parish picnic, and an assortment of godforsaken utensils dating back to the Nixon administration. And there's always a cabinet full of puke green clunky ashtrays. If you like to chain-smoke while making a cheese soufflé with a rusty hand whisk, this is your lucky day!

So here's a call to action: Take Back the Kitchen! Take matters into your own hands (or yellow rubber gloves). Get a group of hearty friends, hire a dumpster, get a blowtorch, and start scrubbing and throwing things out. It is spiritually cleansing to toss out bags and bags full of useless junk that no one will ever miss.

Just make sure you do it in the middle of the night. If you get caught by the current crop of church pillars, you'll be eaten alive.

How Many Episcopalians *Does* It Take to Change a Lightbulb?

Occasionally lightbulbs actually do need to be changed in churches. Yes, we have the whole Light of Christ thing, but groping around in the dark doesn't make for good liturgy unless you're attending the Easter Vigil.

I have reverently compiled a list of Episcopal lightbulbs jokes to save you from having to log onto the Internet yourself. You can use the time you've gained to tell these jokes to people at the office who will give you a blank stare and say, "What's an Episcopalian?"

How Many Episcopalians Does It Take to Change a Lightbulb?

- Change?!? What do you mean "change?" My mother donated that lightbulb.
- None. We always use candles instead.
- None. The old one is complete and sufficient unto itself, and should not be changed according to the world's whims.
- Three. One to call the electrician, one to mix the drinks, and one to talk about how much better the old one was.
- Four. One to change the bulb, one to bless the elements, one to pour the sherry, and one to offer a toast to the old lightbulb.
- Four. One to call the electrician, one to clear it with the vestry, and two to argue about how much better candles were.
- Six. One to change the bulb and five to form a society to preserve the memory of the old lightbulb.
- Eight. One to call the electrician and seven to say how much they liked the old electrician better (the old lightbulb, too).
- Ten. One to actually change the bulb and nine to say how much they liked the old one.
- Twelve. One to do the work and eleven to serve on the committee.
- Three hundred. A sexton to change the bulb. The rector, the assistant rector, deacon, and seminarian to lead the ceremony blessing the new bulb. The church secretary to make up the special bulletin insert with the bulb-blessing ceremony, including congregational responses: "Do you, the people of St. Swithin's, promise to support this bulb in its work on behalf of this church?" "We do!" The choirmaster/organist to write and arrange a special Blessing of the Bulb Anthem: the "Phos 100-Watt GE Soft White" and twelve choir members to sing it. An acolyte and two torch-bearers to sit around looking bored and making faces at each other. And 278 people in the pews thinking to themselves, "Is this service EVER going to end?" PLUS—6 of those 278 (about 2 percent) will form a Society for the Preservation of the Lightbulb, and 2 of

those people will leave the parish, and try to find someone who will let them use the Real Lightbulb of their forefathers.
- The entire General Convention. One to move that the bulb be changed while the others debate until the room spins.

Complaint Department

A young neighbor of mine recently told me about the "Rejection Hotline." Basically, it's a phone number young ladies can give to gentlemen suitors who are persistent yet undesirable. When the young lad is ready to follow up on his "success," he calls the number and, instead of reaching his potential new girlfriend, he hears a mocking recorded message telling him that he has been rejected.

Mean-spirited? Funny? I guess it depends on your point of view—and whether or not you've ever been unlucky enough to be handed the number on a napkin. But somehow it got me thinking about a new voice messaging system for the rector's phone.

Thank you for calling the Church of St. John the Beheaded. Please listen to the following menu items:

- *To complain about the rector, please press one.*
- *If you would like to return to the 1928 Prayer Book, press one.*
- *If you wish the rector's spouse would join the altar guild, press two.*
- *If you are displeased with the behavior of the rector's children during church, press three.*
- *If you feel the rector's sermons are too long, press four.*
- *If you feel the rector's sermons are too short, press five.*
- *If you think the rector never visits parishioners, press six.*
- *If you are tired of deviled eggs at coffee hour, press seven.*

- *If you think the rector talks too much about money, press eight.*
- *If you think the rector needs to talk more about money, press nine.*
- *If you do not like the rector's new haircut or have other issues with his personal hygiene, press ten.*
- *To reach the associate priest to triangulate the rector, please press two.*
- *To commiserate about the rector's poor preaching, press one.*
- *To complain about any of the above topics, press two.*
- *To leave an anonymous complaint about typos in the bulletin, please press three.*
- *For all other negative comments or "brainstorms" on how to make the liturgy more relevant, please stay on the line to listen to this menu over and over again.*

How Not to Use Your Smartphone in Church

Texting and driving is a bad thing—anybody who's ever been rear-ended knows this. But what about texting/tweeting/surfing the web during a church service? This is where the great generational divide kicks in.

For younger churchgoers, it's a form of evangelism to live-tweet a Sunday sermon or let their friends know they're at church by "checking in" on Facebook. For older folks, cell phones should neither be seen nor heard. Ironically enough, it's often an older person's phone that goes off with the volume all the way up playing "Hot, Hot, Hot" during the veneration of the cross on Good Friday. Or at least that's my experience since this actually happened to me one Holy Week.

If you insist on bringing your smartphone to church, either turn the volume off, put it in airplane/sanctuary mode, or use it to surf the web during one of those endless nine verse hymns. To model digital decorum, I thought I'd offer a few suggestions on how not to use your cell phone in church.

- Don't take a selfie with the crucifer as she processes down the aisle during the opening hymn.
- I don't care that you have a peal app on your iPhone. It's not appropriate to use it as the sanctus bell.
- Holding up the flashlight on your phone rather than a candle during the singing of *Silent Night* on Christmas Eve will make you look like a hippie who would rather be at a Grateful Dead concert.
- Using that vulgar app that makes farting noises should not be used every time the celebrant sits down.
- Googling a picture of Gene Simmons of Kiss fame sticking out his tongue and then holding your phone in front of your face as the priest approaches to give you communion is less amusing than you'd think.
- Calling the rector to test whether or not he/she accidentally left a cell phone in his/her pocket is not fair.
- Live-tweeting rubrical violations and bulletin typos is bad form.
- Taking a photo of the wafer before consuming it and then tweeting it out with the hashtag #jesusisinthehouse is not in the spirit of the Last Supper.
- No, playing the *Rocky* theme song during the gospel procession will not "get the crowd fired up."
- If you take pictures during a baptism, know that the ushers have been specially trained to toss your phone into the baptismal font. #oops

The New Narthex

There are certain churchy phrases that annoy me. That's probably not a news flash to those who know me, but of late I can't seem to get several of these out of my head.

Many of these phrases or words convey profound meaning and are deeply inspirational to those who use them. My intent isn't to belittle or demean anyone's personal spiritual experience. Really. Rather it's to highlight the fact that we often get so caught up in our insider language of faith that most people have no clue what we're talking about.

To me this small collection has become the "new narthex"—the spiritual equivalent of archaic phrases describing church architecture (words that I adore, mind you). For instance, telling the church visitor how to get to coffee hour: "It's easy. Just go through the narthex, past the sacristy, and then down to the undercroft." Huh?

So here's my little list:

Thin Place. This isn't slang for the local Weight Watchers. Nor does it refer to the space between the high altar and the free-standing altar that was put in place in 1978. It's meant to convey the "thinness" of the veil between heaven and earth in certain inspirational places. Visitors to the isle of Iona off the coast of Scotland often refer to it as "a thin place." In many church pews it might also describe the amount of padding on the kneelers.

Traveling Mercies. You'll see this phrase on Facebook comment threads when someone posts that they'll soon be leaving for a church conference or heading out to the Grand Canyon with the family in the Buick station wagon. It was the title of a popular Anne Lamott book (yes, I read it a few years ago and liked it) and I think it has been a popular phrase among Episcopalians ever since. In my opinion "Godspeed" suffices.

Namaste. Oh don't get all bent out of shape, yoga fanatics. I tried yoga recently and had a Sam-I-Am experience—shockingly I liked it. Nonetheless, this word annoys me. It means something like "let the light inside of me shine in you" which is just a bit too new-agey for my taste. Plus, anyone who says it suddenly seems to crave a soy, half caf latte from Starbucks.

Liminal. In addition to rhyming with "minimal" (I really should pen a limerick), this word means "the space between." How vague is that? Used spiritually, it's kind of synonymous with "thin place." In liturgy, it refers to a transitional state when a rite has begun but has not yet been completed. In other words, it's a good word to throw around when you want to confuse people. Note to seminarians: use this word in a sermon and prepare for the silent treatment at coffee hour.

Fellowshipping. This is not a real verb! If you hear someone using it, run for your life or be forever committed to making a monthly coffee cake or at least picking up the Entenmann's version. And I don't want to hear from anyone interested in dialoguing about this.

Missional. This word gets thrown around so much in church circles, yet no one can actually define it. Seriously. Ask the next person you hear use it what it means and they'll bolt your presence like a man on a mission(al).

The Eighth Sacrament

Let's just make it official and declare coffee the Church's eighth sacrament. It functions de facto as such and without coffee the church would collapse. You think I'm being overly dramatic? Consider this: without coffee, church attendance would plummet, the Anglican tradition would be lost, and liturgical chaos would ensue.

Without an early morning jolt of java, fewer parishioners would make it out of bed and out the door on a Sunday morning. The hardy souls who did make it to church would be in no mood to greet one another, let alone newcomers. "Coffee Hour" without coffee would be a bust and the exalted fellowship time would be nonexistent. So much for church growth.

The church would also unleash a new cadre of ill-trained clergy who, without coffee, would never have made it to those early morning Hooker classes at seminary. The famed three-legged stool of Anglicanism, the integration of Scripture, tradition, and reason, would undoubtedly lose a leg and come crashing to the floor.

The liturgical consequences would be equally troubling. Most directly impacted would be 8:00 a.m. services. Without coffee, the services would start late, not because the priest couldn't get there on time but because he or she would be unable to spit out the opening acclamation in a timely fashion. And could you imagine saying, "the innumerable benefits procured unto us by the same" without first having had a steaming mug of coffee?

Then there's the sermon. It's not that parishioners would nod off and fail to gain the appropriate enlightenment provided by our well-educated priests. That happens regardless of how much coffee is consumed before a service. The real tragedy would be the loss of a true sense of community as the people in the pews wouldn't be awake enough to read the service bulletin during the sermon time.

The dire cost being that without this quality time to read the myriad announcements, attendance at parish events would tumble.

I realize that canonizing St. Joe would be controversial among some Anglicans. After all, tea is the traditional drink of choice for a people whose roots are in the Church of England. But being a cradle American as well as a cradle Episcopalian, I have three words for those bound purely by tradition: Boston Tea Party.

I recently came across a silver tea set at my church. Where is it kept? In the parish safe. The coffee urns, on the other hand, are prominently and permanently displayed in the kitchen, used each week at our lively coffee hour. There's a reason, even in Anglicanism, that it's not called "tea hour." Who would stay?

Even if we convince the archbishop of Canterbury to make this a key item in his agenda, during afternoon tea, one nagging concern remains. The church continues to be a haven for mediocre coffee. I advocate a populist-style insurrection to demand better quality coffee in our parish halls. The church is, after all, God's house, not Maxwell's House. Shouldn't excellence in worship extend to excellence in coffee beans? At Cana, Jesus saved the best wine for last. After years of drinking weak coffee in undercrofts throughout the country, isn't it time to roll out the good stuff once and for all? The very lifeblood of the church depends on it.

The true test of coffee's sacramental potential lies, of course, in the classic definition of a sacrament. We must prove that coffee is an outward and visible sign of an inward and spiritual grace. For those among us who make it to yet another 8 o'clock service on Sunday morning, could there be any doubt?

The Fine Line between Junk and Parish Lore

The dumpster is the church's last great taboo. No one ever feels empowered to throw anything out, which is why many of our parishes feel like grandma's attic. This isn't readily apparent to the average churchgoer since, aside from a stray prayer desk or two, the worship space is generally clutter free. But beware the undercroft and the parish office because here lurk the remnants of the 1950s Sunday school curriculum, that ratty sofa no one bought at the last rummage sale, and the stack of bulletins from 1977 filed under "Historical Documents."

When it comes to the stewardship of parish lore, we are pack rats. No one can recall when the tarnished, unattractive silver-plated ladle appeared in the parish kitchen and it doesn't matter. The object is part of the fabric of the place. So at the risk of offending dear old Helen, who may or may not have bequeathed the item (this is a topic of debate), it stays. And now no one can imagine parish life without that bronze bust of Albert Schweitzer sitting atop the bookcase in the guild room.

Who's to blame? Rectors and parish secretaries don't help. Rectors are terrified of alienating a pillar of the church and anything mimeographed has archival potential. So it stays. The oversensitivity of sextons only adds to the problem. Granted throwing things out, other than the trash, is not in their job descriptions, but there's something about their overall handiness that precludes them from getting rid of things. They no doubt *could* fix that old halogen lamp, but after five years it's probably not going to happen so for God's sake get rid of it.

While Jesus urged us to store up treasure in heaven rather than accumulate treasure on earth, many churches apparently never got the message. Moth and rust are alive, well, and consuming in many parish basements. One of the most innovative ways to deal with the sticky church furniture question was the sexton I knew who created a chapel altar out of the old pew doors. The only problem was what to do with the other two hundred that remained in the basement.

Perhaps the problem is best illustrated by the infamous parish library. Its shelves contain a microcosm of the whole issue. Perusing the library turns up a mix of outdated theology (along with a hidden gem or two), old Sunday school manuals, and shelf after shelf of 1928 Prayer Books. Perhaps the church's greatest rubbish conundrum is what to do with old prayer books since every parish has them stashed away somewhere. No one wants to throw out a Prayer Book, or a 1940 Hymnal, and there's something comforting about the parish as steward of generations of prayers and hymns sent forth. The problem is we don't need three bookshelves' worth.

There is a fine line between rummage and parish lore and in between stands the dumpster. Moth-eaten cassocks don't remind us of days gone by. They are disgusting; get rid of them. Bent forks in the parish kitchen are not holy relics; toss them. And if you brought lasagna to the last potluck supper, please take the chipped baking dish home. I beg you.

PART X

SURVIVING ECUMENISM

What can I say? I grew up in the Episcopal Church. My very first word was "vouchsafe." I'm not very good at working with other denominations, though I did chair our Interfaith Clergy Association for a couple of years while in New York. But if you think I have little patience for poor Anglican liturgy, you ought to sit next to me during an ecumenical baccalaureate service.

On Ecumenical "Worship"

Whenever I attend ecumenical conferences, I must endure the accompanying worship. Generally I'm able to keep my *sotto voce* comments to a minimum. More or less. The Christian Unity folks won't appreciate my comments here, but be that as it may, I will offer you a few things that I detest about ecumenical worship services (but all in the spirit of ecumenism).

1. **The so-called "Call to Worship."** Perhaps those of other denominations can't abide the phrase "Opening Acclamation" but for me "Call to Worship" evokes a 1950s neighborhood mom ringing a dinner bell to call her kids home on a summer evening. Not that there's anything particularly wrong with that except the usual generic Protestant Call to Worship involves a badly composed and contrived call and response between minister and congregation. Change the dinner bell to a gong and I might be interested.

2. **Clapping during worship.** Pardon me, but did your little performance intrude on my worship? Leave the clapping to Carnegie Hall and Lambeau Field. Please.

3. **Standing ovations for the preacher.** My annoyance for this practice is not just because I've never gotten one. It's the message it conveys that worship is more about the bearer of the message than the Message itself. Once the distinction gets blurred, we're all in deep trouble.

4. **What's up with the prominence of the organ?** I like organ music. In fact I adore organ music. But why do all of these Protestant churches put the organ so prominently at the center of the worship space? It makes me want to sneak up to the console and play the "Charge!"

5. **Dramatic readings of Scripture.** It's not that I mind when readers pour their hearts and souls into a text through preparation

and delivery. But, please, read with some sense of humility. It's not as if you wrote it, after all, no matter how much you're enjoying channeling Jeremiah.

6. **Lack of communion.** Okay, so this is a theological and spiritual bias on my part. But worship without sacrament feels empty no matter the venue. Next time I'll just bring my own.

7. **Benediction means "blessing" not nice-words-to-send-you-home-by.** If you're going to offer a benediction, then bless us like you mean it! That means offering a blessing in the Trinitarian fullness of God. If I wanted to hang out with Unitarians, I would do so on my own time.

I won't even get into vesture and liturgical colors. It's not worth it. Though perhaps I'll tack these Seven Theses up on the door of the local Presbyterian church and see what happens.

Top Ten Reasons to Attend the Community Thanksgiving Service

Each November all the local clergy and a disproportionately small number of townspeople gather for the Interfaith Community Thanksgiving Service at the local Congregational church. It's nice to gather, certainly, and I appreciate knowing all the other clergy. But at a completely different level, there are many good (well, ten) reasons to attend such services. Thus, I offer you my:

Top Ten Reasons to Attend the Community Thanksgiving Service

1. When else would you get to hold a bulletin emblazoned with cornucopia clip art?
2. To prove the superior vesture of Episcopalians (or, at what point does an abundance of polyester cassock-albs become a fire hazard?).
3. To get away from the in-laws for an hour while they dispute the ingredients of your late grandmother's stuffing recipe.
4. To worship God in lowest common denominator form (along with several references to Mother Earth).
5. To pray that parishioners from other churches will see the light and join *your* congregation.
6. To enjoy seeing the area clergy being paraded around in front of the congregation like a police lineup ("Hey, you, number two Methodist; stand next to that Presbyterian and sing "Eagles' Wings").
7. To take bets on how many times the hosting cleric will say the word "welcome."

8. To witness hearing all the participating clergy being given a line or two (in the name of inclusion) so it feels like a third-grade play.
9. Since the rest of your family refuses to go, it makes for a contemplative time.
10. To enjoy the postservice store-bought brownies and punch reception (a result of several unnamed Protestant denominations for whom wine is anathema).

As an Episcopalian I look forward to celebrating Thanksgiving with The Great Thanksgiving. All the rest is just icing on the turkey.

When (Not) in Rome

While many are concerned about the declining numbers of mainline denominations, I believe the Episcopal Church will always be just fine as long as Roman Catholics continue to marry Presbyterians. Or United Methodists.

At my parish on Boston's South Shore we have a lot of former Roman Catholics gracing the pews (including my wife). Here are some helpful guidelines for recovering Catholics new to the Episcopal Church. "When in Rome" has morphed into "When in a church that looks vaguely like something you'd find in the English countryside."

- It's "*Ah*-men" not "*Ay*-men." Fonzie was not an Episcopalian. Though many tongue depressor–wielding doctors apparently are.
- When I make a reference in a sermon to "my little boys" it's not something creepy. I really do have two children.
- If the initial shock of seeing a female priest at the altar is too much, we have defibrillators on hand.

- It's okay to dress up a bit for church. Really.
- If you come to the communion rail and stick out your tongue, I will give you the host. But first I might stick my tongue out back at you. Or ask you to say ahhh–men.
- You won't hear me preach about the evils of birth control. The only time I'll bring the pulpit into the bedroom is if you ask me to do a house blessing.
- You can still refer to a liturgy of communion as "mass." Other names are the Holy Eucharist (preferred) or Holy Communion. This is so that I can offer the occasional service of "Mass on the Grass" during the summer. And let's face it, nothing rhymes with Eucharist with the (sort-of) exception of Bucharest.
- Feel free to open the Hymnal and actually sing the hymns. Yes, we typically sing all the verses. Sorry. Fortunately most of us are pretty good singers or, if not, our choirs know all the tunes.
- If your grandmother insists that you'll go to hell if you step foot inside another church besides St. Stanislaus, feel free to wear a disguise when you arrive. It's easier than getting into a conversation about theology. Plus, your secret's safe with me.
- You see? Stained glass doesn't have to be ugly! When we refer to our church being built in the '60s, we mean the *1860s*.

I hope this little primer will help anyone with a Roman Catholic background who is curious about trying out worship in the Episcopal Church. Oh, and one more thing: yes, you are welcome to receive communion at any one of our many branch locations.

That's NOT in the Bible? Nope.

Recent surveys have shown biblical illiteracy at an all-time high. And, no, Gallup wasn't just polling Episcopalians. What's most disturbing to me isn't that people have no idea who or what Moses did; it's the number of quotes they *think* are biblical but actually are not.

To clear up any confusion, I've compiled a list of the most common nonbiblical clichés. Perhaps over time, in the name of God and country, we can root out these insidious scriptural misquotes. And then everyone can live happily ever after and return to their previously scheduled programming.

- *"What doesn't kill you makes you stronger."* Perhaps not. Although in extreme cases you may end up as a vegetable.
- *"God never gives us more than we can handle."* Talk to Job. Or anyone else who has ever been overwhelmed by the circumstances of life. That's not to say that God isn't in the midst of it all, but God isn't intentionally heaping weights upon our shoulders to help us identify our own breaking points.
- *"To thine own self be true."* Just because it's written in Elizabethan English doesn't mean it's Scripture. It is, however, a line from Shakespeare's *Hamlet*.
- *"The lion shall lay down with the lamb."* In Isaiah, the wolf lives with the lamb and the leopard lies down with the kid but the lion and the lamb? Never the twain shall meet. "The wolf shall live with the lamb, the leopard shall lie down with the kid, the calf and the lion and the fatling together" (11:6) and "The wolf and the lamb shall feed together, the lion shall eat straw like the ox" (65:25).
- *"Cleanliness is next to godliness."* Slobs of the world rejoice! While the saying may have its roots in an ancient, nonbiblical Hebrew proverb, the earliest example in English comes from Francis Bacon in 1605.

- *"God works in mysterious ways."* Duh. And U2 sings "God *moves* in mysterious ways." But as true as this may be, it's not in the Bible.
- *"Do unto others as you would have them do unto you."* Psych! The Golden Rule actually *does* come from the Bible if not in this precise wording. See Matthew 7:12. In fact, this call to ethical reciprocity predates the Bible and can be found in nearly every world religion.
- *"God helps those who help themselves."* Perhaps, but God also helps those who cannot help themselves. This phrase seems to have originated in one of Aesop's Fables—the Waggoner. It shouldn't be surprising that since Aesop lived in the sixth century BC the original phrase was "The gods help those who help themselves."
- *"Money is the root of all evil."* There's a similar saying in 1 Timothy: "For the love of money is a root of all kinds of evil." But that's completely different—money itself is not evil! Remember that distinction come stewardship season.
- *"It's a long way to the top, if you want to rock 'n roll."* What? This isn't in the book of Revelation? Nope, it's AC/DC.

So there you have it. A little biblical literacy to get your blood flowing. And if you didn't like anything about this? "This too shall pass" (again, not biblical).

CONCLUSION

I hope you've enjoyed this little dash through our communal life as people seeking to follow Jesus as best we can. If we can't laugh at ourselves and some of our nonfoundational traditions, we have serious problems. I want to end with two questions. First, is snark un-Christian and second, is Jesus funny? You surely know by now where I stand on these topics, but I think they're worth a brief exploration.

Is Snark Un-Christian?

"Snark" is one of those wonderful terms born of the Internet. It reminds me of some of the great Yiddish words that sound like what they mean—like klutz, shlep, and schmuck. The word is basically a synonym for sarcastic, an amalgamation of "snide" and "remark." Depending on your perspective, to call someone "snarky" is either a compliment of the highest order or a derogatory term for an overly negative person.

Snark often plays out on social media as a sort of public gallows humor. You can spot it on Facebook, though it's more prevalent on micro-blogging sites like Twitter that offer opportunities for real-time back and forth repartee.

Some church folks are particularly adept at snark, making cutting comments about everything from liturgy to church meetings to the seven habits of the highly dysfunctional. At its best, snark highlights in a humorous manner the deeper truths that bubble just beneath the surface while also exposing self-serving hypocrisy. When engaged in a lighthearted rather than angry way, snark can be a delightful respite from the profound responsibilities of ministry. Indeed, I'd contend that true snark, while at times acidic, is never without a degree of levity.

Christians with a predilection for online snark occasionally encounter pushback from those who don't think it's appropriate. The best snark comes right up to the line without crossing over it and that can push buttons for people who expect more positive output from their clergy and lay leaders.

This all begs the question: Is snark un-Christian?

If you get back to the original definition of "sarcastic," I don't think you have to look much further than Jesus himself for validation. While it's rarely put this way, Jesus had a wicked sense of humor that made extensive use of both hyperbole and sarcasm. If Jesus was

Tweeting, I'm pretty confident he'd be a master of the medium (though I doubt he'd have as many followers as Justin Bieber).

Here are some examples:

- "Let the dead bury their own dead." (Matt. 8:21–22)
- "How can you say to your neighbor, 'Let me take the speck out of your eye,' while the log is in your own eye?" (Matt. 7:4)
- About John the Baptist: "What then did you go out to see? Someone dressed in soft robes? Look, those who put on fine clothing and live in luxury are in royal palaces." (Luke 7:25)
- Upon his arrest: "Have you come out with swords and clubs to arrest me as though I were a bandit?" (Mark 14:48)
- "Beware of the scribes, who like to walk around in long robes, and to be greeted with respect in the marketplaces, and to have the best seats in the synagogues and places of honor at banquets! They devour widows' houses and for the sake of appearance say long prayers." (Mark 12:38–40)
- About the scribes and Pharisees: "You blind guides! You strain out a gnat but swallow a camel!" (Matt. 23:24)
- About profaning the holy: "Do not give what is holy to dogs; and do not throw your pearls before swine, or they will trample them under foot and turn and maul you." (Matt. 7:6)

There are countless other instances of Jesus using a cutting remark to make his point and, yes, he also got a lot of flak. Obviously I'm not comparing snarky Christians to Jesus but there is a place for snark and edgy humor in the Church. Snark, like all humor, simply looks at life and faith and ministry from a slightly different angle and we all need that. Ultimately it's about taking our faith but not ourselves too seriously—which is critical to the health and vibrancy of the Church.

So snark on, friends. You're in good company.

Is Jesus Funny?

There's nothing worse than a humorless Christian. They're grim, sanctimonious, and judgmental. Yet a more nuanced reading of Scripture leads us irrevocably away from holier-than-thou solemnity and back to joy. Jesus uses humor to teach, to heal, to convert, and, ultimately, to redeem. In the process he shows us that laughter and profundity are not mutually exclusive.

But is Jesus funny? This question has long confounded theologians. Maybe it's all in how you define "humor." The Gospels aren't funny in the traditional sense. It's not slapstick comedy; there are no pratfalls or disciples saying "nyuck, nyuck, nyuck." The humor of Jesus is subtle, nearly imperceptible at first glance.

The Sermon on the Mount doesn't begin with a joke to warm up the crowd, though Jesus does display great wit, command of the language, a gift for irony and word plays, and his timing is impeccable—all hallmarks of great comedians. And, after all, the aim of the Evangelists was not to record Jesus's sense of humor. The Gospels are passion narratives, not anthologies containing "The Wit and Wisdom of Jesus Christ." But then the story of our salvation, the death and resurrection of our Lord, is serious business—our very life depends upon it.

Which is precisely why Jesus made his message accessible. Parables, with their use of common language and commentary on everyday situations, spoke directly to people. So, while Jesus's messages held the keys to salvation, they were couched in language people could understand. A master storyteller would never forsake humor as a means to reach an audience. Jesus, who spent much of his ministry breaking down barriers between people, knew that humor does exactly this. Humor disarms and unites; it sets people at ease and leaves them receptive to the speaker's message.

Since God created humor, it makes sense that Jesus would use humor to communicate with humanity. Without humor, life would be unbearable. Humor serves as a means to deal with the burdens of life while making light the yoke of sin, death, and human frailty. Jesus was sensitive to the important role it can play in discussing grave matters, recognizing that humor is as much a part of the human condition as suffering and joy. It is integral to the human condition, and Jesus embodied this just as much as he embodied forgiveness, compassion, and hope. Laughter is simply good for the soul and it allows us to confront the darker sides of life with grace and composure.

If humor is a gift from God, it's no wonder Jesus had a wonderfully vibrant sense of humor. But his humor is employed not merely to "get laughs." It is humor that seeks to inform and convert. Even when the humor is directed at a certain group, such as the Pharisees, it is still a humor borne of love and compassion. Jesus mocks the self-righteous even while calling them to open their eyes, repent, and see. And Jesus exposes our human foibles not to embarrass or condemn but to illuminate and transform. When we take ourselves too seriously, we commit perhaps humanity's greatest sin: trusting in ourselves rather than God. Jesus shows us the absurd consequences that invariably result.

The examples of Jesus's irony and wit are plentiful. Take, for instance, his relationship with Peter. Naming this impetuous, overly eager apostle "the rock" is amusing. You can almost envision the sly smile as Jesus says, "Upon this rock I will build my church." Time after time, Peter was anything but a rock in difficult situations and the irony must not have been lost on the other disciples. And yet, it indeed was upon this "rock" that the Church was built. With Jesus, the line between the deadly serious business of faith and the human attempt to live out this faith blurs and, because there is some of Peter in all of us, it becomes untenable to take ourselves too seriously. Which is precisely Jesus's point.

Perhaps we can view the humorless Pharisees as the ultimate straight men for Jesus. Throughout the four Gospels the joke, it seems, is on them. Their somber rigidity is paralyzing and their hypocrisy and self-righteousness keep them from true relationship with the divine. They are the perfect foils to Jesus's message of love. Jesus continually meets their scorn and contempt with quick wit and perfect timing. The encounters with the Pharisees are full of brilliant one-liners such as, "Give therefore to the emperor the things that are the emperor's, and to God the things that are God's." (Matt. 22:21), a perfect response dripping with irony. The blind leading the blind is, of course, a comical visual image and a pointed commentary on the religious leaders of the day (Matt. 15:14). And think about the hilarious image of straining out a gnat while eating a camel (Matt. 23:24). His hearers certainly chuckled at this purposefully ludicrous image and it invariably stuck with them.

There are hosts of other wonderfully amusing moments in the Gospel accounts. There is irony and humorous exaggeration, phrases that would have brought smiles to the lips of his hearers, if not full belly laughs. Explaining the efficacy of prayer he asks the twelve, "Is there anyone among you who, if your child asks for a fish, will give a snake instead of a fish? Or if the child asks for an egg, will give a scorpion?" (Luke 11:11–12). "It is easier for a camel to go through the eye of a needle than for someone who is rich to enter the kingdom of God" (Mark 10:25). That's a memorable image. What fool *would* place a lamp "under a bushel basket, or under the bed, and not on the lamp stand?" (Mark 4:21). And the list goes on and on if we are open to reading the Gospels through the hermeneutic of humor

It is a bit odd that within the Church the humor of Jesus is so roundly ignored. Maybe we're afraid to laugh in the presence of the divine. We tend to shy away from visions of our Lord smiling and joking and engaging us in laughter. Yet there is great evidence that Jesus desires this important piece of our humanity to shine forth. One obstacle may be that Jesus's mastery of words is literally lost in translation. Our Scripture is a translation of the Greek, which is a translation of Jesus's own Aramaic. Without knowledge of Jesus's native tongue, certain wordplays are simply lost to us. For instance, an added layer of Matthew 23:24 is that the Aramaic word for gnat is *galma* and the word for camel is *gamla*. We are blind to this aspect of the exchange.

We also lose the facial expressions and tone of voice so crucial to successful comedy. Jimmy Fallon can make us laugh with a simple facial expression or the inflection of his voice. A manuscript of his show wouldn't be nearly as amusing as seeing it live. Unfortunately the Gospels have been handed down to us as manuscripts rather than YouTube videos.

The point here is not to place Jesus in the Comedy Hall of Fame. Jerry Seinfeld cannot be hailed as the new Jesus (though they *are* both Jewish). Rather it is to encourage us to see and hear the message of our Lord with fresh eyes and ears; to discover a new aspect of his divine brilliance; and to meet him with renewed joy and laughter in our hearts.

AFTERWORD

As I was putting the final touches on this manuscript, word arrived that comedian Robin Williams died. I've always loved his iconic list "Top Ten Reasons to Be an Episcopalian." While I have no insights into his spiritual life, the former *Mork & Mindy* star grew up an Episcopalian and his list is absolutely brilliant.

Just to refresh your memory here it is:

Top Ten Reasons to Be an Episcopalian (according to Robin Williams)

10. No snake handling.
9. You can believe in dinosaurs.
8. Male and female God created them; male and female we ordain them.
7. You don't have to check your brains at the door.
6. Pew aerobics.
5. Church year is color-coded.
4. Free wine on Sunday.
3. All of the pageantry—none of the guilt.
2. You don't have to know how to swim to get baptized.

And the number one reason to be an Episcopalian:

1. No matter what you believe, there's bound to be at least one other Episcopalian who agrees with you.

Oddly enough, less than a week before his death, I had the audacity to update his list on my blog. Sure, it was the ultimate act of hubris, but I was on vacation and . . . what the heck? Humility is in the eye of the beholder—I think that's in the Bible somewhere.

Here's my list. If you'd like it permanently affixed to your back, we have tattoo artists standing by. Enjoy!

More Top Ten Reasons to Be an Episcopalian (according to Father Tim)

10. The only thing we take literally is "coffee hour."
9. All of the sacraments—none of the indulgences.
8. Gay and straight God created them; gay and straight we marry them.
7. Bouncers don't check your ID at communion.
6. Fire and incense, not fire and brimstone.
5. Guilt-free royal watching—because we're Anglicans.
4. Vestments cover a multitude of wardrobe malfunctions.
3. No "second collection."
2. Washington National Cathedral? Yeah, that's ours.

And the number one reason to be an Episcopalian:

1. We're the only ones God trusts enough to take the summer off.

the**facts**

Alzheimer's and other dementias

JULIAN C. HUGHES

Consultant in Old Age Psychiatry,
Northumbria Healthcare NHS
Foundation Trust
and Honorary Professor of
Philosophy of Ageing,
Institute for Ageing and Health
Newcastle University, UK

OXFORD
UNIVERSITY PRESS

OXFORD
UNIVERSITY PRESS

Great Clarendon Street, Oxford OX2 6DP

Oxford University Press is a department of the University of Oxford.
It furthers the University's objective of excellence in research, scholarship,
and education by publishing worldwide in

Oxford New York

Auckland Cape Town Dar es Salaam Hong Kong Karachi
Kuala Lumpur Madrid Melbourne Mexico City Nairobi
New Delhi Shanghai Taipei Toronto

With offices in

Argentina Austria Brazil Chile Czech Republic France Greece
Guatemala Hungary Italy Japan Poland Portugal Singapore
South Korea Switzerland Thailand Turkey Ukraine Vietnam

Oxford is a registered trade mark of Oxford University Press
in the UK and in certain other countries

Published in the United States
by Oxford University Press Inc., New York

© Oxford University Press, 2011

The moral rights of the author have been asserted

Database right Oxford University Press (maker)

First edition published 2011

British Library Cataloguing in Publication Data

Data available

Library of Congress Cataloguing in Publication Data

Data available

ISBN 978-0-19-959655-3

10 9 8 7 6 5 4 3 2

Typeset in Plantin
by Cenveo, Bangalore, India
Printed in Great Britain
on acid-free paper by
Clays Colour Press Ltd, Gosport, Hampshire

While every effort has been made to ensure that the contents of this book are as complete, accurate
and up-to-date as possible at the date of writing, Oxford University Press is not able to give any
guarantee or assurance that such is the case. Readers are urged to take appropriately qualified
medical advice in all cases. The information in this book is intended to be useful to the general
reader, but should not be used as a means of self-diagnosis or for the prescription of medication. The authors and the publishers do not accept responsibility or legal liability for any errors
in the text or for the misuse or misapplication of material in this book.

Foreword

Only in recent years have Alzheimer's disease and other dementias risen in public awareness. While once the subject seemed never to make the news, today it seems hardly to be out of it. The raised awareness is in part due to the activities of organisations like *Alzheimer's Society,* which has campaigned for the rights of those living with dementia, and in part due to demographics. Today there are 750,000 people with dementia in the UK but that number will reach one million by 2021. Of those of us who live beyond the age of 65, one in three of us will end our lives with dementia.

The next step is to improve everyone's understanding of dementia, to help us reduce stigma and enable everyone to be better prepared to face the challenge that it presents to our society. To begin that we need much more and much clearer information about dementia, as well as the impact it has on the 100,000 people who develop the condition each year and those who care for them.

That is why *Alzheimer's Society* welcomes this contribution from Professor Hughes, which will enable many more people to understand what dementia is, what the impact is and the challenges it presents.

The greater understanding will also enable us to make better judgments on ethical issues, some of which Professor Hughes raises in his book. This will encourage us all to understand that enabling the person with dementia to continue to live the life that they choose, in an independent way, will allow them to flourish, doing the sort of things we all do to feel fully human. It means remembering the person, remembering they wish to be known as the person and not for their dementia.

(Prof) Clive Ballard
Director of Research
Alzheimer's Society
London E1W 1JX
www.alzheimers.org.uk

Preface

The aim of this book is to set out the important facts about dementia in a way that is accessible to the non-specialist. As with many diseases, the complexity around dementia is huge and there are numerous facts to be considered. These move from facts about how many people suffer from the disease to facts about the different types of dementia. Underlying these different types of dementia, there are different causes. The causes themselves are multiple. For instance, there is no doubt that genetics can cause some cases of dementia, and make a contribution to almost all causes of dementia, but there are also environmental reasons to explain why people suffer from dementia. Moreover, social attitudes—stigma—can add to the distress suffered both by people with dementia and by their carers.

Much of the first half of the book is concerned to explain what dementia is and the different types. Much of the second half concerns how people with dementia should be treated or cared for. But the process of care starts with good assessment. There might be little more to be said about a disease, as long as the causes, assessment, and treatment are discussed in broad enough terms. Dementia, however, raises somewhat unique concerns. The link with ageing means that dementia poses a startling and huge challenge to the world as our population ages. The implications of dementia in an ageing world are immense. At another level, dementia raises questions of a fundamental nature about our standing as human beings in the world: it poses a threat to personhood, one which needs to be grasped properly.

Hence, there is an inevitable sense in which discussion of the facts to do with dementia cannot avoid discussing the values-based judgements that have to be made in order to try to help both people with dementia and their carers. So, this book will deal with the facts, but will set these facts within the context of a broader understanding of dementia as a condition that stems from the challenges of ageing and requires us to rethink our standing as human beings who live in an interdependent world.

Julian C. Hughes
Newcastle upon Tyne

Acknowledgements

I have tried to keep the referencing to a minimum for the sake of clarity. The book does, however, contain references where the material is taken directly from other sources. Many of the facts recorded have been derived from or checked against a variety of sources. My two main references have been the excellent *Oxford Textbook of Old Age Psychiatry*, edited by Robin Jacoby, Catherine Oppenheimer, Tom Dening, and Alan Thomas, and the equally excellent fourth edition of the definitive textbook *Dementia*, edited by David Ames, Alistair Burns, and John O'Brien. The full details of both books appear in Appendix 2. Readers who require further information about dementia are advised to consult these texts and the other sources listed in Appendix 2. Readers who require more immediate practical advice should contact their local Alzheimer's Society or other relevant support organization. The web addresses for these organizations appear, with other useful contacts, in Appendix 1.

I wish to thank the following for permission to reproduce copyright material: Alzheimer's Disease International for permission to use the material in Box 1.1 and to adapt material for Figures 1.1 and 1.2; the Alzheimer's Society for permission to adapt the material for Box 10.1; the Nuffield Council on Bioethics for permission to use Box 14.2 and to adapt the information in Box 14.3; and Quay Books for permission to adapt the contents of Box 11.1 and to use the information in Box 14.1. I should particularly like to thank Professor John O'Brien for providing me with the brain scans that appear in Chapters 4 and 9.

I must thank Nicola Wilson and Jenny Wright, with the rest of the staff involved at Oxford University Press, for their encouragement and consistently helpful advice. Finally, I wish to thank Lindsay Turner for her excellent secretarial help and my wife, Anne, for her proof-reading skills and ubiquitous support.

Disclaimer

Any opinions expressed in the book are entirely those of the author and do not necessarily reflect the views of any organizations with which he is associated. The case histories used in this book are entirely fictional (unless stated otherwise), but are based on reality. Every effort has been made to ensure that the details about and dosages of drugs are accurate, but prescribers are urged to check local, contemporaneous, and authoritative sources before prescribing any medication. Psychosocial interventions should only be used in appropriate contexts under the supervision of properly trained and registered practitioners.

Contents

1

Setting the scene

➡ Key points

◆ The number of people with dementia is growing as the world population ages: dementia is not a part of normal ageing but it is a manifestation of ageing.

◆ Almost 5 percent of people over 60 years have dementia; over the age of 95 years, the prevalence is above 30 percent; dementia affects younger people too.

◆ Dementia costs about 1 percent of the total amount that the world produces, but the costs are not equitably spread across the world.

◆ The economic burden of dementia in the UK is about the same as for cancer, heart disease, and stroke added together, yet dementia research is under-funded.

◆ There is a gradual, but increasing, awareness of dementia as a political issue.

◆ We should make sure that stigmatizing attitudes do not themselves disable people with dementia.

Introduction

In the Western world, it is strange if you have not heard of dementia. President Ronald Reagan had it and famously (and movingly) let the world know. Many other famous people have had dementia: the actors Charles Bronson and Charlton Heston, the actress Rita Hayworth, the singer Perry Como, the composer Aaron Copland, the British Prime Minister Harold Wilson, and the children's author Terry Pratchett, to name but a few. The British newscaster John Suchet has spoken movingly about his wife, Bonnie, who has dementia. Iris Murdoch, the novelist and philosopher, also had dementia and was depicted in the film *Iris*, based on the account given by her husband, the academic, John Bayley. Moreover, most people will know someone who has dementia—if not an elderly relative, then the elderly relative of a friend.

And yet, surprisingly, some people do not know about dementia. This is partly because it still carries a stigma. People do not wish to talk about and are ashamed of it. The word 'stigma' comes from the Greek and referred to the sign that criminals or other outcasts might have tattooed on them. People with dementia are often felt to be embarrassing, because of their confusion or behaviour, so it is as if they are marked out by their condition. In fact, it is only recently that people with dementia have started to be open about what they have. So, while Ronald Reagan went public in 1994, Harold Wilson's dementia was largely kept a secret until after his death in 1995. There may be various reasons why people are now more willing to speak out about dementia: people are more open about other diseases too. But it might also be because, as the scientific study of the brain has advanced, the prospect of being able to do something about dementia seems to be closer. So people want to speak out and attract attention to what needs to be done.

I have already touched upon several themes that need to be discussed in more detail later in this book: for instance, the advances in neuroscience and the social reactions to dementia. But this chapter is about setting the scene. Before talking in detail about dementia itself, I want to paint the background context in terms of facts and figures. I must, however, confess to two things I have already done that might paint the wrong sort of picture. First, I started by talking of the 'Western' world, as if dementia is not so much of a problem for other countries. We shall see that this is not the case. Second, I talked about 'elderly' relatives, which is itself a bad thing for two reasons: dementia is not a condition that only affects elderly people; and talk of 'the elderly' can also be regarded as stigmatizing inasmuch as it tends to suggest that all older people can be lumped together in one box. But in doing this we may be stigmatizing 'the elderly' as well, especially if we then tend to link 'them' to dementia. Not all older people have dementia. Older people are as different as younger people and people with dementia are by no means all the same. They retain their unique individual qualities even in the advanced stages of the disease, albeit they also change.

My scene setting will involve looking at the numbers of people with dementia in the United Kingdom and in the world. The significance of these numbers has to be understood in terms of the costs, which are both financial and emotional. Different cultures respond in different ways to dementia, which I shall also consider briefly. I shall touch on the political reaction to dementia, and finally I shall return to the theme of ageing.

Numbers

The number of people with dementia is growing as the world population ages. Alzheimer's Disease International (ADI) is the international federation of Alzheimer societies throughout the world. In their *World Alzheimer Report 2009*, based on the latest figures at the time, they made a number of (sometimes staggering) estimates. Here are just some of them:

- There would be about 36 million people in the world with dementia in 2010;
- There would be over 65 million people with dementia by 2030;
- There would be about 115 million people with dementia by 2050;
- This represents an increase of 225 percent between 2010 and 2050;
- The world population of people aged over 60 years would be about 758 million in 2010;
- Hence, the prevalence of dementia (i.e. the proportion of the population affected) was estimated to be 4.7 percent.

This figure, roughly 5 percent, is usually quoted as the prevalence of dementia in those over 60 years old. In one sense this is quite hopeful, because it means that 95 percent of those over 60 years will *not* have dementia. This hides the fact, however, that the prevalence of dementia increases with age. For those over 80 years the prevalence is higher than 20 percent; and it continues to climb to over 30 percent in those aged about 95 years old. We might still wish to argue that most of the very old will not have dementia, but this ignores the importance of the demographic changes (i.e. the ageing of the population), which mean that the overall number of people with dementia goes up significantly as societies live longer.

Using the UK as an example, whereas in 2007 it seemed reasonable to predict that there would be just over 600 000 people with dementia in the UK by 2010, by the time we arrived at 2010 the figure was 700 000 people. Although up to the age of about 80 years the increase in the number of people with dementia will be slight, after the age of 80 years the numbers start to increase quite markedly. This is because we are all living longer. In 20 years' time there will be many more people living to be 90 or 100 years old and hence, because the prevalence of dementia increases with age, there will be increasing numbers of people with dementia.

We should not forget, however, that there are about 15 000 people in the UK who are under the age of 65 years and yet have dementia. Most of these (about two thirds) will be over 55 years, but dementia can occur in people as young as 30 years old, albeit very rarely. We should remember, too, that many people with Down's syndrome develop dementia at a much younger age than other adults. It has been suggested, for instance, that the average age for a person with Down's syndrome to develop dementia is about 55 years, which implies that many people with Down's syndrome will be below this age when dementia appears. And we should also remember that people with Down's syndrome are themselves living longer, making it more likely that they will eventually have dementia.

To return to the 2009 report from ADI, the prevalence of dementia, worked out on average at about 5 percent, varies to a degree between countries, but most countries lie somewhere between 5 and 7 percent. Overall prevalence figures are brought down by the lower prevalence rates in sub-Saharan Africa, but this probably reflects the lack of studies in this region, which means that the numbers are not as trustworthy as they are in areas where there have been lots of studies (such as in Europe and the United States). Dementia is a world-wide problem, which affects people in similar numbers despite different background cultures. In other words, even if diet, education, and lifestyle generally are important (as we shall see that they are), dementia is powerfully driven by biology. And the most important biological fact is that we age.

The reason for emphasizing the relevance of ageing is that this is having profound effects globally. The number of people with dementia will increase the most in low- and middle-income countries. This is because the poorer countries of the world are predicted to see the biggest increases in terms of their ageing populations. Higher-income countries are also ageing, but not as fast. This is partly because people in higher-income countries already live longer; but also, as better survival occurs in poorer countries, their populations will grow (at least until the birth rate falls). In any case, the fact is that low- and middle-income countries, that is, those that can least afford it, face a steep rise in the number of people they will need to look after. This takes us on to the next bit of scene setting, which is to do with the cost of dementia.

Costs

In 2010, the ADI produced a further report that focused on the costs of dementia. The *World Alzheimer Report 2010* is again filled with arresting and sometimes worrying facts. For example:

- The worldwide costs of dementia in 2010 were estimated to be US$604 billion;
- This is around 1 percent of the world's gross domestic product (GDP), i.e. 1 percent of the total amount that the world produces in terms of goods and services;

- The percentage of GDP ranges from 0.24 for low-income countries to 1.24 in high-income countries;
- Informal care (i.e. unpaid care provided by families and others) accounts for about 42 percent of the costs;
- Direct social care costs (provided by professionals in the community or in long-term care settings) similarly account for 42 percent of the overall costs;
- Direct medical care costs are lower at 16 percent;
- In low-income countries most of the care costs (58 percent) are for informal care, whereas in high-income countries informal care makes up only 40 percent of the total costs;
- Direct social care costs account for almost 50 percent of the costs in high-income countries, whereas they account for only 10 percent in lower-income countries.

The Report makes the point that if dementia were a company, and these figures represented its income, it would be the world's largest company in terms of revenue; if dementia care were a country, it would be the eighteenth largest economy. In short, dementia is a major issue as far as its economic impact is concerned. But whereas, in terms of prevalence, it will be an increasingly big issue for low- and middle-income countries, at the moment the spending on dementia care is skewed disproportionately towards the high-income countries (see Fig. 1.1).

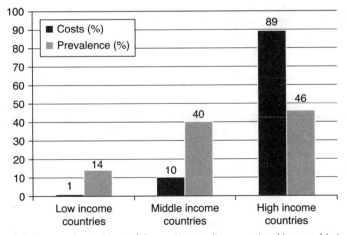

Figure 1.1 Costs and prevalence of dementia according to national income (derived from ADI's *World Alzheimer Report 2010*).

The point of Fig. 1.1 is not that that too much money is being spent in high-income countries. It is that the expenditure is not fairly distributed in terms of the numbers of people affected. In other words, the spending on dementia is not equitable. This is an even bigger worry if the problem is going to worsen in poorer countries as they age more rapidly relative to richer countries. But it does not necessarily mean that we are spending too much money on dementia in the richer countries.

Actually, given that large slices of the cost (or economic impact) are to do with informal care by, for instance, relatives and friends, what these figures reflect is the burden of the disease on society. Remember that the informal care costs are higher in low-income countries (58 percent) than they are in high-income countries (40 percent).

If we want to find out whether we are spending too much or too little on dementia, which in the end must be a political decision reflecting the values of society, we need to make comparisons with other health conditions of a similar nature. This was done in the UK by the University of Oxford, who produced a report in 2010 for the Alzheimer's Research Trust, which is incorporated in the ADI 2010 Report. It estimated that the annual costs to society of dementia were as follows:

- £23 billion for dementia;
- £12 billion for cancer;
- £8 billion for heart disease;
- £5 billion for stroke.

So the economic burden of dementia for the UK is about the same as for cancer, heart disease, and stroke added together. In which case, it would make sense if the funding for research were to reflect this burden. But the situation is just the reverse.

Figure 1.2 shows that, rather than money being spent on research in proportion to the economic burden the particular disease places on society, instead (at least for these conditions) it is the other way around. In the UK, in terms of research, we seem to spend least on the condition that costs us the most.

Political reaction

If the situation is as clear-cut as I have suggested with these figures, in other words, if there is an increasing human problem with a huge economic impact, we might expect that there should have been a political reaction. The good news is that increasingly we are seeing such a reaction. This is, in part, because

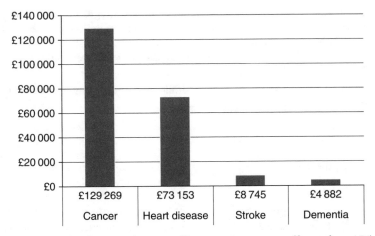

Figure 1.2 Funding for research per £1 million spent on care costs (figures from ADI's *World Alzheimer Report 2010*).

of the advocacy of organizations such as Alzheimer's International, Alzheimer Europe, and the various national Alzheimer organizations, such as the Alzheimer's Society in the UK.

As shown in Box 1.1, Alzheimer's International has produced a Charter of six principles to make Alzheimer's disease a global priority.

Box 1.1 Global Alzheimer's Disease Charter

The following six principles should be adopted to make Alzheimer's disease and other dementias a global priority:

1. Promote awareness and understanding of the disease
2. Respect the human rights of people with dementia
3. Recognize the key role of families and carers
4. Provide access to health and social care
5. Stress the importance of optimal treatment after diagnosis
6. Take action to prevent the disease through improvements in public health

Reproduced from Alzheimer Disease International's *World Alzheimer Report 2009*, with permission

In the UK, for instance, a national dementia strategy, *Living Well With Dementia*, was launched in England in 2009, and was followed in 2010 by Scotland's National Dementia Strategy. There have been similar initiatives elsewhere. The three themes underpinning the National Dementia Strategy for England are as follows:

1. Improving public and professional attitudes and understanding of dementia;
2. Early diagnosis and intervention for all;
3. Good-quality care and support at all stages from diagnosis through to the end of life.

Although these themes are only particular to England, they summarize the main areas of concern if people with dementia are to receive the sort of support and help that they need. Of course, the challenge is to make sure that the detailed objectives of the strategy in England, as in other countries, are achieved. This takes political will, determination, and perseverance, as well as good planning. But there are two particular points to be made about the political agenda.

The needs of special groups

First, it can be considered a duty of the state to look after its most vulnerable citizens, which will include people with dementia and their carers. More will be said about this in later chapters. But any society needs to pay special attention to their minority ethnic groups (which will include indigenous peoples in some countries), particularly because these groups often find it difficult to access the appropriate health services. There may be:

- language barriers;
- lack of understanding among health workers of cultural differences;
- distrust of orthodox (e.g. Western) medicine;
- unhelpful assumptions (e.g. that certain minority groups look after their own and do not require outside help).

Hence, national strategies or programmes need to target particular vulnerable groups. There are other groups that will also require particular attention, such as people with younger-onset dementia and people with learning disabilities, some of whom (as I discussed above) are more prone to dementia.

Individual political action

Second, it is important to remember that politics is not something that other people do! We all contribute. At a national level this may only be by voting (or by deciding not to vote); but we can contribute by our individual actions too.

Increasingly, we have seen people with dementia and their carers becoming more active and more vocal (President Reagan's letter about his Alzheimer's disease was an example). This helps to combat the stigma I alluded to above. It does this partly by increasing our understanding of what it is like to have dementia. Such sharing of experience can also be supportive for people with dementia and for their carers. For example, the Dementia Advocacy and Support Network International (DASNI) provides an internet-based support group for people with dementia and those who care for them. It aims to lessen the isolation some people with dementia feel and, run by people with dementia, it also hopes to increase their own understanding of the conditions that affect them. By attracting attention to the different types of dementia, the problems faced by all concerned can be understood, which will also increase political pressure both regionally and nationally. Hence the importance of support for local and national groups, such as the Alzheimer's Society in the UK and its sister groups elsewhere. Appendix 1 provides the web addresses for a number of helpful organizations, including DASNI.

Conclusion: dementia and ageing

This chapter has been about setting the scene. One of the major bits of scene setting has been to place dementia in the context of our ageing world. I am going to end the chapter by making some points about ageing, because it is important to see the connections between dementia and ageing correctly.

Is dementia a part of normal ageing?

There is an important and simple answer to this question: no! But there is also a more complicated response. The simple answer is 'no' because if you suggest that it is normal to have dementia, then you are saying that the suffering that comes with dementia is normal. Also, most older people do not have dementia, so it does not seem to be the normal way to age. And the answer is important because, if it were normal to experience dementia, then there might be no need for anyone to try to make things better—you can just be told 'it's normal for your age'! Whereas, in fact, dementia is harmful. We can see this when we look at the brains of people with dementia—they are usually very different from the brains of similarly aged people who do not have dementia. We can see it when we compare the person of 70 years with advanced dementia and the person of the same age who continues to be active in the community, as part of a family or by performing voluntary work. For all these reasons, therefore, it is wrong to think of dementia as being normal.

The more complicated response, however, is that dementia is a manifestation of ageing. As we have seen, even though dementia can start at a younger age in some people, it becomes more likely as we age. This is because the changes that occur in dementia are more likely to be found as we get older. The changes in the brain found in people with dementia are also found in older people without symptoms or signs of dementia: the brain changes are more common in older people, even if most older people do not have dementia. To put the point another way, there is no clear biological cut-off between normal and abnormal. Scientists have made up cut-offs—in terms of the amount of pathology that has to be seen in the brain—which are based on understanding how likely it is that a person will have dementia if they have a certain amount of pathology; but the truth is that there is a spectrum. The boundaries are blurred so it is often not possible to be certain whether or not a person has dementia just by looking at the brain. In other words, there is a continuum from normal to abnormal. But, to reiterate, this does not mean that dementia is normal. It just means that what is normal and what is abnormal is decided on different grounds. It is decided by looking at the whole picture: the picture of the whole person.

Should the problems of dementia and the problems of ageing be regarded as similar?

Well, it depends what you mean by 'problems'! In one sense, the problems of dementia are unique to dementia. *Never* being able to remember where they live is not a routine problem for older people. But many older people find it harder to remember *some* things. A general slowing down as we age, both physically and in some aspects of our mental functioning (remember that on some measures of intelligence we reach our peak performance in our twenties), can be regarded as problematic.

But another answer to the question is to reject the very idea that we should think in terms of problems. If we are thinking of scene setting, the question is: must we always see dementia and ageing as being problematic? Yes, there are aspects of getting older that can be a nuisance, but most older people say that they enjoy a good quality of life. Similarly, while some aspects of dementia are very upsetting, not every aspect of being a person with dementia is. Older people continue to live fruitful, useful, and varied lives. In fact, they contribute hugely to the economy, despite the tendency for people to think of the ageing population as an economic problem. People with dementia can also continue to contribute to and participate in their communities in a variety of ways.

This leads to a very important point. It would be discrimination to say to someone that they could no longer drive solely because they had reached a certain age (it would be fine to say this if they were driving badly). It would be unjust to say to someone that they could not have an operation only because they had reached a particular birthday (it would be fine to say that they were not fit enough for the operation). In a similar way, *just because* a person has dementia, it does not mean that they should be prevented from doing certain things and it does not mean that they should be treated differently. We no longer tolerate ageism and we should not tolerate behaviours or policies that discriminate against people with dementia. The important point is this: sometimes the things that other people do and the attitudes they take can make the person seem worse than he or she really is. Just as it has been said that we should celebrate ageing and the possibilities it brings, so too we should celebrate the remaining possibilities for people with dementia. So our scene setting ends on a positive note: people with dementia can still participate in activities that other people enjoy; they can still be creative; they can still engage with those around them; some of them can still drive (under the right circumstances). Many people fear dementia more than any other condition associated with getting old. But this is because the reality of dementia (for many and for much of the time) is not what they think it is. It certainly should not be the case that the actions of others or the attitudes of society make it worse than it needs to be. There is no doubt that dementia, like many other diseases, is cruel. Society should not make it worse. If we focus on the whole picture—the whole person in his or her social setting—we are more likely to get things right.

2

How the brain works

➜ Key points

◆ The complexity of the brain means that small amounts of damage can have profound effects; but there is also the possibility of compensation for damage.

◆ Functions in the brain tend to be localized, although a lot of functions are shared between different sites.

◆ A major division in the brain is between the cerebral cortex, the grey matter of the brain, concerned with higher (cognitive) functions, and the subcortical white matter, which is involved in the transmission of neuronal information between the different parts of the brain.

◆ A brain nerve cell, or neuron, works by an action potential (an electrical nerve impulse) travelling down it to cause the release of a neurotransmitter at the synapse; this in turn activates receptors on the new neuron, which set off a further nerve impulse.

◆ Anything that interferes with the development of an action potential, or the formation or release of neurotransmitters, stops the neuron from working.

Introduction

The brain is an immensely complicated organ, which ultimately controls all that we do. Its intricate convolutions can seem at first sight unlikely to contain much order. Luckily, the structure of the brain can be simplified. And for the purposes of this book we need to be clear about two main issues:

- first, concerning how different areas of the brain perform different functions;
- second, concerning how the brain can go wrong.

While simplifying matters, it is worth remembering that the actual complexity of the brain is staggering. There are said to be between fifty and one hundred billion (10^{11}) neurons (or nerve cells). There are then one thousand trillion (10^{15}) connections between cells, with each cell making thousands of connections to other cells. This complexity has good and bad effects. It means, on the one hand, that slight damage in one part of the brain may have significant effects elsewhere. On the other hand, it means that the brain is able to compensate, to some degree at least, when things go wrong.

The structure of the brain

In this section I shall look at the different parts of the brain and explain what they do. First, it is immediately striking that the brain has two halves, a left and a right. It is then split into different lobes. Table 2.1 gives details of the different lobes of the brain and the functions that are connected to these particular lobes. Figure 2.1 shows where the lobes are located in the brain.

Table 2.1 also records the *dys*function that results from damage to the different lobes of the brain. The table splits the functions according to whether the side of the brain is 'dominant' or 'non-dominant'. The dominant side (or hemisphere) is the side that controls language. In almost all right-handed people, the left hemisphere is dominant. In many left-handed people, the left hemisphere is dominant too. The usually accepted view is that the left side of the brain deals with words and the right side of the brain with music and pictures. Of course, as we might expect, things are not as simple as this and, in fact, both sides of the brain are involved in dealing with most things. They are linked by a huge bundle of nerve fibres called the corpus callosum. The whole brain tends, therefore, to work together. Nevertheless, if a stroke affects one side rather than the other, the difference in terms of symptoms and signs can be quite striking.

Just underneath the main body of the brain is a lobe called the cerebellum. As Figure 2.1 records, it is normally thought of in connection with coordination

Table 2.1 Lobes of the brain: function and dysfunction

Brain lobe	Function	Dysfunction
Frontal	Personality, social behaviour, emotional control, language, motor function, urination	Seizures, paralysis, sexual and social disinhibition, poor motivation and planning, impaired memory, problems with production of speech (expressive dysphasia), incontinence
Dominant parietal	Language, calculation	Problems with speech, calculation, reading, performing complex tasks, recognition, sensory and visual problems
Non-dominant parietal	Constructional abilities, spatial awareness	Problems with constructional tasks, with dressing, with spatial orientation, neglect of body on other side, sensory and visual problems
Dominant temporal	Language, verbal memory, smell, auditory perception, balance	Receptive dysphasia (i.e. problems understanding language), problems reading, poor verbal memory, problems with vision and complex hallucinations
Non-dominant temporal	Melody, pitch and auditory perception, non-verbal memory, smell, balance	Poor non-verbal memory, impaired musical skills, problems with vision and complex hallucinations
Occipital	Visual processing	Visual inattention, difficulty with visual recognition, visual loss and hallucinations
Cerebellum	Motor function, language, executive function and working memory, attention	Incoordination, language problems, poor attention, executive problems (e.g. sequencing)

and balance; but (as suggested in Table 2.1) the reality is more complex and, in fact, it is involved in some 'higher' functions.

On the inner side of each hemisphere, in the middle and forming a circuit around the ventricles (which are the fluid-filled cavities in the middle of the brain), there are a series of structures that make up the limbic system. Table 2.2 presents the names of some of the different parts of the limbic system and suggests their functions.

Once again, it has to be kept in mind that the reality is likely to be much more complicated than Table 2.2 suggests. The limbic system is regarded as being an older part of the brain in evolutionary terms. It controls many of our basic functions, for instance through its control of the organs in the body that release hormones (the endocrine system). The limbic system also has an effect on the

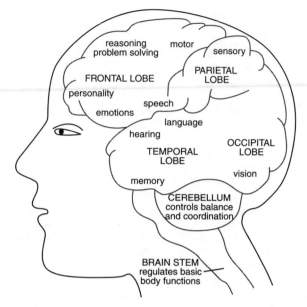

Figure 2.1 The brain. Reproduced from Daisley A, Tams R, and Kischka U (2009) *Head Injury: The Facts*, Oxford University Press, with permission.

Table 2.2 Important structures and functions of the limbic system

Structure	Function
Amygdala	To do with motivation, fear, and reward
Cingulate gyrus	Involved in regulation of autonomic functions (e.g. heart rate and blood pressure) and in cognitive processing (e.g. attention)
Hippocampus	Involved in long-term episodic memories and spatial orientation
Hypothalamus	Controls autonomic nervous system through release of hormones, with influence on blood pressure, heart rate, hunger and thirst, sexual arousal, and the sleep–wake cycle
Mammillary bodies	Involved in memory (affected by severe alcoholism; see Chapter 8)
Parahippocampal gyrus	Involved in spatial memory
Pituitary	Releases hormones to control (among other things) the adrenal glands, blood pressure, fluid retention, the thyroid gland (and thus metabolism generally)
Thalamus	A relay station between the spinal cord and other areas of the brain and the cerebral cortex (e.g. very important in pain perception)

autonomic nervous system. This is the part of the nervous system that controls some basic functions such as heart rate and blood pressure.

These basic (lower) functions are regarded as more ancient. The higher functions of the brain, to do with thought, understanding, calculation, and so on, depend on the cerebral cortex and are regarded as more recent in evolutionary terms. The cortex is a sheet of tissue running over the surface of the brain. This nervous tissue is known as the 'grey matter'. It is only 2–4 mm thick but has six layers. It is contrasted with the 'white matter'. This is formed from the axons of the neurons or nerve cells, which are surrounded by a sheath of material known as myelin. Myelin insulates the nerve cells and allows conduction to take place more quickly along the cells. The white matter is myelinated, whereas the grey matter is unmyelinated. This makes sense if we think that the information being processed in the cortex needs to be transported very quickly to other parts of the brain. It leads to differences between cortical and subcortical dementias. Typically, as we shall see, subcortical dementias, where the white matter is affected, are characterized by slow processing of information.

> We can see, therefore, that *where* an insult occurs in the brain will determine *what sort of problem* the person experiences.

But next we need to consider how the brain actually works and this means understanding how the individual nerve cells or neurons work.

How neurons work

The basic shape of a neuron is that it has a cell body (or soma) along with dendrites and an axon (in fact, neuronal cells will be very different depending on their location). The dendrites are thin branching parts of the cell and can be thought of as the parts that receive incoming information. The axon, which can be extremely long, is the part of the cell that reaches out to communicate with other parts of the body through its terminal branches.

The neuron works because two things happen.

1. An electrical impulse passes down the axon. This is called an action potential. It results from tiny changes in the cell wall of the neuron that allows ions to pass in and out. An ion is an element such as sodium, potassium or calcium, which carries an electrical charge. Sodium and potassium carry one positive charge (Na^+ and K^+), whereas calcium carries a double positive charge (Ca^{++}). Changes in the fluctuation of ions in and out of the cell cause the electrical current to move along the cell body. This detail might not seem important, but given that every nerve cell in the body requires these elements to be at the right concentration, it becomes obvious that too much or too little of these

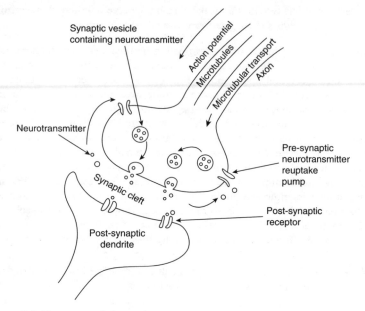

Figure 2.2 Neurotransmission at the synapse.

elements may have a profound effect and stop the neurons from working properly. This is why it is important that blood tests are performed to check these elements during assessments for memory problems (see Chapter 9).

2. The second process that is going on in the nervous system to help it function is that the neurons are communicating with one another by transmitting chemicals. This neurotransmission occurs from the end of the axon. The chemicals, or neurotransmitters, are released in little packets into the gap, known as the synapse, between one nerve cell and the other. Figure 2.2 shows a schematic picture of the synapse.

The chemicals then bind to receptor sites on the new nerve on the far side of the synapse. This in turn sets off a further chain of events in which, with the right amount of stimulation, a further action potential is generated in the new neuron. (Of course, outside the brain the nerve will often terminate at a muscle, so the effect of the release of the neurochemical will be, for instance, to make the muscle contract.)

How do things go wrong?

Having described how the neuron works, it should then become apparent that there are several ways in which things might go wrong. For instance, in order to release the neurotransmitter into the synapse the right chemicals must have been brought to the terminal end of the axon. This requires an effective and efficient transportation system within the cell. The axon contains **microtubules** (see Figure 2.2) along which the neurotransmitters and the chemicals that form the neurotransmitters are conveyed in an orderly fashion. If the microtubules become disrupted, this will not be possible. All of this activity requires considerable energy. If anything affects the production of energy, therefore, the cells will not be able to work as efficiently. This would help to explain why oxygen is so important to the brain. In Chapter 8, I shall mention, albeit briefly, mitochondrial disorders. The **mitochondria** are the organs within the cell that produce the energy to keep the cell working. Finally, it can be seen that if anything has affected the formation of the neurotransmitters themselves, the whole system will not work as it should. As we shall see, in Alzheimer's disease and in dementia with Lewy bodies there is a deficit in acetylcholine, which is one of the neurotransmitters. Although there are drugs that can boost the effect of any remaining acetylcholine, once the source of this neurotransmitter has been severely reduced, the drugs become less effective (see Chapter 12).

Neurotransmitter pathways

Each of the four major neurotransmitters (noradrenaline, dopamine, serotonin, and acetylcholine) have pathways in the brain with specific effects. These are outlined in Table 2.3.

Each pathway is a bundle of nerve cells that has a specific route in the brain to bring about particular effects. Many drugs that are used in connection with dementia are intended to affect, in one way or another, particular pathways. For instance, loss of dopamine neurons in the nigrostriatal pathway, which connects the substantia nigra to a part of the brain called the striatum, is the cause of Parkinson's disease. In addition, antipsychotic drugs block the effects of this pathway and can cause parkinsonism (i.e. the symptoms and signs of Parkinson's disease). A further example would be the cholinergic pathway (that is a pathway which uses acetylcholine as the neurotransmitter), which starts in the nucleus basalis of Meynert, towards the base of the brain, but then runs up to project widely to the cortex. In Parkinson's disease, Alzheimer's disease, and dementia with Lewy bodies, this nucleus degenerates and the loss of acetylcholine correlates with (that is, goes along with) problems with recall and learning new material.

Glutamate: an excitatory neurotransmitter

As I mentioned above, there are millions of interconnections between the neurons. The action of one nerve ending may be to excite the target nerve,

Table 2.3 Major neurotransmitter pathways

Neurotransmitter	Pathway	Function
Acetylcholine	From areas in the base of the brain, e.g. the nucleus basalis of Meynert, to subcortical structures and widely within the cortex	Involved in new learning, memory, level of arousal
Dopamine	From various areas in the base of the brain, there are four pathways: (1) the *mesocortical* pathway goes to the frontal lobe; (2) the *mesolimbic* pathway goes to structures in the limbic system; (3) the *nigrostriatal* pathway goes from the substantia nigra to an area of the brain called the striatum, which is involved in movement and is the pathway implicated in Parkinson's disease and parkinsonism; (4) the *tuberoinfundibular pathway* goes from the hypothalamus to the pituitary	Involved in hormone release, in motor function, cognition, and in the reward (or pleasure) system
Noradrenaline (in USA, norepinephrine)	From the brain stem (the locus coeruleus) and elsewhere to significant proportions of the subcortex, cortex, and spinal cord	To do with arousal and reward
Serotonin	From the dorsal raphe nucleus in the brain stem to widespread areas of the subcortex, cortex, cerebellum, and spinal cord	To do with appetite, mood, body temperature, sleep, and pain

while another nerve ending may inhibit the target nerve's activity. Glutamate is an excitatory neurotransmitter. When glutamate is released from a cell it needs to be taken up again so that it does not cause excess excitation. This process can go wrong, including in Alzheimer's disease. When too much glutamate builds up, calcium ions enter the cells via small channels guarded by receptors called NMDA receptors (which stands for *N*-methyl-D-aspartic acid), which respond to glutamate. This leads to cell damage and eventually cell death. As we shall see in Chapter 12, there is one anti-dementia drug, memantine, which blocks the NMDA receptors and thus stops the calcium ions from entering the cell.

Glial cells

The neurons are not the only type of cell in the brain. The other important types of cell are the glial cells. These cells:

♦ maintain an appropriate environment in which the neurons can work;

- provide a structure to keep the neurons in place;
- supply oxygen and other nutrients to the neurons;
- produce myelin to insulate the neurons;
- clear dead tissue and destroy pathogens.

It can be seen, therefore, that anything that distorts or interrupts the working of the glial cells will affect the way in which the brain works. In addition, the glial cells are very important when it comes to inflammatory responses in the brain. There are various types of glial cells, e.g. astrocytes, oligodendrocytes, and Schwann cells.

Fluids

There are two types of fluid that need to be considered briefly: cerebrospinal fluid (CSF) and blood.

Cerebrospinal fluid

CSF is a clear fluid that circulates within and around the brain and the spinal cord. The brain is covered by layers of tissue called the meninges. The middle layer of the meninges is the arachnoid mater and the layer closest to the brain is the pia mater. The CSF is between these two layers. It also fills the ventricles, the large spaces within the middle of the brain. The details of the CSF do not need to detain us. However, CSF is important if it starts to build up, as it does in (so-called) normal pressure hydrocephalus. This is discussed in Chapter 8. It is also worth noting at this point that when, because of atrophy (that is, the process of cell shrinkage and death commonly seen in dementia) the spaces in the brain, such as the ventricles, enlarge, it might be tempting to think this is caused by excess fluid, whereas it is more commonly the other way around. In other words the CSF fills the increasingly available space.

Blood

The blood supply to the brain comes from the two vertebral arteries and from the two internal carotid arteries. The details of the blood supply can be found elsewhere. As we shall see in Chapter 5, however, problems with the blood supply are a potent cause of dementia. Normally there is very strict control of what can pass from the blood to the brain. This is called the 'blood–brain barrier'. It can be affected by disease. Perhaps the other important point to note is that many of the small arteries in the brain are called 'end arteries'. This means that the artery is the only supply of blood to that particular bit of brain tissue. Hence, if the end artery is compromised, the particular area of the brain served by the artery is in danger.

Conclusion

The brain is the most complicated organ of the body. The complexity means that small changes can have significant effects, but also that the brain can sometimes compensate when there is damage. How the brain works is known in outline, but the details are still far from clear.

3

Defining dementia

Key points

- Dementia is an acquired, chronic, usually progressive disorder, which affects multiple parts of the brain, and can lead to symptoms and signs that involve higher cognitive functions, activities of daily living, emotional and social behaviours, and physical abilities.

- The main types of dementia are Alzheimer's disease, dementia with Lewy bodies, vascular dementia, mixtures of vascular dementia and other types, and frontotemporal dementia.

- There are many rarer types of dementia, which can be more common in younger-onset dementia, but Alzheimer's disease is still the commonest form even in this group.

Introduction

Having set the scene in Chapter 1, I still have not said what dementia is. In this chapter, dementia will be defined and I shall end by mentioning the main types of dementia before describing them in more detail in subsequent chapters.

Dementia: an umbrella term

Dementia describes a syndrome. A syndrome is a collection of symptoms and signs. Symptoms are the things that we notice and complain about as patients. Signs are the aspects of the illness that other people, especially our healthcare professionals, notice when they examine us. A person with dementia may present with the symptom of poor memory. The doctor may then also notice that there are some abnormalities in the way that the person's nerves

23

> ## Box 3.1 Definition of dementia
>
> Dementia is a syndrome due to disease of the brain, usually of a chronic or progressive nature in which there is disturbance of multiple higher cortical functions, including memory, thinking, orientation, comprehension, calculation, learning capacity, language and judgement. Consciousness is not clouded. Impairments of cognitive function are commonly accompanied, and occasionally preceded, by deterioration in emotional control, social behaviour, or motivation.
>
> Source: *ICD-10 Classification of Mental and Behavioural Disorders: Clinical Descriptions and Diagnostic Guidelines*. Geneva: WHO; 1992

are working, which could be a sign of dementia. But what is it? Box 3.1 gives the definition of dementia from the *International Classification of Diseases* (ICD), which is produced by the World Health Organization (WHO).

Higher functions

The first thing to note about dementia is that it is a disease of the brain. But it is a disease of the brain that affects the 'higher' functions. So, for instance, a stroke might leave someone with weakness in his or her arm, but not affect the person's ability to think. This is not dementia. As we shall see, however, a stroke in another part of the brain might have profound effects on the person's ability to remember words or to calculate sums. It is loss of these higher functions that we call dementia.

Chronic, acute, and delirium

The word 'chronic' implies that this is a condition which lasts a long time. The opposite is 'acute', meaning that it is a condition with a short history. 'Confusion' is an imprecise word, but it can be a useful way to describe a loss of coherence or clarity of thought. In connection with the words 'acute' and 'chronic' the notion of confusion helps to make a useful distinction:

- An **acute** confusion is called **delirium**;
- A **chronic** confusion is called **dementia**.

Thus, if someone comes to hospital and the story is that two days ago he had all of his faculties, but now he has become very confused, this will not be dementia. This sounds more like a delirium. A common cause of a delirium would be something like an infection. For the story to be the story of someone with dementia, the history must be 'chronic': she must have had the confusion for some months. Usually, but not always, it starts gradually and slowly gets worse. In other words, as the WHO definition suggests, it is 'progressive'. Dementia normally gets worse, not better. But we shall see there can be exceptions, albeit very rarely.

Acute on chronic

Before leaving the notion of delirium behind, it is worth saying that it is possible to have a dementia that is very mild, but is gradually progressing, and then to suffer a bad infection that makes the person seem as if they have hugely deteriorated. In fact, it may be that the dementia has not worsened. It may be that the person has simply picked up an infection, which has caused a delirium. Sometimes doctors call this an 'acute on chronic' confusion. Once the infection, or other cause of the delirium (e.g. a mix-up of tablets), has settled or been treated, the person will often return to how they were before. In the more advanced forms of dementia, or if the cause of the delirium is severe, sometimes the person is not as well as they were before the delirium.

Acquired

One word the WHO definition does not use is 'acquired'. The reason this word is sometimes used to define dementia is because it is not generally something you are born with. It is something that comes on later in life. However, as we shall see in Chapter 8, there are inherited conditions in which dementia only appears later in life. In Chapter 1, I said dementia can sometimes come on surprisingly early. But dementia is not a 'congenital' condition, one you are born with, even if the inherited causes are already present at birth. The conditions that involve loss of higher brain functions from the time of birth are called learning disabilities. Cerebral palsy, for instance, which is present at birth, can cause learning problems. (Like a stroke, it is also possible to have cerebral palsy that causes physical disabilities without affecting mental abilities.) Conditions which are present at birth and affect the person's ability to learn are not called dementia. This points to one of the features of dementia, which is that it leads to a loss of skills that the person once had. Learning disabilities, such as Down's syndrome, on the other hand, are to do with defects that are present from the time of birth. It is possible, of course, that the person with Down's syndrome, having picked up a host of skills during his or her life, might then start to lose them if dementia is acquired in later life.

Multiple

The definition states that multiple cognitive domains must be affected. Cognitive functions are those higher functions to do with the brain's ability to acquire knowledge and understanding. If a person simply has a limited problem affecting only one higher function, say the ability to recall things from a few minutes ago, a diagnosis of dementia cannot be made. Dementia requires multiple cognitive domains to be involved, that is, not just a problem with recall but also, for example, a problem copying pictures (i.e. a visuospatial or constructional problem). This means there must be multiple areas of the brain involved.

Consciousness

The WHO definition mentions that consciousness must not be clouded. This is another way of excluding the possibility of delirium, which is partly defined by the presence of 'clouding of consciousness'. This refers to a lack of alertness or problems with the ability to concentrate. In the extreme, when consciousness is profoundly affected, a person would be in a coma. But at the milder end, the person may simply have passing moments where he or she is not able to focus properly on the environment. This is 'clouding of consciousness' and is typical of delirium. It should not be present in dementia. However, in this respect the WHO definition is looking a little dated. Since the publication of the tenth version of the ICD (ICD-10) in 1992, it has become clearer that at least one type of dementia (dementia with Lewy bodies, see Chapter 6) does sometimes involve clouding of consciousness.

Non-cognitive symptoms of dementia

The WHO definition finally talks about 'emotional control, social behaviour, or motivation'. Another way in which this definition now seems dated, perhaps, is that it leaves these points to the end almost as an afterthought. But, in fact, it is often these 'non-cognitive' symptoms and signs that cause people the most problems. Being forgetful is one thing, but changes in personality—becoming aggressive, for instance—are often much more devastating for the family carer. These behaviours are now often summarized as '**behavioural and psychological symptoms of dementia**' (BPSD) and are increasingly being studied in their own right. The list of all the behaviours and psychological symptoms (although, given what I said above about symptoms and signs, many of them should more properly be called signs!) that might occur is long. The most common are listed in Box 3.2.

Much more could be said about BPSD, for instance in connection with treatment (see Chapters 11 and 12). But it is worth noting two things immediately. First, they cannot all be lumped together as if they are one thing, because (for example) shouting is a very different thing from apathy. Moreover, each individual 'symptom' can probably be split up into different types of behaviour.

Box 3.2 Behavioural and psychological symptoms of dementia

Aggression	Agitation
Anxiety	Apathy
Delusions	Depression
Disinhibition	Eating behaviours
Euphoria	Hallucinations
Irritability	Movement disorders
Shouting	Wandering

The most obvious example of this is 'wandering', which is a word that covers a number of different behaviours. I may 'wander' because, for example:

◆ I need exercise and like getting out; or

◆ I need to know where my wife is otherwise I become anxious, so I like to stay near her and constantly follow her; or

◆ I want to get home and do not recognize the place where I am now as my home (even if it is).

'Wandering' is a term which many people now try to avoid, because it seems to imply, in the context of dementia, that the behaviour is confused. It is better to recognize that the behaviour *has a purpose* and so can be understood and dealt with accordingly.

The second point to note is that adding BPSD to cognitive impairment still does not cover everything that can occur in dementia (in another sense, then, the WHO definition is not as full as it could be). In particular, the number of physical symptoms and signs that can occur, especially as dementia progresses, is itself significant: epileptic fits, incontinence, odd movements, swallowing problems, weight loss, and so on. This emphasizes that dementia, although it is a brain disorder, is one that profoundly affects the whole body and the whole person.

Summary

Hence, in defining dementia, we can say that it is an acquired, chronic, usually progressive disorder, which affects multiple parts of the brain, and can lead to symptoms and signs that involve:

◆ higher cognitive functions;

◆ activities of daily living;

◆ emotional and social behaviours;

◆ physical abilities.

Concluding thought

Having defined dementia and explained the significance of a number of elements of the definition, there is one more point to make. Perhaps the word 'dementia' is unhelpful. As I have said, it does not define a disease—it is an umbrella term for a number of diseases—and it is not particularly useful because, as we shall see, the way these diseases show themselves can be quite varied. The word 'dementia' does not tell us what the cause of the condition is, nor even the exact nature of the symptoms. But more than this, the word, which comes from the Latin suggesting the person is out of his or her mind, actually adds to the stigma of the condition. To call someone 'demented' is to insult them. Some experts in the field have suggested that the word should be replaced. But at the time of writing it is not clear what the alternative might be. In America various committees are looking again at the *Diagnostic and Statistical Manual* (DSM), currently in its fourth edition (DSM-IV), but about to be in its fifth (DSM-5). The drafters of DSM-5 are considering the possibility of replacing the word 'dementia' with the term 'major neurocognitive disorder'. My own inclination is to agree that 'dementia' is defunct, but I prefer the term 'acquired diffuse neurocognitive dysfunction' on the grounds that this is a better description of the syndrome. But this is for another day. Meanwhile, if dementia is an umbrella or syndromal word, what are the actual types of dementia?

Types of dementia

The most common type of dementia is Alzheimer's disease. As Fig. 3.1 shows, when the brains of people with dementia are looked at after death, Alzheimer's accounts for just over 50 percent of the cases in terms of the pathology (i.e. the changes in the brain that cause the different types of disease with their different symptoms and signs).

Figure 3.1 also shows that in many cases of dementia there is a mixture of Alzheimer's disease and vascular pathology. 'Vascular' implies something to do with the blood vessels. Blood vessels can either get furred up (which is known as atherosclerosis) or they can leak (in other words, bleed or haemorrhage). According to the studies of the pathology upon which Fig. 3.1 is based, dementia with Lewy bodies is the second most common type of dementia. Studies of people in the community have also found that about 20 percent of people with dementia have the Lewy body type. This can seem surprising, because it is the least known of the major types of dementia. It may be, however, that because

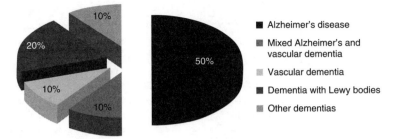

Figure 3.1 Prevalence of different types of dementia according to pathology.

it is relatively new it is still under-detected by clinicians. (There is more information on all of these conditions on various websites in Appendix 1, which includes the website of the Lewy Body Society.) It should be added that the prevalence of the mixed type of vascular and Alzheimer's disease varies in different studies and may be more common than we think.

The number of other types of dementia is huge. The most common is frontotemporal dementia. This can be seen in old age, although it mostly starts between the ages of 50 and 60 years. Like many of the rarer forms of dementia, it is more common in the younger-onset dementias. In fact, it is the second commonest type of dementia in those presenting under the age of 65; Alzheimer's disease remains the most common form even below 65 years. Some estimate that frontotemporal dementia accounts for about 5 percent of late-onset dementias (i.e. those starting after 65), although there is, again, the worry that some cases are not diagnosed or are misdiagnosed as Alzheimer's disease.

In the next four chapters I shall describe the clinical features of the four main types of dementia (Alzheimer's, vascular, Lewy body, and frontotemporal) in a little more detail. Then, in Chapter 8, I shall briefly describe some of the rarer forms of dementia.

The interested reader could refer to the websites listed in Appendix 1 for more information or to the more detailed texts listed in Appendix 2. Dementia as a subject is simply vast and encompasses a good deal of highly specialized knowledge. Fortunately, the main facts surrounding the most common types of dementia can be set out more briefly.

4

Alzheimer's disease and mild cognitive impairment

Key points

* As well as being the most common form of dementia, Alzheimer's disease presents in the typical way that people tend to imagine, with gradually progressing memory impairment.

* Eventually the disease affects every aspect of a person's mental functioning and of their physical state too.

* Mild cognitive impairment is a new 'pre-diagnosis' that might help to predict progression to dementia and provide the opportunity for early treatment.

* There are international criteria for a diagnosis of Alzheimer's disease, which may be improved by using biomarkers.

* The two key hallmarks of Alzheimer's pathology are amyloid plaques and neurofibrillary tangles (which involve a protein called tau).

* Some genes have been identified for early-onset Alzheimer's disease, but most cases do not have a known genetic basis. However, ApoE status seems to be a marker of risk.

Introduction

As we have seen, the most common type of dementia is Alzheimer's disease, which is the underlying cause in about 50 percent of late-onset cases. The person with Alzheimer's presents in the way that most people imagine dementia occurs. In other words, there is a gradual onset of symptoms. Initially the changes might be subtle, but they become more obvious and difficult to ignore. Sometimes an event occurs (such as a fall), which seems to highlight the symptoms, and many carers will say that the event caused the problems. It is always difficult to be sure how important a particular event might have been, especially given that the causes of most illnesses are probably a complex mix of biological, psychological, and social factors.

In the boxes below, I have set out three different stories, which could all be typical of Alzheimer's disease. The thing to note is that there is a gradual onset of symptoms, which tend to start with memory difficulties, but then broaden to include other mental functions. I shall use each case to highlight particular issues under the headings: diagnosis and mild cognitive impairment; family support and bereavement; infections, inflammation, and disease progression. I shall then go on to outline diagnostic criteria for Alzheimer's disease and mention different types of memory, before concluding with a brief review of the pathology and genetics of Alzheimer's disease.

Diagnosis and mild cognitive impairment (MCI)

📄 Case study

Mr Humphrey—early signs

Looking back, the family felt that Mr Humphrey was probably 72 years old when the first signs of Alzheimer's disease appeared. He had long been bad at remembering names, but one day he became really confused about the names of his grandchildren and daughters-in-law. They thought this was a bit of a joke, but soon afterwards he went out to the shops and came home empty handed because he'd forgotten what he wanted to buy. He was quite upset. Then it became more obvious that he was forgetting things over a very short space of time: going into the kitchen and then not knowing what he was doing there. Gradually he also started to have problems remembering the right words. When he got lost whilst out driving, the family became very worried and persuaded him to see the doctor.

First, the case of Mr Humphrey raises a question about diagnosis. He had been forgetful for some time. These are the circumstances under which people sometimes go to their general practitioner (GP) and are told that the problem is simply to do with their age. Of course, as I have discussed at the end of Chapter 1, it is *something* to do with the person's age; but there will be a degree of forgetfulness that might well benefit from further investigation. Mr Humphrey reached a point at which he wanted help. But this is not always the case and it can be difficult for those caring for a person with memory problems to know at what point to encourage the individual to seek help. Issues around assessment will be discussed further in Chapter 9.

If, however, Mr Humphrey had been referred sooner to a memory clinic, he might have been given the diagnosis of **mild cognitive impairment** (MCI). The notion of MCI is increasingly being used to describe a state in which a person is experiencing problems with memory, but it is not felt that this amounts to dementia. The importance of MCI is that if it is a pre-dementia state, and if it could be identified as such, then it would (a) be a good time for the person to start planning for the future, and (b) be a good time to start treatments that might be able to slow the disease or stop it (if such treatments were available—at the time of writing, no such treatments are available). There has been an increasing amount of research to try to identify MCI in an exact manner. This has included neuroimaging, genetic studies, the use of other biomarkers (which means anything biological that can be measured, such as proteins in the cerebrospinal fluid (CSF), in an attempt to provide clear evidence of the condition), and so on. (The CSF is the fluid which circulates around the brain and the spinal cord.) By making the criteria for MCI tighter (i.e. by defining MCI in a more precise way) it has been increasingly possible to state the probability that someone with MCI will go on to develop dementia. In particular, the type of MCI that is mostly to do with memory problems (the sort that Mr Humphrey may have had), so-called amnestic MCI, seems to be better at predicting Alzheimer's disease than other types of MCI. In broad terms, the criteria for the amnestic type of MCI are as follows:

◆ Memory complaint, preferably supported by an informant;

◆ Test to show memory impairment relative to age and education;

◆ Normal general cognitive function;

◆ Intact activities of daily living;

◆ Failure to satisfy criteria for dementia.

The conversion rate from MCI to dementia is around 10–15 percent per year. In other words, if 100 people are given a diagnosis of MCI this year, between 10 and 15 of them will have dementia next year. In ten years' time, between 65 and 81 of them will have dementia (all other things being equal). But this also means that most of them will *not* have dementia next year; and, even in ten years' time, between 19 and 35 of them will still *not* have dementia. And this highlights one of the controversies to do with MCI, which is that being told you have MCI may or may not mean that you will go on to have dementia. Hence, the 'diagnosis' of MCI may simply cause anxiety for no good reason. Your view on this will rather depend on whether or not you think there are benefits to early diagnosis and how significant those benefits might be, which I shall also discuss in Chapter 9.

There is a final important practical point to be made about MCI. The figures above come from, and the continuing efforts to refine the criteria for MCI are to be found in, academic centres of excellence. Many ordinary clinicians are now also using the terminology MCI, but not always in such a precise way. In many cases this will mean that the person actually already has dementia, but it is so mild the clinician has not felt it appropriate to tell the person, or perhaps there is still some doubt about the type of dementia. We shall have to wait to see how the term MCI comes to be used in routine practice in the future.

Family support and bereavement

📄 Case study

Mrs Aggarwal—moderate ('hidden') impairment

When Mr Aggarwal died many felt that Mrs Aggarwal had dealt with her loss very well. Her family did not live locally, but as they became more involved again with their mother they soon realized that there was a problem. They initially thought that her problems were a type of bereavement reaction. Sometimes she seemed to believe their father was still alive. And she seemed rather bland in her response when they tried kindly to remind her that he had died. But their alarm was really over the extent to which she could not look after herself. She didn't seem able to cook. They soon realized that her personal hygiene was poor. Now that they thought back they recalled that about four years ago, for no obvious reason, Mr Aggarwal had taken over the cooking. They also remembered that their father and mother had stopped visiting them about two years ago and, now they thought about it, they realized that, albeit their mother had been previously shy in company, their father had done all the talking even when it was just the family. He'd been answering all the questions and Mrs Aggarwal had tended simply to agree with what he'd said. They suspected that, in his usual way, he'd wanted to protect her from the illness that had been progressing for some years.

The story of Mrs Aggarwal is very common. Often family members have suspected a slight problem but have not realized the extent of the problem because the spouse has been 'covering up'. Another possibility is that the person really does deteriorate at the time of the bereavement. This might be as part of a bereavement reaction, but it might also be that the person's normal supports, in this case supplied by Mr Aggarwal, have suddenly disappeared, leading to disorientation and increased confusion.

Bereavement reactions in dementia can be various. Here Mrs Aggarwal is portrayed as being somewhat bland in terms of her responses. This might either be because she is still in a state of shock and denial, or perhaps her Alzheimer's disease has had a partial effect on the frontal lobe of her brain, which has led to a degree of apathy and disinterest. In other cases of bereavement in dementia, the person forgets the news that the person has died and has to be reminded. Each time the person is reminded there is renewed distress. For understandable reasons, this sort of reaction will often lead families to avoid discussing the loss with the person. In general, this is not a good tactic. First, it can be argued that the person has a right to know what has happened. Second, the person will, if not told, potentially become more distressed not knowing where the dead person has gone. Third, even though it may take a while for the person to come to terms with his or her grief, this is important emotional work and allows others to deal with the person in a straightforward manner.

The final point to draw from the story of Mrs Aggarwal is the reminder that these events place an enormous burden on the families of those involved. More will be said about this later. But there are two things to note: first, that families can find it particularly stressful to have to look after someone when they live at a distance; second, that families are often having to deal with their own grief, in this case at the loss of their father, while at the same time coming to terms with the need to care for their mother.

Infections, inflammation and disease progression

📄 Case study

Mrs Brighton—severe decline

Mrs Brighton had received a diagnosis of dementia many years before, which had gradually worsened. She was now really quite confused and dependent on staff in the care home for help with all of her basic needs. But she was content and happily pottered around, often sitting to look into the garden. One morning, however, she was found to be suddenly agitated and much more confused. She became aggressive when the care staff, whom she knew well, tried to help her after she had been incontinent. She seemed to be very scared and one member of staff wondered whether she was hallucinating. A urine sample was tested and she was found to have an infection. Within two days of starting an antibiotic she became much calmer. But two weeks later the same thing happened again. There was another infection. Although she picked up following further treatment, she seemed to have deteriorated significantly. Her speech became much worse, she did not seem to recognize her family when they visited and gradually, after a further urine infection two months later, she stopped walking altogether.

I want to use the case of Mrs Brighton to highlight three points.

First, her case demonstrates the sort of physical decline I mentioned previously. In the more advanced stages of Alzheimer's (as in other types of dementia), the disease affects not only the brain but the whole body. The pathology is solely in the brain, but the brain and the nervous system have profound effects on everything we do. People with severe Alzheimer's disease require a good deal of physical nursing. A general observation is that, in the advanced stages of any dementia, because of the physical deterioration, the conditions start to look very similar and it becomes increasingly difficult to distinguish the different types of dementia.

Second, Mrs Brighton's case demonstrates the sort of 'acute on chronic' confusion that was mentioned above. Her infection gives her a delirium, which explains the sudden (acute) deterioration in her behaviour. She may well have been hallucinating, which could account for her apparent fear. The treatment was quite correct: once the infection was treated her behaviour settled.

But the third aspect of her case to comment upon is the way in which the infections seem to lead to a sudden worsening of her general state. There are reasons to believe there might be a sort of negative feedback loop in which a disease such as Alzheimer's makes it more likely that the person will become frail and susceptible to infections, and each such infection (with its resultant inflammation) makes the person frailer and more susceptible. Meanwhile, there is an increasing mental deterioration too, which may itself be a result of inflammation in the brain. As the science of this continues to be worked out, the clinical observation—that people in the advanced stages of dementia are prone to infections (e.g. because they are immobile) and deteriorate both physically and mentally as a result—is common.

Criteria for a diagnosis of Alzheimer's disease

In 1984, following a working group of the National Institute of Neurological and Communicative Disorders and Stroke (NINCDS) and the Alzheimer's Disease and Related Disorders Association (ADRDA), McKhann and his colleagues in the USA published criteria in the journal *Neurology*, to make the diagnosis of Alzheimer's disease more uniform. A summary of these criteria appears in Box 4.1. The criteria have become known as the McKhann criteria or the NINCDS-ADRDA criteria, and have been used extensively throughout the world.

Box 4.1 Summary of NINCDS-ADRDA criteria for a clinical diagnosis of Alzheimer's disease

1. PROBABLE Alzheimer's disease requires:

— an established diagnosis of dementia supported by neuropsychological testing;

— deficits in two or more areas of cognition;

— progressive worsening of memory and other cognitive functions;

— clear consciousness;

— onset between the ages 40 and 90, most often after the age of 65 years;

— absence of other disorders that could account for cognitive deficits.

2. SUPPORTIVE features:

— progressive deterioration in terms of language (aphasia), motor skills (apraxia), and perception (agnosia);

— impaired activities of daily living and altered patterns of behaviour;

— family history of similar disorders;

— normal specialized investigations (some of which will be mentioned in Chapter 9 on assessment);

— evidence of progressive cerebral atrophy (i.e. shrinkage of the brain) on computed tomography (CT) brain scanning (which is a type of X-ray).

3. CONSISTENT features:

— plateaus in the course of progression of the illness;

— associated symptoms of depression, insomnia, incontinence, delusions, illusions, hallucinations, catastrophic verbal, emotional or physical outbursts, sexual disorders and weight loss;

— other neurological abnormalities in some patients, especially with more advanced disease, including motor signs such as increased muscle tone, myoclonus (i.e. jerkiness) or gait disorder;

— seizures (i.e. epileptic fits) in advanced disease;

— CT scan normal for age.

4. The diagnosis of PROBABLE Alzheimer's disease is UNLIKELY if:

— there is a sudden, apoplectic onset;

— there are focal neurological findings such as paralysis, sensory loss, visual field deficits, and incoordination early in the course of the illness;

— seizures or gait disturbances at the onset or very early in the course of the illness.

5. There are also criteria for a diagnosis of POSSIBLE Alzheimer's disease, i.e. where the features are not as certain.

6. A DEFINITE diagnosis of Alzheimer's disease requires:

— the clinical criteria for probable Alzheimer's disease; and

— histopathological evidence obtained from a biopsy or autopsy (where 'histopathology' means that the relevant cells or changes in the brain tissue (see below) have been seen down the microscope).

More recently, a group of experts has updated the NINCDS-ADRDA criteria on the basis of advances in the scientific understanding of dementia. These new criteria share several features with the old. For instance, to some extent the diagnosis of Alzheimer's disease is based on the *exclusion* of other diseases that might cause similar problems. Thus, if there is anything that would raise the suspicion of a stroke (such as paralysis early in the disease), Alzheimer's is less likely as a diagnosis. Points to highlight in the new criteria are, first, an emphasis on the core feature of a gradually progressive disturbance in episodic memory lasting more than six months; and, second, supportive abnormalities in biomarkers. I shall deal with memory first and then discuss biomarkers.

Memory

There are three broad types of memory:

◆ **Episodic memory** is, as the term suggests, our memory for episodes, for events that occurred at a particular time. My memory of an event on the beach at Bognor is an example of episodic memory.

◆ **Semantic memory** is our store of knowledge, which is not linked to particular events. The fact that I know what a beach is (what the word means)

and that Bognor is a seaside town on the south coast of England are examples of semantic memory.

◆ **Procedural memory** is memory of how to do things. That I can remember how to drive my car, for instance to Bognor, is an example of procedural memory.

All three types of memory can be affected by Alzheimer's and they are affected by other types of dementia as well. But the typical feature in Alzheimer's disease is that problems with episodic memory are noted first.

As an aside, it is also commonly noted that the person initially forgets recent things, but can still remember things from a long time ago. Gradually the things remembered become more and more distant. This can explain the upsetting experience that many children or spouses have of being forgotten. When the husband remembers his wife, he can only recall the woman who was with him on his wedding day. This means that he does not know who this older woman is who visits him, although he may feel she is familiar (or he may shun her in favour of the younger woman—his daughter—who looks like the young woman he married).

Biomarkers

The second key feature to highlight is that the new (research) criteria stipulate that the core feature of loss of episodic memory should be supported by an abnormal biomarker. A number of such biological markers for Alzheimer's have been identified in recent years. How sensitive or specific some of these biomarkers are for Alzheimer's is still being worked out. In other words, it can still be the case that the absence of a particular marker does not mean you do not have the condition; but nor does the presence of a particular marker mean you do have the condition—you may have another type of dementia, or no dementia! But the expert group felt that there was enough evidence to say that the following would support a diagnosis of Alzheimer's disease:

◆ Atrophy of the medial temporal lobe on magnetic resonance imaging (MRI) brain scans (i.e. shrinkage of the part of the brain that is most to do with episodic memory—see Fig. 4.1);

◆ Abnormal CSF biomarker, i.e. substances in the CSF which might indicate Alzheimer's, such as amyloid or tau—where CSF is obtained by a lumbar puncture (i.e. a needle inserted into the lower back);

◆ Specific patterns on functional neuroimaging with positron emission tomography (PET) (i.e. a particular type of brain scan that will be mentioned in Chapter 9);

◆ A proven Alzheimer's disease autosomal dominant genetic mutation within the immediate family (i.e. where a very rare Alzheimer's gene in one

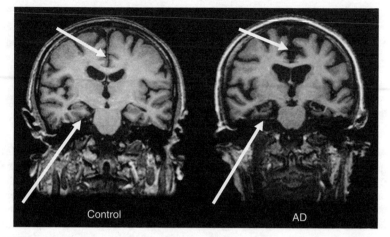

Figure 4.1 MRI scans of normal brain (left) and brain of person with Alzheimer's disease (AD) (right) (courtesy of Professor John O'Brien, Institute for Ageing and Health, Newcastle University).

parent will mean that offspring have a 50 percent chance of inheriting the condition).

How good these new criteria are at picking out Alzheimer's disease rather than any other type of dementia will have to be seen.

Figure 4.1 shows the potential benefits of good-quality brain scans, the sort which are available from magnetic resonance imaging (MRI) scanners (see Chapter 9). Both pictures show brains as they are seen from the front. The picture on the left shows a normal scan of someone the same age as the person scanned on the right who has Alzheimer's disease. In Chapter 2 we discussed how different parts of the brain have different functions. The longer arrow points to the medial temporal lobe (which contains the hippocampus). This bit of the brain is associated with the recall of information and is affected early. In this scan it is very clear that the affected brain has lost most of the medial temporal lobe. It is called 'medial' because it is the bit of the temporal lobe that is in the middle. Remember that the brain is symmetrical, so the loss of the medial temporal lobe is seen on both sides.

But it is not just the temporal lobe that is affected. The whole of the brain in Alzheimer's eventually shows atrophy, which means shrinkage. The shorter arrow indicates a part of the brain that shows much less brain tissue and, therefore, more black on the scan. (Where the scan is very black, this is air; where it is slightly fuzzy but still black, it is fluid, in this case CSF, described in Chapter 2.)

So the whole of the brain in Alzheimer's shows this wasting or atrophy, but the medial temporal lobe shows it more markedly. This can happen in other types of dementia as well, e.g. Lewy body dementia. So it is important to put the scan together with the history in order to come to a diagnosis. Nonetheless, Fig. 4.1 shows clearly how useful a scan can be as part of the process of making a diagnosis. It also helps to emphasize the extent to which this is a *disease*, one in which the distressing symptoms can be explained, but one which also requires as much attention in terms of care, treatment, and research as any other.

Pathology of Alzheimer's disease

The two main features that Aloïs Alzheimer (1864–1915) described, just over one hundred years ago, when he looked down the microscope at the brain of his former patient Auguste Deter, were amyloid plaques and neurofibrillary tangles. I shall describe these and some of the other findings in the brains of people with Alzheimer's disease. One striking finding, without the microscope, is (as shown in Fig. 4.1) that the brains are smaller and atrophied. We now know that there is considerable loss of cells in the brains of people with all the various sorts of dementia.

Amyloid plaques

Amyloid is a protein. It comes in different forms but is derived from a bigger protein, the amyloid precursor protein (APP). A protein is a molecule made up of amino acids. The amino acids are the basic building blocks, where the building process is controlled by genes. One of the interesting things about Down's syndrome, which I shall discuss in Chapter 8, given that Alzheimer's disease occurs early in Down's, is that the gene for APP is on the same chromosome (chromosome 21) that causes most cases of Down's syndrome.

APP is a normal substance in the body. It can be found in the membranes of neurons, particularly around the synapse (see Chapter 2). It is thought to be involved in repair and regeneration of the nerve cells, among other things. The APP molecule is broken down into smaller fragments by substances called secretases. The smaller fragments are known as beta-amyloid or Aβ. Some of the normal amyloid fragments are soluble and appear to cause no harm (these are the result of the work of α-secretase breaking down APP). But the version with 42 amino acids ($A\beta_{42}$), which results from γ-secretase cleaving APP at a particular point, is insoluble and seems to be especially toxic to neurons. There is also a β-secretase that forms a slightly shorter Aβ fragment ($A\beta_{40}$), which is also insoluble and with $A\beta_{42}$ forms the core of amyloid plaques. These plaques are slightly different in different parts of the brain. But the theory is that Aβ is deposited in the brain as an early event in the process that leads to Alzheimer's disease. It should be said that amyloid plaques can be found in 'normal' ageing brains, but it is the pattern and profusion of the plaques that marks out typical cases of Alzheimer's. The dense amyloid core of the plaques is surrounded by neuritic processes, mainly composed of another protein called tau, which will be discussed below. In any event, the deposition of Aβ is disruptive to the normal functioning of the brain.

Neurofibrillary tangles (NFT)

Again, NFTs are not specific to Alzheimer's disease: they occur in other diseases and to a lesser extent in normal ageing brains. In Chapter 2, I discussed the microtubules that form the skeleton of the axon of the neuron and help to transport chemicals towards the synapse for neurotransmission. The tau proteins help to stabilize this neuronal cytoskeleton, i.e. the microtubules (see Fig. 2.2), which are made up of tubulin, another protein. Tau is partly given some structure by phosphorus. In NFTs, however, the phosphorylation of tau is excessive (i.e. there is hyperphosphorylation of tau) and the result is that microtubules become destabilized and form tangles, which disrupts their normal functioning. In addition, the tau is covered in another protein, called ubiquitin, which is also thought to have regulatory functions. NFTs are, therefore, intracellular (i.e. within the cell) inclusion bodies made up of phosphorylated and ubiquinated tau, but they can be found outside the cell, presumably when the cell dies. There are also thread-like and curly fibres found as dementia worsens in the cortex. They are very similar to NFTs.

Granulovacuolar degeneration

Granulovacuolar degeneration consists of small holes (vacuoles) within the cell body. Inside the vacuole there is a granule. It turns out this is made up of most of the constituents of the NFT: tubulin, neurofilaments, tau, and ubiquitin. It looks as if the cell has swallowed up these remnants. So this finding may just be a marker of previous damage.

Hirano bodies

The significance of these round bodies is not clear and they appear in normal brains as well as in other pathological conditions. They may also contain tau, among other things.

Inflammatory changes

There is evidence of inflammation—glial cells (see Chapter 2) such as astrocytes become active—around other areas of pathology, such as amyloid plaques and NFTs, as well as in connection with vascular changes, for instance in the white matter of the brain.

Vascular pathology

Just as Aβ is found in plaques, so too it is found in the blood vessels of the brain. Vascular amyloid causes the vessel walls to become fragile. It is common in Alzheimer's disease. There can be small bleeds (haemorrhages). In some cases, this form of angiopathy is inherited: autosomal dominant familial cerebral amyloid angiopathy is, however, very rare.

Posterior cortical atrophy

Before discussing genetics further, it is worth saying that there is a small group of patients who do not show global atrophy, but do have the typical features of Alzheimer's pathology. Posterior cortical atrophy (PCA) is the best described finding in this group. For these people, memory and speech can be good, but there is a progressive and marked loss of skills to do with vision and related to language, such as spelling, writing, and arithmetic. There are variations on the typical pattern of PCA, including in terms of pathology, so that not everyone is convinced it is a type of Alzheimer's disease. It may be a condition in its own right.

Genetics of Alzheimer's disease

Alzheimer's disease is an inherited familial disorder in probably less than 5 percent of cases. There are more cases of inherited Alzheimer's disease in people with early-onset disease. Most cases of early-onset autosomal dominant familial Alzheimer's disease are accounted for by mutations in three genes:

♦ APP gene—on chromosome 21;

♦ PS1 gene—on chromosome 14;

♦ PS2 gene—on chromosome 1.

The effect of the mutation on the APP gene is to increase the amount of $A\beta_{42}$. There are two presenilin (PS) genes. PS1 leads to earlier manifestations of the disease. The mutations on chromosome 14 are thought to account for about 70 percent of early-onset familial cases (i.e. those few cases where there is a clear genetic component). PS1 is also said to be more aggressive than the disease caused by PS2. The number of families known to be affected by all three genes is only a few hundred. Indeed, these particular inherited forms of Alzheimer's disease probably account for only about 0.1 percent of all the cases at any age.

Most cases of Alzheimer's occur, of course, after the age of 65 years and there is no clear pattern of inheritance. But studies using twins with older-onset disease suggest that the genetic influence is quite strong. If your first-degree relative has dementia, your chances of having dementia go up by two- to six-fold compared with someone without this family history. The clearest genetic risk factor in older age is linked to apolipoprotein E (ApoE).

ApoE

The gene for ApoE is on chromosome 19. There are three possible variants of the *ApoE* gene: ε2, ε3, and ε4. We each carry a pair of genes for ApoE (each one is called an allele). They might both be the ε4 allele, in which case we are said to be *homozygous* for ε4; or we might have one ε4 and an alternative (e.g. ε2), in which case we are *heterozygous* for ε4. The protein, ApoE, is important for the metabolism of cholesterol. It is important, therefore, in heart disease. But it is also very important for neurons. After neuronal damage ApoE is released from astrocytes to help in repair. But the different alleles are more or less good at this, ε4 being poor at it. More than this, ε4 turns out to be a risk factor for Alzheimer's disease:

- Having the ε4 allele increases the risk at any age;
- Being ε4 heterozygous (where one allele is ε4) doubles the risk;
- Being ε4 homozygous (where both alleles are ε4) increases the risk by six to eight times;
- ε4 increases the risk of Alzheimer's disease after stroke;
- ε4 increases the risk after head injury.

Meanwhile, the ApoE ε2 allele may confer some protection against Alzheimer's disease.

Having said all this, it is still not recommended that ApoE should be used clinically as a marker for Alzheimer's, because it is not a good enough predictor.

There are now other potential markers for increased risk of Alzheimer's disease, but research remains at an early stage. For instance, α2-macroglobulin is connected with amyloid plaques; and an enzyme involved in transport of proteins (where there is also a link to APP) in connection with mitochondria is also known to be deficient in Alzheimer's disease (it is called translocase of mitochondrial membrane 40).

Putting it all together

There may be ways in which the pathology links together. It used to be thought that the main issue in Alzheimer's disease was the loss of the neurotransmitter acetylcholine, but treatments which boost this neurotransmitter have shown that this is not the underlying cause of Alzheimer's disease. The current favourite theory, however, is to do with amyloid.

There may be a link between amyloid plaques and NFTs provided by the enzyme (i.e. a protein that speeds up or encourages some other reaction within the body) glycogen synthase kinase 3 (GSK3). GSK3 has a number of roles, which include helping to keep the intracellular microtubules stable. But if the enzyme overworks, it also causes hyperphosphorylation of tau, which (as we saw) leads to NFTs. This effect is blocked by insulin. It turns out that insulin also has an effect on amyloid, both by encouraging α-secretase (the good secretase!) as well as by encouraging the breakdown of Aβ. And one particular form of GSK3 is implicated in increased Aβ production (so excess activity by GSK3 is bad, but insulin is good).

There is also a theory that too much Aβ might cause damage to mitochondria (and in Chapter 8 we shall see that mitochondrial disease has been identified as a possible cause of dementia). This in itself might increase Aβ_{42} and the phosphorylation of tau. Meanwhile, another alternative is that the inflammation that is seen in Alzheimer's disease, partly through the action of the excitatory neurotransmitter glutamate (see Chapter 2) and its effects on zinc, might lead to the increased production of Aβ.

Hence, we can see that a mixture of genetic and molecular mechanisms could help to push the formation of APP into Aβ, which would lead both to plaque formation and to vascular amyloid pathology. In addition, there are environmental influences such as obesity (as well as diabetes, smoking, heart disease, and atherosclerosis—which are also risk factors for vascular dementia). Meanwhile, the damage caused by amyloid deposition (plus perhaps other risk factors) could lead to cell changes that encourage the formation of NFTs. The details of this hypothesis need working out, but the central role of amyloid is now the focus of therapeutic efforts (as we shall see in Chapter 12).

5

Vascular dementia

Key points

- Vascular dementia can follow large strokes or small strokes, which may be caused by blockages in the blood vessels or by bleeding.

- There is often either an abrupt onset or obvious neurological events (e.g. loss of consciousness) that precede the emergence of symptoms and signs.

- Sometimes, however, there are multiple, very small strokes that do not cause obvious problems until the onset of memory problems.

- Executive dysfunction may be an earlier sign than memory problems; there may be a greater preservation of the personality; but depression is more common than in other forms of dementia.

- Prevention may be possible by attention to risk factors in middle age.

- There is a rare inherited form of vascular dementia known as CADASIL.

Introduction

Vascular dementia comes in various forms. Sometimes it follows a large stroke. A stroke is caused either by a blood vessel becoming completely blocked up (an ischaemic stroke, where the word 'ischaemia' means there is an inadequate blood supply), or by a bleed from a blood vessel in the brain (haemorrhagic stroke).

Ischaemic strokes are more common. They can be caused by 'furring of the arteries' (atherosclerosis) or by a clot or other substance coming from somewhere else in the body to block up a small artery in the brain (an embolism). But vascular dementia can also result from a series of very small strokes, where the person may not even realize that they are occurring. These are sometimes called 'mini-strokes'; the medical term would be multi-infarct dementia (where an 'infarction' implies that tissue—in this case brain tissue—has died because of a local lack of oxygen). An alternative is simply that the blood vessels become furred up and damaged even though they are not actually blocked. This might still be enough to cause damage to the surrounding brain tissue. People often know that they have had TIAs, that is, **transient ischaemic attacks**. A TIA is where the blood supply is cut off only for a short while or partially, causing passing (transient) symptoms, such as problems with vision or dizziness. A TIA is a warning that the person is in danger of having a larger stroke. Whatever the circumstances, the upshot of a poor blood supply to the brain is damage, because there is a lack of oxygen and the brain is very sensitive to this (e.g. we soon faint if our oxygen supply is cut off).

Pathology of vascular dementia

The description above already indicates the types of pathology that can be found in vascular dementia. But matters can be summarized in this way:

- There can be large vessel disease and large infarctions (i.e. strokes);
- There can be disease of the small blood vessels (microvascular disease), which can take various forms involving:
  - weakening of the blood vessel walls;
  - narrowing of the blood vessels by arteriosclerosis;
- There can be small infarctions (microinfarctions) and lacunar infarcts.

Having multiple microinfarcts (mini-strokes) is probably the most common cause of vascular dementia in older people and tends to be progressive with a poor outlook. Similarly, lacunar infarcts are also commonly found and associated with a poor outcome. A lacuna is an unfilled space and lacunar infarcts may represent the site of an old microinfarction. They mostly occur in the subcortical white matter, as well as in other subcortical structures such as the thalamus, basal ganglia (e.g. the substantia nigra and striatum), and brain stem (see Chapter 2 for clarification of these terms). Cortical microinfarcts can occur too. There can also be a loss of neurons and consequent inflammation caused by poor blood supply to the neurons. The sort of cerebral amyloid angiopathy referred to in Chapter 4 can also be found, sometimes without significant evidence of other Alzheimer's pathology.

Mixed pathology and severity

I shall briefly highlight two points about vascular dementia. First, it often occurs with other types of dementia and may explain the differences in terms of *severity*. Two people may have the same amount of Alzheimer's pathology, but one might seem much more impaired, which may be explained by the amount of vascular damage. This might then affect the person's response to treatment.

Prevention and vascular dementia

Second, although there is a lot of talk about cures for dementia, it may be that, especially in connection with vascular dementia, we should focus on *prevention*. Vascular dementia probably results from the same sort of risk factors that cause heart disease: raised blood pressure, high cholesterol, smoking, lack of exercise, diabetes related to obesity, and so on. It may well be that lifestyle changes could have a significant impact on the prevalence of vascular dementia.

Patterns of presentation

The following two cases illustrate the differing patterns that vascular dementia can take.

Case study

At the age of 71 years Mr Hurst, who up until that point had enjoyed good health apart from his raised blood pressure, suddenly suffered a stroke that left him paralysed down his right side. It also affected his speech, which became very slurred. After six weeks of rehabilitation, he could mobilize independently, albeit with difficulty, and friends said he was back to his old self. But he still required a good deal of practical help. Within a couple of months, although his speech had mostly recovered, it was noted that he was having increasing difficulty finding the right words. This caused him a good deal of frustration and he would sometimes burst into tears. His family felt he was depressed. They also noted that he was not so good at remembering names and appointments.

Mr Hurst's case demonstrates very clearly some of the key points required to establish a diagnosis of vascular dementia:

◆ There is definite **evidence of a stroke** and, therefore, of cerebrovascular disease (i.e. disease affecting the blood vessels of the brain);

◆ There is a clear connection between **the timing of the stroke** and the fairly **abrupt onset** of the symptoms and signs of dementia;

◆ He exhibits **deficits in a number of cognitive domains**: expressive dysphasia (difficulty finding the right words), with evidence of memory problems, including episodic memory problems, as well as poor recall of names.

There are, as with Alzheimer's disease, formal sets of criteria to diagnose vascular dementia (e.g. that developed on behalf of the National Institute of Neurological Disorders and Stroke and Association Internationale pour la Recherché et l'Enseignement en Neurosciences (NINDS-AIREN) and published in *Neurology* in 1993). In addition, in 1975 Hachinski and his colleagues published (in *Archives of Neurology*) a scale based on symptoms and signs that were likely to indicate ischaemic damage (i.e. damage caused by poor blood supply to the brain, e.g. because of a stroke). The Hachinski ischaemia scale has often been criticized, but it has also stood the test of time and remains a useful tool. For instance, Mr. Hurst potentially scores quite high on the Hachinski scale, because of the abrupt onset of his condition, the preservation of his personality, his possible depression and definite emotional lability, along with his history of hypertension and stroke, as well as his neurological symptoms and signs. Thus, the diagnosis of vascular dementia would seem to be fairly certain. There was no hint of a gradual onset of memory problems before the stroke. Whereas in Alzheimer's the person's personality can change as the dementia worsens, in vascular dementia it may be that the personality remains intact despite increasing problems with various other functions. It might be that Mr Hurst's speech becomes worse and worse, but his feelings and understanding of what is happening to him do not similarly deteriorate. In other words, he continues to have insight into what is happening to him, which can be very distressing. The link between depression and vascular damage in the brain, which is strong, is discussed further in Chapter 11. The exact pattern of symptoms or signs depends on which parts of the brain have been affected. As vascular dementia deepens, however, it becomes increasingly likely the pattern of impairments will look more global.

📄 Case study

Mrs Brunton's diabetes was diagnosed when she was 63 years old. The doctor said it was to do with her being overweight. But he was also concerned about her smoking and hypertension (high blood pressure). She was treated for her hypertension and also for the raised cholesterol which was discovered at about the same time. Mrs Brunton managed to lose some weight and when, four years later, she was diagnosed with angina she stopped smoking. It was explained to her that angina was caused by poor blood supply to the heart, which in all likelihood was made worse by her smoking. Four years later, aged 71, she had started to have dizzy spells, but she tended to ignore them. Once or twice she almost fell. During the course of the next year her family felt that she had become a little more vacant and vague. She found it difficult to concentrate on things. In fact, she became noticeably bad at doing household chores: she often could not motivate herself and, if she did, she would do things wrongly, *e.g.* putting the tea bag straight into the kettle instead of into the teapot. There were times when she seemed very bright and then times when she seemed more confused. There were occasions when she could not recall what she was meant to be doing. But she always recognized her friends and family. At this point she was referred to the memory clinic. She had a brain scan and she and the family were told that there were extensive blockages in the small blood vessels of the brain and that she had had at least one small stroke at some point, if not two. It was not clear when these strokes had occurred.

Mrs Brunton's case reinforces the point made above about *prevention*. If it had been possible for Mrs Brunton to have adjusted her lifestyle in her early middle age and if her risk factors had been treated sooner, she might have fared better. Both her heart and her brain suffered from the poor state of her blood vessels, caused by smoking, hypertension, diabetes, and raised cholesterol (hypercholesterolaemia). Her case also shows why it can be difficult to make the diagnosis of vascular dementia, because clinically there was no good evidence of a stroke. The onset of cognitive problems was not particularly abrupt. Indeed, in the absence of further information, she would score fairly low on the Hachinski scale. She would score positively for the fluctuations in her mental state, for her hypertension and because of the evidence of atherosclerosis elsewhere. This is why more detailed criteria for vascular dementia emphasize the importance of brain scanning: it is surprising how often vascular damage is found. There are, however, two points to keep in mind:

1. Vascular damage often occurs with other types of dementia;
2. Some degree of vascular damage can also be found in normal older people.

In Mrs Brunton's case, however, it might be argued that the evidence of stroke disease on neuroimaging, along with the risk factors and history, make the diagnosis of vascular (multi-infarct) dementia seem quite likely. Her problems are certainly not normal.

Executive dysfunction and subcortical ischaemic vascular dementia

A further point to make is that this case shows how, in vascular dementia, the main problem is not always initially to do with memory. A typical feature is that she has problems with **executive functions**. These will be discussed in more detail in the next chapter. In Mrs Brunton's case, this is shown by her problems with motivation (e.g. her difficulty getting going with things) and with sequencing (her problems making the tea and getting things in the wrong order). In other words executive function is to do with being able to plan and to execute a plan. To suffer executive *dys*function is to lack such skills. Damage to blood vessels in the white matter of the brain is often associated with hypertension and can cause executive dysfunction. A similar picture used to be called **Binswanger's disease**. Experts are now trying to define a specific type of vascular dementia, which would incorporate Binswanger's disease, called **subcortical ischaemic vascular dementia**. It is 'subcortical' because it does not involve the cortex, the grey matter, of the brain (see Chapter 2). But its effect is to upset the way in which different parts of the brain communicate (via the white subcortical matter). Subcortical ischaemic vascular dementia is characterized by:

◆ dysexecutive problems (to do with planning, initiation, sequencing, and so on);

◆ slowed thinking;

◆ general problems with attention;

◆ memory difficulties mainly affecting recall, and, to a lesser degree, recognition.

CADASIL

It is interesting that an extremely rare, hereditary form of vascular dementia has been identified. It is called cerebral autosomal dominant arteriopathy with subcortical infarcts and leukoencephalopathy (more simply known as CADASIL). As mentioned in Chapter 4, autosomal dominant means that it occurs in 50 percent of the offspring. An autosomal recessive form has also been found, in which—if both parents carry the gene—there is a 25 percent chance of being affected and a 50 percent chance of being a carrier. The word 'arteriopathy' means damage to the arteries and 'leukoencephalopathy' implies damage to the white matter of the brain (Figure 9.1 in Chapter 9 shows a good example of white matter changes on a brain scan). While it is of tremendous interest in terms of research, it should be said again that CADASIL is fortunately rare. It affects about 2 per 100 000 people, that is about 1 200 people in the UK.

6

Dementia with Lewy bodies

> ## ➲ Key points
>
> ◆ Dementia with Lewy bodies is characterized by fluctuating cognitive function, which often affects visuospatial abilities earlier than memory; visual hallucinations; and features of parkinsonism.
>
> ◆ Lewy bodies are round inclusion bodies which appear inside the cell and are mainly made up of α-synuclein, making this one of a group of conditions called the α-synucleinopathies, which includes Parkinson's disease.
>
> ◆ In Parkinson's disease the Lewy bodies tend to be confined to the base of the brain, whereas in dementia with Lewy bodies they are more scattered, including in the cortex.
>
> ◆ There are several important factors to consider in Lewy body dementia: people can present with falls; there can be profound autonomic problems and REM sleep disorder; sensitivity to neuroleptic drugs is common.
>
> ◆ Diagnosis can be aided by a specific brain scan called a DAT scan.
>
> ◆ People with dementia with Lewy bodies often respond well to cholinesterase inhibitors.

Introduction

Descriptions of cases that specifically linked the finding of cortical Lewy bodies with dementia first appeared in 1961. Friedrich Lewy (1885–1950) had described the roundish bodies that appeared in the neurons (i.e. nerve cells) of parkinsonian patients in 1912. More serious research was underway by the end of the 1980s and the first international consortium on dementia with Lewy bodies (DLB) met in October 1995 in Newcastle upon Tyne. This helped to identify the three core features of DLB:

* fluctuations;
* visual hallucinations;
* spontaneous motor features of parkinsonism.

Pathology

DLB is a primary degenerative dementia, like Alzheimer's disease, and was once thought to be a variant of it. It is closely related, as well, to Parkinson's disease. Lewy bodies were known to be found in the subcortical nuclei (in particular, the substantia nigra) in connection with Parkinson's disease. Nuclei are discrete areas in the brain in which neurons meet and coordinate functional activity. Lewy bodies are round, inclusion bodies in the neuronal cell's cytoplasm, which is the material in the cell body (apart from the nucleus). In DLB, cortical Lewy bodies are also found. These are less well circumscribed and their discovery was aided by new staining techniques. This involved using antibodies to the protein ubiquitin (mentioned in Chapter 4) and to a substance called synuclein. The antibodies can be labelled and they then seek out the particular substances that they are primed to find. These techniques have shown that Lewy bodies can be found throughout the brain, including in the cortex. They do not solely occur in DLB and they can occur in normally ageing brains. In addition, Lewy bodies are not the only pathology in DLB, where there is frequently Alzheimer's pathology to be found—particularly amyloid plaques and less frequently NFTs—as well as vascular pathology.

It turns out that the major filamentous protein in Lewy bodies is a type of synuclein called α-synuclein. The synucleins are a family of proteins. It is not exactly known what their function is, although they seem to be involved in the synaptic membrane and α-synuclein may be associated with the microtubules of the neurons (see Chapter 2). However, there are now several conditions linked under the heading **α-synucleinopathies**. These include: DLB, Parkinson's disease, autonomic failure (see below), and Lewy body dysphagia (this is a swallowing problem where Lewy bodies are found in the brain stem nucleus that controls swallowing, but the person has neither Parkinson's disease nor dementia). The full significance of α-synuclein in connection with DLB is yet to be determined.

A final point in terms of pathology is that the two neurotransmitters, acetylcholine and dopamine, are both reduced in DLB.

◆ The reduction in dopamine mirrors the reduction in this neurotransmitter in Parkinson's disease, which accounts for the movement problems in parkinsonism.

◆ The loss of acetylcholine mirrors the reduction of this neurotransmitter in Alzheimer's disease, but the loss of activity is greater in DLB. This may explain why the cholinesterase inhibitors are more effective in DLB (see Chapter 12).

Key issues

The case below highlights some of the other issues that arise in DLB.

📑 Case study

For two years Mrs Thornton had noted that her husband sometimes seemed just to switch off. He would become vacant, as if dreaming, and then would not quite remember what had happened. But it was not much of a concern to them at the time—it just seemed eccentric. Things became more worrying when Mr Thornton developed a chest infection and started to hallucinate, but the GP said it was the infection and, indeed, it settled once he was given antibiotics. But from about this time he started to be bothered by bad nightmares, during which he would occasionally hit out; during the day he was then drowsy. A little further on and Mr Thornton was becoming increasingly confused, although there were times when he was quite 'with it'. But he was very prone to becoming lost and he started to suffer from falls when he was out. At about the same time he also became convinced that small people had infiltrated the house. He would shout at them and become quite agitated. The initial medication given by the GP, designed to calm him down, simply led to a major decline in his physical state. He was unable to walk and could hardly speak. His body was rigid. It was not possible for Mrs Thornton to cope and Mr Thornton had to be admitted to hospital. Eventually, following a brain scan, a diagnosis of dementia with Lewy bodies was made.

There are several distinctive points about DLB.

1. The problems with cognitive function fluctuate and do not obviously, initially at least, involve memory. Visuospatial tasks, such as copying complex pictures, rather than tasks which involve recalling information (such as words), are more likely to be impaired when the person comes to the doctor.

2. In addition, cognitive function fluctuates. This can change in the space of a few minutes, or over hours or days, but is seen at some point in the illness in most people with DLB. This often involves (a lack of) attention.

3. The visual hallucinations are said to be 'complex' in that they are of people and animals. Patients with DLB might start making drinks for the numerous people who have come into the house. Although hallucinations can occur in delirium, in DLB they tend to persist. But the mixture of problems with attention, cognitive fluctuation, and perceptual disturbance are common in DLB and look very similar to delirium (see Chapter 3).

4. In Parkinson's disease the three core features are tremor, rigidity, and slowness of movement. In DLB, parkinsonism is a core feature too, but tremor is less common. Patients will often show a lack of facial expression and be somewhat 'mask-like'. The link between DLB and Parkinson's disease will be discussed further, including in Chapter 8.

Consensus criteria

Box 6.1 sets out the most recent criteria for a clinical diagnosis of DLB. These came from the Third Consortium on DLB held in 2003, led by Professor Ian McKeith and recorded in the journal *Neurology* in 2005.

Some elements of these criteria require further comment:

◆ REM sleep behaviour disorder: rapid eye movement (REM) sleep, which occurs when we are dreaming, is a normal part of the sleep cycle. During REM sleep, we essentially become paralysed because our muscles lose their normal tone. In REM sleep behaviour disorder, however, muscle tone remains and so we act out our dreams. This can lead to shouting or punching or more complicated movements, which are extremely upsetting for any bed partner.

◆ Severe neuroleptic sensitivity: neuroleptic drugs are also called antipsychotics and they are often the right drugs to use for psychotic experiences (i.e. where the person's experiences have lost touch with reality) such as hallucinations. However, people with DLB can react very badly to these drugs—as in the case of Mr Thornton—and deteriorate very quickly. As we shall see in Chapter 12, there are other reasons for being cautious with these drugs in other types of dementia.

◆ Low dopamine transporter uptake in the basal ganglia: this is the DAT scan, which will be described in Chapter 9, but in brief it is the scan that shows the problem in terms of the neurotransmitter dopamine that also accounts for the symptoms of parkinsonism.

◆ Autonomic dysfunction: the autonomic nervous system is part of the peripheral nervous system (i.e. it does not involve the brain or spinal cord).

Box 6.1 Summary of criteria for a clinical diagnosis of DLB

1. **Central feature**: Dementia with noticeable deficits in terms of attention, executive function, and visuospatial tasks.

2. **Core features**:

— fluctuating cognition with pronounced variations in attention and alertness;

— recurrent visual hallucinations which are typically well formed and detailed;

— spontaneous features of parkinsonism.

3. **Suggestive features**:

— REM sleep behaviour disorder;

— severe neuroleptic sensitivity;

— low dopamine transporter uptake in basal ganglia shown by brain scanning.

4. **Supportive features**: include repeated falls and faints; severe autonomic dysfunction; other types of hallucinations and delusions; depression; and a variety of findings on specific scans.

5. A diagnosis of DLB is **less likely** if there is evidence of stroke disease or anything else that might explain the symptoms and signs; it is also less likely if parkinsonism only appears for the first time when the person has severe dementia.

6. **Temporal sequence of symptoms**: DLB should be diagnosed when dementia occurs before or at the same time as parkinsonism (if it is present). A one-year rule stipulates that the onset of dementia within 12 months of the onset of parkinsonism qualifies as DLB; if there is more than 12 months of parkinsonism before the dementia starts, the diagnosis is Parkinson's disease dementia (PDD) (see Chapter 8).

It (i.e. the autonomic nervous system) controls the functioning of a variety of our internal organs without our being conscious of it. For example, autonomic nerves control the pulse rate of the heart. Autonomic dysfunction is seen in DLB in a variety of ways. For instance, there may be sudden drops in blood pressure, especially when the person stands up (orthostatic hypotension), as well as disturbances to the functions of the bowels and bladder. This may explain one of the other supportive features of a diagnosis of DLB, namely the tendency to fall.

Conclusion: the importance of the diagnosis

There are several reasons why DLB is important.

* First, the diagnosis can be easily missed or confused with some other form of dementia. For instance, it would be perfectly possible for someone to arrive at casualty having had a fall and having seemed confused, but is then found to be lucid and, on a test of memory, to do well. The person might then be sent home. But a test of visuospatial skills, if it had been performed, may well have proven more problematic. At other times the person may still be quite confused. And in this example the fall is as yet unexplained. It is understandable (perhaps) that a busy casualty department might decide not to look into this any further, but simply advise the person to seek further help if there were to be further problems.

* Second, the mixture of increasing physical disability and neuropsychiatric symptoms (i.e. visual hallucinations), as well as worsening cognitive function, means that people with DLB pose particular problems for professionals (who cannot use neuroleptic medication for the hallucinations) and for the family carers.

* Third, however, there is good news in that people with DLB often respond noticeably well to cholinesterase inhibitors (discussed in Chapter 12), even if the effects wear off.

7

Frontotemporal dementias

> ## ➲ Key points
>
> ◆ There are three clinical presentations of frontotemporal lobar degeneration: the frontal (behavioural) variant; semantic dementia; and progressive non-fluent aphasia.
>
> ◆ The frontal (behavioural) variant presents with insidious changes in personality, affecting behaviour (e.g. causing disinhibition) and executive functioning.
>
> ◆ In semantic dementia the person loses word meaning.
>
> ◆ In progressive non-fluent aphasia, speech production is affected.
>
> ◆ Pick bodies and cells are characteristic pathological findings in many cases and involve tau; but tauopathies (Pick bodies and neurofibrillary tangles) only account for 45 percent of the pathology; most of the rest is accounted for by transactive response DNA binding protein (TDP-43).
>
> ◆ Mutations on the genes on chromosome 17 which code for tau and progranulin account for 20 percent of frontotemporal lobar degeneration.

Introduction

We have already seen that frontotemporal dementia (FTD) is relatively uncommon, but is a more common form of younger-onset dementia. The terminology is not straightforward, but is summarized in Fig. 7.1.

The unifying feature of the three ways in which frontotemporal dementias can present is that they all show the same pathology, which is captured by the term frontotemporal lobar degeneration (FTLD). The frontal variant of FTD is probably the form of these disorders that receives the most publicity. This is because (as mentioned in Chapter 2) the frontal lobe is to do with social behaviour and personality, and problems in these areas can be a cause of considerable strain for the families of those involved. If there are changes in behaviour or personality, the diagnosis of dementia is often delayed. In what follows I shall focus on the frontal form of FTD, before dealing with the other two types more briefly.

Diagnostic criteria: frontotemporal dementia

Once again, international diagnostic criteria have been developed, which were reported in the journal *Neurology* in 1998. The core features for the frontal form of FTLD are shown in Box 7.1.

In addition to the core features in Box 7.1, there are numerous supportive diagnostic features, covering behavioural problems, abnormal aspects of language and speech, physical signs, as well as abnormal investigations. The following case illustrates many of these features.

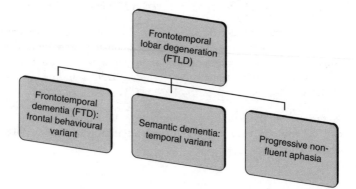

Figure 7.1 Frontotemporal dementias.

Box 7.1 Core diagnostic features of the frontal (behavioural) variant of FTLD

Insidious onset and gradual progression

Early decline in social interpersonal conduct

Early impairment in regulation of personal conduct

Early emotional blunting

Early loss of insight

Case study

At the age of 54 years Mr Wallace was reprimanded by his boss in the bank for sending an inappropriate email to a younger female member of staff. He said it was just a joke. But within a short space of time he had done something similar. When he was given a formal warning, he became verbally aggressive with his senior colleagues (which was most out of character) and stormed out. At home he was increasingly irritable with his wife. When she tried to have a conversation with him about what had happened, he shouted at her. When she cried, he just stared at her and did not seem affected by her tears. She felt that he must be unwell and asked him to see the doctor. He would not go. She went to the doctor herself and the GP suggested marriage counselling. Mr Wallace would not consider this idea. He spent days pacing around the house. Eventually, with persuasion from the children, who were also becoming concerned, Mr Wallace went to the GP. It was noted that he was unemotional in his responses, that there had been a slip in terms of his personal appearance, and given he had suffered the loss of his job, it was surmised that he might be depressed. An antidepressant tablet was started. But Mr Wallace, if anything, started to get worse. He seemed to cheer up when his adolescent children's friends were around, but they became embarrassed by the sexual nature of some of his comments. Mr Wallace seemed to have developed rituals, which involved taking all of his books from their shelves in order to re-stack them. He sometimes did this several times a day and he would swear quite violently (which he would not have done before) if any of the books were disturbed. One of their neighbours complained quietly to Mrs Wallace that her husband had been seen urinating in the garden. Mr Wallace's eating habits were becoming difficult to live with: not only did he eat very quickly, and sometimes copious amounts of cake or anything else sugary, but he had also seemingly lost his social graces. Mr Wallace was starting to show evidence of speech problems: he would sometimes seem to get stuck on a word. He was gradually unable to converse with the family and did not seem to understand all that they said to him. They had to call the doctor to see him. Mr Wallace then became threatening towards the doctor. In the end, Mr Wallace had to be detained under the Mental Health Act and taken into hospital for tests.

Family carers of people with FTD often complain about how long it can take for the diagnosis to be made. They frequently feel quite bewildered by the changes that occur in someone they have known and loved for many years. Socially disruptive behaviour can easily lead to police involvement. Cognitive problems, such as memory impairments, are sometimes overlooked by families who are understandably more concerned by odd behaviours. Repetitive behaviours and speech, a tendency to put things in the mouth (hyperorality) and to like sugary food, incontinence, and (in the later stages) physical effects, such as rigidity or muscle weakness, are but some of the signs that can suggest the diagnosis, which is made considerably more certain by brain imaging showing defects in the frontal lobe.

Semantic dementia

The main problem that characterizes this rare type of dementia is a gradual and progressive loss of word meaning. The person affected cannot remember the names of things and cannot understand things that are said. There may also be a loss of the ability to remember familiar faces (prosopagnosia). But people with semantic dementia can still repeat words spoken to them and can copy, read aloud, and write some words to dictation. There may also be behavioural signs, such as a loss of sympathy and a narrowing of the person's preoccupations.

Progressive non-fluent aphasia

This is again a relatively rare form of dementia. The speech problems can dominate for several years before behavioural problems are seen. Whereas in semantic dementia the person can still speak fluently, but is just losing words, in this form of aphasia (which implies a problem with speech) the person's speech is non-fluent. In other words, they make numerous mistakes as they speak so that their powers to converse diminish. At its most severe, people can become mute. Early on, however, they can still understand the meaning of words; and even late on there may be evidence of good memory and visuospatial orientation, which allows them to continue to function relatively well in the community. This can be compared to people who have lost speech in Alzheimer's disease, where other cognitive functions would also be profoundly affected so that they would not be able to function apparently so normally.

Pathology

The pathology of FTLD used to be characterized in terms of the lesions (i.e. the areas that have suffered damage) found in 1892 by Arnold Pick (1851–1924). The condition was called **Pick's disease**. Pick cells are neurons that have expanded or ballooned and contain bundles of neurofilaments that turn out to contain tau (see Chapter 4 for a fuller description of tau). When these filaments are condensed to form a small inclusion body in the cell, they are called Pick bodies. These findings, however, do not correspond in a helpful way with the classification outlined in this chapter and the term Pick's disease tends not to be used now.

Some generalizations can be made about the different types of FTLD and their individual pathological appearances:

- In *FTD* (the frontal, behavioural variety) there is bilateral atrophy (i.e. shrinkage) of the frontal and anterior temporal lobes (i.e. the front parts of the temporal lobes);

- In *semantic dementia* there is bitemporal atrophy (i.e. shrinkage affecting both sides), but the atrophy is often worse on the left and tends to be anterior rather than posterior;

- In *progressive non-fluent aphasia* there is marked asymmetry, most often affecting the left hemisphere around the area that serves speech production (see Chapter 2).

Although approximately 45 percent of cases of FTLD show evidence of tau in the brain, either as NFTs or as Pick bodies, the further 55 percent (approximately) of cases can be accounted for by a type of pathology known as FTLD-U, because instead of tau it contains a protein that stains for ubiquitin. This protein is called the transactive response DNA binding protein, abbreviated to TDP-43. The details of the TDP-43 protein do not need to concern us here. Together, the pathology caused by tau (tauopathies) and the pathology linked to TDP-43 account for 95 percent of all cases of FTLD. A very small proportion of cases is accounted for by other proteins.

Genetics

The observation that in many families (perhaps 40 percent) these conditions appear to show an autosomal dominant pattern of inheritance has led to a search for the responsible gene or genes. The most significant findings to date relate to chromosome 17. This is the chromosome that codes for tau. And, indeed, mutations (i.e. changes in the genetic code) have been found in the tau gene, which is known as the *MAPT* gene (which stands for microtubule-associated protein tau). Further mutations were then found in the progranulin gene (*PGRN*). Progranulin is connected with tissue remodelling or repair, and seems to be important for neuronal survival. The *PGRN* gene is very close to the *MAPT* gene. But together the *MAPT* and *PGRN* mutations only account for about 20 percent of all cases of FTLD. Work continues in this field.

Conclusion

FTLD is, after all, fairly rare. It is more common that people with other pathologies—Alzheimer's disease, vascular dementia, or DLB—present in a way that is described as 'frontal', meaning that there are changes in personality, such as disinhibition, or dysexecutive signs. For, by definition, dementias are 'global' (see Chapter 3) and in some cases there will be an impact on the frontal lobe. But the importance of FTLD is that it has given a number of unique insights into the ways in which the brain changes as a result of disease and of how this might be controlled.

8

Other dementias

➲ Key points

♦ There are many causes of dementia, which range from common (e.g. heavy alcohol consumption and head trauma) to rare (e.g. prion disease or some inherited metabolic disorders).

♦ Rarer forms of dementia are often accompanied by striking physical symptoms or signs, some of which can be diagnostic (e.g. the chorea of Huntington's disease).

♦ The course of these dementias varies greatly: they can be slowly progressive (as is often true in Parkinson's disease) or rapid (e.g. death in six months in CJD).

♦ Part of their importance is that some of them can be prevented with treatment (e.g. thiamine in alcohol-related conditions), some respond well to treatment, especially if this is given quickly (e.g. shunting in normal pressure hydrocephalus), and some are more or less reversible (e.g. certain infections and inflammatory conditions).

The list of possible causes of dementia is long. In this chapter I shall give very brief descriptions of some of the main features of these rarer dementias. There are two caveats: first, the dementias discussed here could all be discussed at considerably greater length; second, there are further possible causes of dementia: those described here are simply a sample. Readers who require further details will need to consult the texts in Appendix 2.

Alcohol-related dementias

Alcohol is poisonous to the nervous system (neurotoxic) and—as is commonly known—the brain does not work so well under the influence of alcohol. High alcohol consumption is a risk factor for cognitive impairment.

◆ Among those who misuse alcohol, between 10 and 24 percent have detectable dementia.

◆ In people with dementia, it is estimated that alcohol abuse or dependence (i.e. addiction) is a significant factor in between 9 and 22 percent.

It has been suggested that there is a specific alcohol-related dementia. But it has been difficult to pin down a specific pathology to go along with such a state. It is possible to demonstrate effects of alcohol on most parts of the brain, but frontal executive dysfunction has often been noted. (Equally, it is possible to demonstrate a reversal of brain atrophy if someone who has been dependent on alcohol subsequently abstains.) Rather than identifying a specific alcohol-related dementia, it is easier to point to other states that alcohol can cause which lead to dementia:

◆ Alcohol is implicated as a cause of **hypertension**, which in turn causes vascular dementia.

◆ **Diseases of the liver** caused by alcohol can lead to a build-up of toxins that affect the brain and lead to a dementia syndrome, i.e. **hepatic encephalopathy**.

◆ Of course, alcohol misuse commonly leads to **falls**, and **head injuries** can be a potent cause of dementia (see below).

◆ There are rarer conditions, linked to alcohol dependence, which can lead to dementia, e.g. **Marchiafava–Bignami disease** and **central pontine myelinolysis,** both of which affect structures near the centre of the brain and involve loss of the myelin sheaths that help to insulate the nerve fibres and speed up conduction of nerve impulses.

◆ Chronic alcoholism is linked to a number of dietary deficiencies, which themselves cause dementia. A rare example now is **pellagra**, a skin condition caused by lack of **niacin** (vitamin B3), which eventually causes dementia. Better known is the syndrome that results from a deficiency of **thiamine** (vitamin B1): **Wernicke–Korsakoff syndrome**.

Wernicke–Korsakoff syndrome

This syndrome, caused by lack of vitamin B1 (thiamine), is said (although the reality is more complex) to have an acute phase (Wernicke's) and a chronic phase (Korsakoff's). The pathology again involves midline structures in the brain, such as the mammillary bodies and thalamus (see Chapter 2).

In *Wernicke's encephalopathy*, which is potentially reversible if detected and appropriately treated with vitamin B1, the following can be seen:

- confusion;
- a variety of signs in the eyes (e.g. abnormal movements and differences in the sizes of the pupils, with slow pupil responses, etc.);
- poor coordination (ataxia);
- coma and death if untreated.

Korsakoff's psychosis also results from lack of vitamin B1 and may follow Wernicke's, although this is not always obviously so. It is a chronic condition mainly characterized by:

- anterograde amnesia: loss of the ability to form new memories;
- retrograde amnesia: loss of previous memories;
- confabulation: stories made up to fill gaps in memory;
- lack of insight: no realization that there are problems;
- apathy: a general disinterest in things.

Alcohol as a protective factor

Although the dangers of alcohol misuse must always be emphasized for the sake of public health generally, and although older people are more susceptible to the bad effects of alcohol (because of changes in their metabolic abilities), nevertheless it can be cautiously stated that a moderate alcohol intake throughout life may protect against dementia in later life.

- Moderate alcohol consumption here means 20–40 ml of ethanol per day.
- In the UK, this would equate to 2–4 units of alcohol per day (where a unit is ½ pint of ordinary strength beer, lager or cider, a small pub measure (25 ml) of spirits, or 50 ml of fortified wine, such as sherry or port).
- However, the recommended safe limit for drinking alcohol in the UK for men is 21 units per week (so to drink 4 units every day would be to go over the safe limit). (It should be noted that different countries define a unit of alcohol differently and also have different recommendations for 'safe' limits.)
- For women, the recommended safe limit in the UK is only 14 units per week.
- Furthermore, other factors (e.g. liver disease, hypertension, and older age) may alter what is safe for an individual.

Down's syndrome and learning disabilities

In Chapter 1, I mentioned the increased prevalence of dementia at a younger age in people with Down's syndrome. As well as the clinical significance of this observation, it also has considerable scientific importance. Down's syndrome is caused, in 95 percent of cases, by a genetic defect known as trisomy 21, which means there is a third copy of the genetic material of chromosome 21. The importance of this is that chromosome 21 contains the APP gene (see Chapter 4). Hence, it is not surprising that four to five times the normal amount of amyloid is produced. The theory is that this then leads to early and excessive deposition of amyloid in the brain, causing Alzheimer's disease. Indeed, it has been shown at post-mortem that the brains of people with trisomy 21 have typical Alzheimer's pathology (both amyloid plaques and neurofibrillary tangles) by the age of 40 years. Bearing in mind the prevalence of dementia is about 5 percent in the general population over 60 years of age, the approximate prevalence of dementia in Down's syndrome is:

- 9 percent up to 49 years;
- 18 percent from 50–54 years;
- 32 percent from 55–59 years;
- 26 percent above 60 years.

The slightly lower prevalence over 60 might reflect increasing mortality.

Alzheimer's disease tends to be diagnosed in Down's syndrome between the ages of 50 and 55 years. The diagnosis, as well as being based on cognitive tests, is also based on changes in personality and behaviour.

Finally, it has to be kept in mind that Down's syndrome is not the only learning (or intellectual) disability in which there is an increased prevalence of dementia. This is a complicated area because many people with mild intellectual disabilities are not diagnosed as such. In old age the diagnosis of a decline in cognitive abilities is difficult. Such a decline may be predisposed by a variety of other factors (i.e. the cause is not necessarily the learning disability itself). These may be biological (e.g. greater rates of cardiovascular risk) or psychosocial (e.g. poorer educational opportunities or an impoverished social environment).

Infections

A variety of infections (viral, prion, and bacterial) can cause dementia. Our ability to treat these types of dementia is as good or bad as our ability to treat the underlying infection. Once again, I have not mentioned every type of infection that might cause dementia, but simply given well-known illustrative examples.

HIV-associated dementia

Human immunodeficiency virus (HIV) is the type of retrovirus that causes acquired immunodeficiency syndrome (AIDS). The development of highly active antiretroviral therapy (HAART) has increased the anticipated lifespan of those with HIV (at least in those countries and for those people able to afford the medication). Because of longer lifespan there has been an increase in the number of people acquiring neurocognitive disorders as a result of HIV. In most cases this amounts to mild neurocognitive disorder rather than full-blown dementia. However, HAD tends to develop and, if untreated, is progressive. Nonetheless, it can sometimes respond so well to HAART that it can be regarded as a reversible form of dementia.

HIV-associated dementia (HAD) presents with a mixture of cognitive, behavioural, and motor signs and symptoms. The dementia can be subcortical, with slowing of cognition, difficulties with complex tasks, and effects on mood and motivation, as well as cortical, with effects on language and memory. In addition, there can be various neurological symptoms and signs from problems with gait unsteadiness, clumsiness, and tremor to abnormal reflexes.

Prion diseases

A prion is a proteinaceous infectious particle. A prion is an infectious agent, although it is only a 'mis-folded' protein. Once inside a new host, the prion makes the existing normal forms of protein change into the prion variety, which then induces further such changes. Prion disease affects the brain in humans. It has a long, silent incubation period, perhaps as long as 50 years. It can be transmitted by surgical instruments or by blood products. It is not eradicated by routine sterilization procedures and is hard to detect in asymptomatic carriers. There are also various genetic, inherited types of prion disease, which are rare and not discussed further here.

Creutzfeldt–Jakob disease

Creutzfeldt–Jakob disease (CJD) is the best known of the prion diseases. It can present with initial features of a rather non-specific nature, such as fatigue, headache, depression, and so on. But the disease is a rapidly progressive dementia affecting multiple neurocognitive functions. It is accompanied by myoclonus, i.e. spasmodic, jerky muscle movements. Most people present between the ages of 45 and 75 years, but most in their early sixties. The disease progresses to akinetic mutism (i.e. where the person can neither move nor speak), and death follows in less than six months. There are various other neurological signs. The diagnosis is helped by neuroimaging and by electroencephalography (EEG). The EEG is a recording made by placing electrodes over the scalp to detect the electrical activity over the surface of the brain. In around 70 percent of cases of CJD it shows a helpful characteristic appearance: pseudoperiodic sharp wave activity.

Variant Creutzfeldt–Jakob disease

Dramatic events occurred in the UK in 1995 when several cases of CJD in adolescents were reported and it became apparent that these represented transmission of bovine spongiform encephalopathy (BSE) to humans through food.

This 'new variant' of CJD (now simply vCJD) often presents initially with behavioural features to psychiatrists, along with symptoms of anxiety and depression.

- Delusions and other psychotic symptoms, such as hallucinations, can also occur.
- Abnormal sensations and limb or face pain can be a persistent feature.
- Usually after some months, neurological symptoms develop, such as a lack of coordination and unsteadiness, as well as dementia.
- The disease progresses to akinetic mutism and death.
- Myoclonus is again a feature.
- The mean age at onset is about 28 years.
- Median survival is 14 months—longer than in typical sporadic CJD.
- The EEG is abnormal, but does not usually show the characteristic feature of typical sporadic CJD.
- Although CT scans may be normal, a more specific MRI scan finding in the posterior thalamus has come to be called the 'pulvinar sign'. More recently this has also been reported in typical sporadic CJD too.

The big question has always been whether there will yet be an epidemic of vCJD. The worry is that many people may have eaten contaminated foodstuffs, but we know that the infection can be clinically silent for years. The good news is that the number of cases of vCJD has been small and is falling in the UK; and anonymous sampling of tissue from appendix and tonsil operations puts the prevalence as low. The bad news is that it might have spread further without detection and will only emerge in due course. The UK National Prion Clinic (web address in Appendix 1) gives advice and up-to-date information. Numerous other countries have now also had cases of vCJD.

Syphilis

Syphilis has never gone away and has again increased, which includes cases of neurosyphilis, sometimes in conjunction with HIV. General paralysis (or paresis) of the insane (GPI) was the old name for neurosyphilis. It tends to affect people between the ages of 35 and 50 years. It appears many years after the initial infection with the bacterium *Treponema pallidum*: the incubation period can be 10 to 25 years. There are gradual changes in personality and cognition. Psychiatric symptoms then appear, such as mania, delusions, and paranoia. Neurological signs include ataxia (poor coordination), disturbed speech, and abnormal pupils.

A conclusive diagnosis requires blood tests or CSF. Treatment with penicillin can be curative if given soon enough, but delayed treatment can lead to irreversible changes.

Inflammation

Inflammation is the body's response to injury or insult. Inflammation involves changes to the blood vessels (e.g. increased permeability) to allow the constituents of the inflammatory response (e.g. white blood cells) to get out to repair the damage or fight the infection. Unfortunately there are conditions in which the inflammation is itself harmful. Inflammation (which involves swelling) in the brain is potentially life-threatening because the brain has little room to swell within the skull. The swelling itself compromises brain function, for instance by impeding the blood supply.

Cerebral vasculitis describes a group of conditions in which the inflammation is in the blood vessels of the brain. This can occur as a result of another inflammatory condition affecting the rest of the body, such as systemic lupus erythematosus (SLE), or, very rarely, as part of an inflammatory condition that only affects the blood vessels of the brain, such as primary angiitis of the central nervous system (PACNS). This condition is important because it is treatable and reversible, but if untreated the dementia is rapidly progressive. The diagnosis is difficult, but headache and confusion, with other neurological signs, and sometimes seizures, can point in the direction of cerebral vasculitis.

Two other types of inflammatory condition are linked to dementia. Again they are important because they can progress rapidly but they can also be treated, so the dementia is reversible. They are interesting as well because of their links to illnesses elsewhere in the body. In **limbic encephalitis** there is inflammation in the limbic system of the brain (see Chapter 2). Some forms of limbic encephalitis occur as a result of autoimmune conditions (where the inflammatory response is aimed at the person's own tissue rather than at foreign tissue (e.g. infections) or at injury from outside); but mostly limbic encephalitis has been linked with cancers, e.g. of the lung, testis, or breast. Hence, these conditions are often called **paraneoplastic**, implying the connection with neoplasms (i.e. new growths or tumours). Treatment tends to be immunosuppression (i.e. to stop the damage caused by the inflammation, which is an immune response) and removal of the underlying malignant tumour. In **Hashimoto's encephalopathy**, which also presents with a variety of neurological and psychiatric symptoms and signs, there is a link with autoimmune thyroid disease. **Anti-thyroid antibodies** are the hallmark of the condition (i.e. the body is attacking its own thyroid tissue); whether or not they cause the condition is another matter (they may just be markers of the underlying inflammatory problem). Treatment, which involves steroids to suppress the inflammation, is very successful.

Inherited metabolic diseases

We tend to think of inherited diseases as appearing at birth or early childhood, but there are some that can appear in adolescence or in young adulthood. Strictly speaking these are not, therefore, acquired (because they are inherited). But, nonetheless, they are not apparent in early life and do represent a loss of functions and abilities that had been present. The number of such metabolic conditions is large, for example **Gaucher disease, metachromatic leukodystrophy, Niemann-Pick disease type C**, and **Wilson's disease**. If they mainly affect the grey matter of the brain, they can present with dementia and seizures; pathology in the white matter can cause muscle weakness, rigidity, or ataxia. Many of these conditions can now be treated with enzyme or dietary replacement (to restore the metabolic dysfunction).

Metabolic disorders

Just as inherited metabolic disorders can cause dementia, so too there are other metabolic conditions, often acquired in later life, which can cause cognitive impairment. In theory, treatment of these conditions could reverse dementia. In practice, hardly anyone ever presents with a dementia where the sole cause is a correctable acquired metabolic disorder. Nevertheless, even if treating these conditions does not cure dementia, treatment will often improve some symptoms (sometimes caused by the more general effects of the deficiency, e.g. lethargy), and it seems sensible and right to maximize the person's physical state. Hence the importance of screening for these deficiencies during assessment using blood tests. Here are four of the possible metabolic abnormalities which might cause or contribute to dementia, and which are routinely checked during assessment:

* folic acid deficiency;
* hypothyroidism (i.e. low thyroid hormone levels);
* hypercalcaemia (i.e. raised calcium in the blood);
* vitamin B12 deficiency.

Of course, there are other examples, such as niacin (vitamin B3) deficiency, which was mentioned in connection with alcohol and dementia. We also know that high homocysteine levels in the blood pose a risk of cardiovascular disease. Vitamins such as B6 and B12 play a role in lowering homocysteine. All of these metabolic conditions have other physical and mental effects, which may make management of cognitive impairment more difficult.

Mitochondrial disorders

A mitochondrion is an organelle found within cells that have a nucleus (eukaryotic cells). The mitochondria are the main source of energy for the cell. So a whole host of metabolic work is done by the mitochondria. But they probably have broader functions too, in terms of coordinating the action and life cycle of the cell. They are, for instance, implicated in cell death. There is a huge raft of conditions that arise as a result of mitochondrial dysfunction. Mitochondrial disorders mainly affect the skeleton and the nervous system. They present with a wide range of neurological symptoms and signs, which include ataxia, epilepsy, migraine, movement disorders, and stroke-like episodes. In addition, there can be psychiatric manifestations, such as psychotic phenomena and dementia. Specific connections between Alzheimer's disease and mitochondrial disease have also been suggested.

Neurological disorders

There are a number of neurological conditions in which dementia is either a key feature or one that is likely to appear if the person lives with the condition for long enough. I shall not try to describe the conditions themselves in any detail. Readers will need to consult more detailed texts on the particular neurological diseases if required.

Huntington's disease

Huntington's disease is an autosomal dominant condition. It begins in mid-life with movement disorders, typically chorea, which consists of abrupt, short, irregular muscle movements. There is also cognitive dysfunction and emotional disturbance. The exact pattern varies, but prognosis includes death within about 20 to 30 years. There are major issues concerning genetic testing for Huntington's, given the dominant pattern of inheritance (for further information, see the Huntington's Disease Association website listed in Appendix 1). The dementia is typically subcortical. In other words, there are memory problems, accompanied by slowing (which affects thinking and practical skills), apathy, and depression. Executive function, visuospatial skills, and language are all affected. The cognitive problems can appear before the physical symptoms. There are also other psychiatric manifestations such as depression, obsessive-compulsive symptoms, psychotic phenomena, and irritability.

In the later stages the person becomes completely dependent because of the mixture of physical signs (e.g. rigidity) and dementia (e.g. affecting communication and activities of daily living).

Multiple sclerosis

Again, for further information about multiple sclerosis (MS), details of the MS Society can be found in Appendix 1. It is a relapsing and remitting, chronic, progressive disease of the central nervous system (CNS). It can show itself in a variety of ways and its course is quite variable. Cognitive impairment tends to affect frontal executive functions and also has a subcortical pattern, with impairment in attention and processing speed. Verbal memory is also affected. It can be difficult to distinguish on MRI scans between vascular disease in old age and demyelination, which is the main pathological finding in MS.

Multiple system atrophy

There is some controversy over whether or not multiple system atrophy (MSA) involves full-blown dementia. Its main symptoms and signs, which appear in a person's fifties, include autonomic dysfunction, unsteadiness, and lack of coordination (ataxia), as well as features of parkinsonism. There can also be REM sleep behaviour disorder. The dementia is, however, usually mild and the deficits, as in MS, are frontosubcortical in nature. The controversy concerns whether dementia in MSA might actually be Alzheimer's disease or DLB.

Normal pressure hydrocephalus

This is a misnomer, because the pressure in 'normal pressure hydrocephalus' (NPH) is actually slightly raised! 'Hydrocephalus' refers to an excess of CSF in the skull. This is either caused because too much is produced (which is rare), absorption is impeded, or the flow of the CSF is obstructed. So the two main types of hydrocephalus are:

+ **obstructive hydrocephalus**, where the flow of CSF is blocked; or
+ **communicating hydrocephalus**, where the flow is not blocked, but the absorption by the arachnoid granulations is impeded.

The arachnoid granulations are valve-like protrusions of the thin second membranous layer that covers the brain (the arachnoid) through the thick outer layer (the dura mater). They allow the CSF to drain into the blood. It is communicating hydrocephalus that is also called NPH on the grounds that an early study showed normal pressures (but the pressure can vary). NPH can be secondary to other conditions that damage the arachnoid granulations (e.g. meningitis). The cause of the problem in primary (or idiopathic) NPH is not known.

The condition normally presents with a triad of:

* gait disturbance;
* cognitive impairment (subcortical);
* urinary urgency, frequency, and incontinence.

The diagnosis is helped by typical brain scan appearances. The treatment is to place a ventriculo-peritoneal shunt—a tube which drains CSF from the brain ventricles to the abdomen. In some neurosurgical units, before such a shunt is used, a dynamic test is performed in which CSF is drained by lumbar puncture (LP) with measurements of gait and cognitive function being performed before and after the drainage. If shunting is then used, the gait disturbance is the feature most likely to improve. The milder the dementia, the more likely it is to improve. At least in theory, then, this is another possibly reversible form of dementia.

Parkinson's disease

Parkinson's disease (PD) is a condition that affects about 1.5 percent of those aged 65 years or older. The main features of PD are resting tremor, bradykinesia (i.e. slowness in movements), and rigidity. As we have seen, DLB is closely related to PD. In PD the pathology, which includes Lewy bodies, is (in the early stages) generally restricted to the area of the brain associated with the abnormal movements of PD (i.e. the pars compacta of the substantia nigra in the basal ganglia). In DLB, on the other hand, Lewy bodies are scattered throughout the brain, including in the cortex. Mild cognitive impairment is quite common in PD. But the prevalence of dementia gradually increases as PD progresses, hence the notion of Parkinson's disease dementia (PDD). In PDD, cortical Lewy bodies are likely to be found (albeit this is also increasingly true as time passes in PD patients without dementia), as well as Alzheimer's and vascular pathology.

Here are some facts about dementia and PD:

* Roughly 31 percent of those with PD have dementia;
* In people with PD, the risk of developing dementia is raised relative to people without PD;
* In the general population, PDD may account for 3–4 percent of patients with dementia;
* On average, about 10 percent of PD patients develop dementia per year;
* After 20 years about 75 percent of people with PD have dementia.

The assessment of dementia in PD is difficult because of the slowing caused by PD and because of apathy. But there is evidence that people with PDD may respond well to treatment with the cholinesterase inhibitor rivastigmine (see Chapter 12), which is a drug used to treat the symptoms of Alzheimer's disease. One trial showed improvements in cognitive function, activities of daily living, and neuropsychiatric symptoms. Some neuropsychiatric symptoms, such as visual hallucinations and confusion, can be caused by anti-parkinsonian medication. If it is not possible to reduce anti-parkinsonian medication, a cholinesterase inhibitor may be a suitable alternative. There are reasons to believe that memantine, another anti-dementia drug, might also be useful in PDD.

It is worth noting that there are other parkinsonian diseases, such as cortico-basal syndrome and corticobasal degeneration, that can also feature dementia. (Further general information and support are available from Parkinson's UK, whose web address is in Appendix 1.)

Progressive supranuclear palsy

Progressive supranuclear palsy (PSP; formerly known as Steele-Richardson-Olszewski syndrome) can often be misdiagnosed, for instance, as PD. It tends to start in the person's sixties. Its main features are difficulty with eye movements and, in particular, with downward gaze, swallowing and speech problems, muscle rigidity in the neck, with parkinsonism, and dementia. The dementia can again be characterized as subcortical, with slower processing, apathy, and poor abilities at abstract thought. Depression is also not uncommon. However, the main problems are physical and the dementia is not usually severe.

Trauma

Any significant head injury, e.g. from a fall, could cause dementia if the damage to the brain were to be extensive enough to affect several domains of cognition, as well as activities of daily living, behaviour, emotions, and so on. However, more than the straightforward direct results of injury, it is now well established that trauma can lead to Aβ amyloid being deposited in the brain.

For similar reasons, perhaps, **boxing** is associated with dementia: so-called 'dementia pugilistica'. This is thought to be a type of chronic traumatic encephalopathy with a long latency, perhaps reflecting diffuse injury to the nervous tissue of the brain. Some people have also commented on the seemingly greater number of cases of dementia in older **professional footballers**, who used to have to 'head' extremely heavy leather balls.

Finally, head trauma may lead to bleeding in the skull. Some types of bleeding will have sudden and dramatic consequences, such as an extradural (arterial) bleed following a blow to the head, which may well lead to immediate loss of consciousness, but if treated need not cause dementia. In a subdural bleed (one between the dura mater and the arachnoid), which may follow a fairly mild trauma in an older person, the fragile veins can be torn so that there is a slow accumulation of blood and clot (a subdural haematoma). The symptoms can be less obvious, such as gradually increasing confusion, which may be mistaken for an already established dementia naturally worsening. Hence the importance of brain scans for older people who fall if there is any suspicion of head injury, increased confusion, or signs that might suggest neurological damage.

Tumours

Whether tumours arise in the brain (primary) or have spread to the brain from elsewhere (secondary), their bad effects stem mostly from the way they are likely to cut or compress important tracts or areas of the brain. As such, their effects might be various, from purely neurological, to behavioural, to cognitive. If they cause raised intracranial pressure there will eventually be altered consciousness, with disturbances of breathing and finally death. Tumours may cause dementia-like symptoms depending on their location. Gliomas (which are malignant, but can be low or high grade) and meningiomas (which are mostly benign) are the most common primary brain tumours likely to cause dementia. Cerebral metastases (i.e. secondary tumours), which are usually multiple, are also likely to cause mass effects (i.e. to exert compressive effects) compromising cognitive and other brain functions. Depending on their site and size, tumours might be amenable to neurosurgery, radiotherapy, or pharmacological treatment: oedema (i.e. swelling) caused by the tumours may be symptomatically treated with steroids and seizures can be treated with anticonvulsants. Some tumours (e.g. some meningiomas and some low-grade gliomas), however, are so slow growing that neither neurosurgery nor other forms of treatment are required.

9

Assessment

➔ Key points

♦ The assessment will entail a history, physical and mental state examination, and investigations, which will include special investigations, such as brain scans.

♦ Assessment at an early stage allows the person to make any necessary plans and allows support and treatment to start as soon as possible if it is required.

♦ The person being assessed should normally attend a memory clinic with an informant who knows them well.

♦ Testing of cognitive function can be upsetting, because it reveals the person's deficits, so it must be undertaken with skill and empathy.

♦ Different brain scans give different types and quality of information.

♦ Being told the diagnosis can also be upsetting; people need to be given adequate information and support as they need it.

Introduction

This chapter describes the process of assessment for any possible form of dementia. In most cases assessment will be because of concerns about memory problems. But it may be, for instance, that the initial worries are about a change in personality. In any event, the assessment needs to be thorough and broad.

When?

An assessment should take place when there is concern. This is not straight-forward, however, because the concern may be on the part of the person with the presumed problem, or, alternatively, may be on the part of that person's family or close carers. It may be that the person with the perceived problem is not keen to be assessed. The ideal is that assessment should be *timely*: it should occur when difficulties are starting to emerge. (This was one of the recommendations of the report by the Nuffield Council on Bioethics, which is referenced in Appendix 2.) It may be that this will require some negotiation, not only between family carers and the person involved, but also with the GP. The first step, indeed, should be for an initial assessment to take place between the person and the GP in order to try to gauge whether a more specialist assessment is required. When problems are emerging, however, it can be argued that the further specialist assessment is timely.

Early assessment

Many people are now encouraging the view that early assessment of memory problems should be pursued. Indeed, early assessment may well be very help-ful, but it still has to be remembered that individuals differ and some may not feel that an early diagnosis is going to be particularly helpful. There are a number of reasons, however, for believing that an early assessment and diag-nosis may be helpful.

- An early diagnosis allows people to plan for the future and to seek assist-ance early. This could involve, for instance, advice about finance. But it might also involve decisions about future care. Advance care planning will be discussed in Chapter 13.

- People will have different concerns at the time of assessment. The assess-ment process should allow these concerns to be checked. Some people may have very valid concerns, but it might also be that they are worried about things they do not need to worry about and the early assessment allows such matters to be settled.

- Whether or not a diagnosis of dementia is made, the assessment proc-ess should also allow general health information to be given so that the person's physical state is optimal both in the present and for the future.

- Finally, early assessment and diagnosis at least make it possible that any relevant treatments can be started early. At the time of writing, there are no specific treatments for mild cognitive impairment (MCI) that have been shown to be beneficial; drug treatment of dementia itself is only modestly effective (see Chapter 12). But the situation might well change in the future.

Where?

In the UK, as part of the National Dementia Strategy, there is a move to encourage assessment in **memory clinics**. These are clinics specially set up to allow detailed assessment as quickly as possible, with as many tests performed during the minimum number of visits so that a diagnosis can be given swiftly. Inevitably, this will usually involve several visits: first for the initial assessment; second, for appropriate brain scans to be performed; and third, for the diagnosis to be discussed with the person and his or her family or carers.

Some people may find it difficult to attend a memory clinic, or it may be that the memory clinic is not well developed in a particular area. It is possible under such circumstances for the assessment to take place in a person's own home. Many old age psychiatry services in the UK still routinely see people in their own homes. This can make some of the more formal tests a little trickier and it does decrease the potential for physical examination. On the other hand, it allows the clinician to take note of the home environment, which may provide clues as to how the person is routinely functioning.

By whom?

In a memory clinic it is quite likely that the assessment will be by different professionals from the multidisciplinary team. A doctor will normally perform physical examinations, but a psychologist or suitably trained nurse may perform the more detailed neuropsychological tests. The doctors involved may be old age psychiatrists, or neurologists, or physicians specializing in medicine for older people. In the UK, most older people with a memory problem are probably assessed by an old age psychiatrist, whereas a younger person presenting with memory problems, especially if there are physical signs, may well initially be assessed by a neurologist. Whoever performs the assessments, there should be an experienced clinician overseeing the process with knowledge of who to involve once the diagnosis is made. There is no particular reason why other professionals, such as occupational therapists or speech and language therapists, should not be involved at this assessment stage. When it comes to treatment, however, it becomes even more necessary to involve all the professionals of a multidisciplinary team (see Chapter 10).

Exactly who performs which tests might also be determined by local cultural, ethnic, or religious differences. A female patient may require a female doctor. It may also occur that a translator is required. This can make some aspects of assessment more complicated, but every clinical service should have access to appropriately trained translators.

With whom?

It is normal practice that an assessment for memory problems would tend to involve someone in addition to the person who is presumed to have the problem. The story given by the person who may have a memory problem needs to be checked with others who can confirm whether or not the person's memory of events is true. The person providing this collateral history, however, needs to be someone with whom the person with the presumed problem feels relaxed. Practice is different in different places, but it is likely that there will be parts of the assessment that the person must undergo alone and parts where he or she can be seen with the friend or family carer. Ideally, therefore, there would be a good deal of trust between the person concerned and his or her friend or family member. When the clinician is interviewing the person with the possible memory problem and the attending member of the family or close friend at the same time, it is important that everyone's voice is heard and that no one is made to feel they are being overlooked.

History

Every medical student should be able to say, if asked how they would arrive at a diagnosis, that they would take a history, examine the patient, and then perform tests, including special investigations. They should add that the most important part of this process is the history. From the descriptions of the different types of dementia already given in this book, it should be apparent that the clinician needs to ask very carefully about every aspect of the person's story. The doctor, nurse, or psychologist will wish to know when the symptoms started, exactly what the symptoms and signs were, whether they have changed, improved, or worsened, and so on. The history should cover the possibility of cognitive symptoms, such as memory problems, but also the possibility of more functional difficulties. For instance, there may be difficulties in activities of daily living. Perhaps the person has lost the ability to perform some practical tasks around the house. The person concerned may not always recognize this, which is why an informant needs to be interviewed as well. There may be other non-cognitive symptoms, including changes in behaviour or personality. Again, an informant will be very useful. In addition, partly because of the changes that might be occurring and because of the worry, it may be that there are various emotional problems emerging, such as anxiety or depression.

Having heard the story of the problem, the clinician will wish to ask questions about the person's background. This will include the individual's personal history. It may not be apparent why the clinician wishes to know about schooling, except that there is evidence that educational status can have an effect on cognitive impairment. Questions about the person's previous medical history and current physical state will seem more relevant. The clinician would be interested, in particular, in a history of cardiovascular disease, such as heart problems or hypertension. Neurological symptoms, from visual disturbances to movement disorders or even seizures, would also be regarded as very important. Recent infections, along with any drugs that are being taken, might explain acute confusion (i.e. delirium). One other area of concern for the clinician would be if there were risk factors, such as smoking or high alcohol intake, which might explain or worsen cognitive impairment. Finally, the history should include details about the person's normal support mechanisms, about whether or not they live with anyone else or receive outside help.

In short, a person going to be assessed should expect to have a very broad history taken, covering not only recent but also past events.

Mental State Examination

The clinician would also be looking for any evidence in the person's appearance, behaviour or speech of any other form of psychiatric disturbance, such as anxiety or depression. Any delusions, or evidence that the person was making things up to cover gaps in memory (confabulating), would also be noted. Evidence of illusions or hallucinations would be very important too. There may be other signs, for instance if the person were repetitious or obviously forgetful, that might be in keeping with the diagnosis of dementia.

Cognitive examination

The most important part of the Mental State Examination, however, where there is possible dementia, is probably the examination of the person's cognitive function. This part of the assessment involves formal questions to test particular cognitive abilities. This is in addition to any general observations that might indicate forgetfulness or other cognitive problems. Table 9.1 gives examples of how particular cognitive functions might be tested.

Numerous researchers have put together various specific tests, such as the examples in Table 9.1, to form a schedule of tests. These then become known by specific (usually abbreviated) names. The most famous of these tests is probably the Mini-Mental State Examination (MMSE). This is marked out of 30. It is said that scores below 24 indicate the possibility of dementia, but in fact it is known that scores between 24 and 27 probably also indicate cognitive impairment (this partly depends on age and education). The MMSE tests orientation to time and place, registration, attention and concentration, recall, naming, the ability to follow a three-stage command, to repeat a simple phrase,

Table 9.1 Examples of tests for particular aspects of cognitive function

Aspect to be tested	Test	Comment
Attention and concentration	The person is asked to spell a word forwards and then backwards; or asked to subtract 7 from 100 and to keep on subtracting 7	The first test obviously tests language skills (i.e. spelling) and the second tests arithmetical skills as well as concentration. Cognitive tests often test different functions at one time
Executive or frontal lobe functions	The person is given proverbs to interpret (e.g. 'people in glass houses shouldn't throw stones'), or asked in what way certain things are similar (e.g. a car and a bike); the person is asked to copy a drawing with an alternating sequence of triangles and squares, which they must continue	Frontal lobe problems can cause problems with abstract thinking leading to a rather 'concrete' type of thought (e.g. 'it means you shouldn't throw stones …'); there can also be problems with set shifting (i.e. moving from one thing to another), which leads to perseveration (where the person gets stuck on one response); in this case the person may not be able to alternate between squares and triangles
Language	The person is asked to repeat something, to read, to follow a command, to write, to name pictures	These tests look at the person's ability to use and to understand language (i.e. expressive and receptive skills), and to process language in various ways, as well as testing the store of words
Memory	The person is asked: to repeat some words or a name and address, and then, after a distracting test, to recall the words or address; to recall recent news; to recognize familiar objects or pictures; to state as many words as possible in one minute that are the names of animals or words that begin with a particular letter	There are many different types of memory (see Chapter 4). Recognition is different from recall. Memory for past events (retrograde memory) is different from memory for new material (anterograde memory). Listing words or names in one minute is a test called 'verbal fluency'; it tests semantic memory (our knowledge of meaning), but the planning aspect of the task also tests the frontal lobe

Praxis (the ability to perform a task)	The person is asked to point to the window and then to the door, or to follow some similar command (e.g. to take a piece of paper, fold it in half, and put it on the table)	This is not a test of the person's physical abilities—although if they have problems (e.g. arthritis or paralysis) they may not be able to do it—it is intended as a test of their mental ability to execute the task
Perceptual skills	The person is shown pictures of familiar objects from unusual angles and asked to name them; or asked to count dots in a square without touching them	Again this may be difficult because of (e.g.) problems with vision, but the test is really one of the mental ability to perform the task
Visuospatial skills	The person is asked to copy a complex figure; or to draw a clock face and to set the hands to a particular time	Drawing a clock face is a screening test in itself. Although it tests visuospatial (or constructional) skills (a parietal lobe function), it also tests multiple areas of the brain: planning is a frontal function; understanding and non-verbal memory are temporal lobe functions; vision depends on the occipital lobe; the cerebellum is involved in aspects of coordination and execution of the task

to understand a written statement, to write, and the ability to copy a complex figure. There are, however, some specific problems with the MMSE. The technicalities need not detain us here, but the main problem is that it does not test the frontal executive functions to any great extent. Some tests have been developed to allow very brief screening (for instance by a GP), others are intended to give much more detailed information; some rely on the information given by an informant, others are based on the observations of carers. Some tests are now computerized. For those interested, further details on cognitive assessment are contained in the books listed in Appendix 2 (and especially, for those wanting more detail, in the book by Professor John Hodges).

But one more important thing needs to be said: cognitive testing can be very upsetting for the person concerned. It reveals the person's problems in a stark way. It needs to be undertaken with care and under the right circumstances. It is important that the things the person can still do should also be emphasized.

Physical examination

The aim of the physical examination is to detect any other conditions that might contribute to cognitive impairment or dementia. Given the large number of conditions that might be relevant, the physical examination should itself be thorough and cover every system of the body. Once again, the clinician will be looking particularly for evidence of heart disease or neurological disorders. There may, for instance, be evidence of high cholesterol, as shown by xanthalasma, which are greasy deposits under the skin; or arcus senilis, where there is a ring around the iris said to be caused by cholesterol. Equally, the clinician would be on the look-out for signs of liver disease, or endocrine disorders such as hypothyroidism, and so on (see Table 9.2).

Special investigations

There are a number of routine tests that should be performed to screen for the causes of cognitive impairment or dementia. These include a mid-stream urine (to rule out a cause of delirium), a full blood count, erythrocyte sedimentation rate or C-reactive protein (both test for inflammation), vitamin B12, folate, thyroid function, urea and electrolytes (which test kidney function), calcium, liver function tests, and glucose. There are then some optional tests, which would only be performed if there were clinical symptoms or signs that alerted the physician to the possibility of something else being wrong, e.g. tests for syphilis or HIV, blood lipid (i.e. fat) levels, a chest X-ray, an electrocardiogram (ECG) or an electroencephalogram (EEG), which measure the electrical activity in the heart and brain respectively, or a lumbar puncture.

Table 9.2 Possible physical tests used in assessment of dementia

Test[1]	Comment
Mid-stream urine (MSU)	Mainly to rule out delirium
Blood tests: full blood count, erythrocyte sedimentation rate or C-reactive protein (both test for inflammation), vitamin B12, folate, thyroid function, urea and electrolytes (test kidney function), calcium, liver function tests, glucose, syphilis (optional), lipids (optional), HIV (optional)	'To exclude a potentially reversible or modifying cause for the dementia and to help exclude common misdiagnoses including delirium'[2]
Chest X-ray	Optional: only performed if there is a clinical indication; but remember paraneoplastic syndromes (see Chapter 8)
Electrocardiogram (ECG)	Probably only required to ensure drug treatment would be safe (see Chapter 12)
Electroencephalogram (EEG)	Not routinely used, but important in (e.g.) CJD (see Chapter 8), and in cases where odd behaviour might be thought to represent seizure activity
Lumbar puncture (LP)	Not currently part of routine clinical practice, but if biomarkers for particular types of dementia become more commonly used and prove to be useful in research, may become more standard
Brain scans	See Table 9.3

[1] Based on the NIC E-SCIE *Guideline on Dementia* (see Appendix 2), paragraph 1.4.2 and page 151.

[2] From the NICE-SCIE *Guideline on Dementia* (see Appendix 2), page 151.

Finally, the clinician would have to consider whether a brain scan might be useful. In the UK, it would now be considered routine practice to carry out some sort of neuroimaging. The different types of scan are described in Table 9.3.

The *NICE-SCIE Guideline on Dementia* (see Appendix 2) recommended MRI scans (although CT scans were also regarded as acceptable) for their better sensitivity, particularly at picking up changes in the subcortical white matter. Figure 9.1 is an example of a MRI scan of the brain, looking down onto the brain from above.

Figure 9.1 shows two types of white matter change. First, there are changes around the ventricles (the lower arrow), known as periventricular hyperintensities. Second, there are deep white matter hyperintensities (shown by the

Table 9.3 Brain scans

Types of scan	Clinical uses	Pros and cons for patients
CT: Computed tomography	Mostly useful as a means to exclude other diagnoses, such as stroke or tumour. Over time the pictures have become more useful (e.g. with angulated views to show the medial temporal lobes; and now 3-D reconstruction is possible). Relatively cheap	Can be quite quickly performed with little likelihood of claustrophobia, but involves X-rays and risks associated with radiation
MRI: Magnetic resonance imaging	Gives a better view of the medial temporal lobes, which are particularly affected in Alzheimer's disease, but can be affected in other types of dementia, such as DLB (see Chapter 4). Allows closer scrutiny of ischaemic damage to the white matter of the brain. Although mainly used for structural imaging (i.e. to show the anatomy), functional MRI is now possible	Non-ionizing radiation, so safer. The powerful magnetic field means the subject must not have ferromagnetic implants: pacemakers, intracranial aneurysm clips, cochlear implants, neurostimulators; also danger if potential magnetic material in the eye; orthopaedic implants are not a problem. Claustrophobia can be a problem in 5–10 percent of people. The whole procedure can take 40 minutes. Sometimes a contrast medium is used, which requires a needle to be inserted into the arm, and which can sometimes cause reactions
SPECT: Single photon emission computed tomography	SPECT (like PET) scans are functional images, which show how the brain works and not just what it looks like. They can be useful at detecting e.g. frontal lobe disorders. There are particular patterns that suggest other types of dementia. For instance, biparietal, bitemporal hypoperfusion (i.e. poor uptake of the radioactive marker on both sides of the brain in the parietal and temporal regions) is thought to be more typical of Alzheimer's disease; whereas deficits in perfusion in the occipital lobe can be indicative of DLB. SPECT scans are much cheaper than PET scans	Involves an injection of a radioactive substance that has to be taken up by the brain before the scan is performed. The dose of ionizing radiation is less than that in a CT scan or chest X-ray. Takes time (10–20 minutes) for the tracer to get to the brain. The scan itself may take 20 minutes

PET: Positron emission tomography	Better resolution images. Often used for research. Expensive	Small doses of radiation, but not available routinely in the UK's NHS
DAT or FP-CIT: A SPECT scan of the Dopamine transporter, which uses ^{123}I-radiolabelled FP-CIT (2 beta-carbomethoxy-3 beta-(4-iodophenyl)-N-(3-fluoropropyl) nortropane)	Used to detect deficiency in dopamine transport in PDD or DLB between substantia nigra and the striatum, as described in Chapters 6 and 8. Mostly useful if there is diagnostic uncertainty	This is a type of SPECT scan. The scan helps to dispel doubt about the diagnosis, which may lead to changes in treatment. These scans are increasingly available, but not routine. The process of waiting for the tracer to be properly taken up takes more time
DTI: Diffusion tensor imaging	Looks at movement of water molecules in tissue. Provides detailed images of white matter pathways	Not used in routine practice, but an exciting research tool

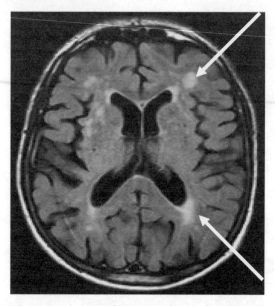

Figure 9.1 MRI brain scan showing white matter changes (courtesy of Professor John O'Brien, Institute for Ageing and Health, Newcastle University).

higher arrow). The hyperintensities show up as small white or pale patches and it can be seen that there are a number of such areas on this scan. The periventricular hyperintensities are referred to as showing cupping of the ends of the ventricles. In this case the cupping is not very extensive. The deep white matter hyperintensities, however, are more marked. There is still a degree of controversy concerning the nature of these lesions. It is known that they can be found in older people who do not have evidence of dementia, but then it tends to be mild. It can also be found in different types of dementia. The lesions do seem to reflect inflammation and vascular changes or damage. As they become more marked and confluent (i.e. joined up), they represent more severe disease and may well include small (sometimes lacunar) infarcts (see Chapter 5). Figure 9.1 shows the benefit of neuroimaging, especially once this sort of picture is put together with the history and other examinations. This scan also shows quite marked atrophy.

There are different types of scan available in different centres. If you have any concerns about a scan you or the person you are looking after is about to have, you should feel free to ask questions. You should, in any case, be given information about the type of scan being used. The length of time the scan will take, for instance, will differ depending on the equipment available.

Conclusion

With the benefit of a full assessment, it is usually possible for the clinicians involved to make a reasonably accurate diagnosis, although in rarer conditions there may have to be more specialized tests, such as genetic testing for possible Huntingdon's disease. The final important part of the process, therefore, is for the person concerned, usually with his or her family, carer, or friend, to be told the diagnosis. This should be done in an empathic way. There are good and bad ways of breaking bad news. Telling someone that he or she has any form of dementia cannot be regarded as good news. People will always have many questions. They do not, however, always come up with the questions at the time the diagnosis is given. This is especially true if they are shocked by the diagnosis. It is, therefore, important that the person should be given appropriate literature and information. If you are attending a clinic, as a patient or as a carer, it is sensible and reasonable to write down any questions you might already have in order to ask the doctor or other clinician while you have the opportunity. Good practice is to make sure that all concerned have appropriate contact numbers so that they can seek further information and support over the coming days and weeks as they come to terms with the diagnosis. An appropriate contact may be at the clinic itself. A follow-up visit may be arranged. Alternatively, in some places immediate support is organized with the local Alzheimer's Society, which is an extremely good source of information about all the different types of dementia and the problems that arise. In some places the local Alzheimer's Society might have direct links with the clinic so that a worker is immediately on hand to give advice and support. In the UK, one of the features of the National Dementia Strategy is that dementia advisers have been put in post. These are people who can be contacted for further advice and support. Part of their function is to signpost relevant services depending on the person's particular problem.

Sometimes the person who is told the diagnosis does not seem to take it in. It may be that the information has to be repeated, but it might also be that this is a defence mechanism. The key thing is there should be the right support for the individual. If appropriate, treatment should now be started. This too will need careful explanation and is likely to lead to many questions.

10

Social approaches to living with dementia

➡ **Key points**

◆ In the UK about a third of people with dementia live in long-term care homes.

◆ Social care is complex: it has to deal with a great variety of personal situations and involves consideration of a raft of issues, from financial, to psychological, to legal, and so on. Hence, it requires close multi-disciplinary working.

◆ Community care can be provided at home, in day care or respite centres, or by the provision of a personal budget.

◆ Assistive technology may help to maintain a person's independence, but also poses a threat to the person's liberty and privacy.

◆ Acute hospitals have to care for large numbers of people with dementia, some of whom will not be able to return home to live independently.

◆ Person-centred care is a philosophy that aims to humanize care, especially in long-term care homes, by keeping the focus on the person and his or her remaining capabilities.

◆ People will sometimes have to be detained or treated against their wishes; different jurisdictions have different laws governing such circumstances.

Introduction

The tendency in many books on dementia, when it comes to discussing management or care, is to start with medical care. Indeed, the last chapter was mainly about medical assessment. We talk of a biopsychosocial approach and, again, the biological approach comes first. The remaining chapters of this book are to do with the care of people with dementia. But I have chosen to start with social care. Why?

◆ Dementia is experienced in a social context. If we are severely ill we may have to spend a lot of time seeing doctors and nurses, but there is no reason to think that the lives of people with dementia should be dominated by medical matters.

◆ If the person is to be understood and helped to live life as he or she would wish, insofar as this is possible, then the individual's story must be fully grasped, which entails grasping the social background.

◆ Whereas the biomedical focus is often on things that are wrong (and I mentioned in the last chapter that neuropsychological testing tends to focus on deficits), attention to the social background in which the person lives will often make it possible to emphasize competencies and remaining capabilities. This theme recurs later in the chapter.

I shall start, however, by asking where people live. I shall then consider the arrangements for social care and the types of care that are available. The chapter will end with a brief word about legislation.

Where do people live?

Estimates suggest that about two-thirds of people with dementia live in the community in their own homes. About one-third, therefore, live in long-term care homes. Figure 10.1 shows the number of people in the UK with late-onset dementia living in care homes compared with those living in the community, for different age groups.

The figures are taken from the Alzheimer's Society report *Dementia UK* (the details of this are in Appendix 2). The report goes on to make the point that the importance of these figures is that the proportion of those people who have dementia and are living in care homes rises with age (Table 10.1).

It should be said, however, that other studies have suggested that over 50 percent of people with dementia live in care homes. If one looks at care homes themselves, then the prevalence of dementia ranges from 40 to 60 percent, depending on the severity of the condition and the type of home.

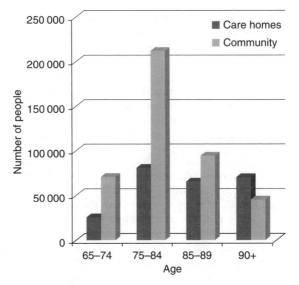

Figure 10.1 Number of people in UK with late-onset dementia in care homes or in the community (adapted from *Dementia UK*; see Appendix 2).

Social care

The aim of social care is generally to keep people living independently in their own homes, since this is what most people would choose for themselves if possible. In the UK and many other countries social care depends on care or case management. In broad terms this involves the following components:

- case finding and screening;
- assessment of needs;
- implementation of a care plan;
- monitoring and review with case closure when appropriate.

Table 10.1 Percentage of people in UK with late-onset dementia who are cared for in care homes

Age group	Percentage in care homes
65–74 years	26.6%
75–84 years	27.8%
85–89 years	40.9%
90 years and over	60.8%

Source: *Dementia UK*; see Appendix 2

Mental health services in the UK pursue care management through the **care programme approach**. The aim is to bring together health and social care. The key components of the care programme approach are the same as care management (assessment, care planning, regular reviews), but the additional component is that there should be a key worker, now referred to as the **care coordinator**. For people with dementia (and for older people in general) there should be a **single assessment process**. It is envisaged that this should involve general assessments as well as specialist assessments, but the idea is that there should be shared information. In practice, this has been hard to achieve.

Before any package of care can be implemented, at least in England and Wales, there has to be a financial assessment and those receiving the services are required to pay at least a proportion. Some believe that health and social care services should be free of charge, as they have been in Scotland, but this is much disputed. The arrangements are different in different countries. There should also be **assessments of carers** in their own right, but again the extent to which this occurs and the benefits that follow are not always clear. Much of this might be changed in the UK by the introduction of **personalized budgets**. The idea is that, rather than services being provided by a limited range of providers who have specific contracts with social service departments, people with dementia and their carers will be given a budget, which they will be free to spend in ways that seem most useful to them. It is hoped this will encourage innovation. For instance, it should be possible for two or three people with dementia living near each other, if they so wish, to use some of their budget to club together to provide a particular type of regular activity, such as a trip out once a week with one or two paid carers.

The multidisciplinary community mental health team

The multidisciplinary team is central to the approach outlined above. Such a team might include:

- community psychiatric nurses (CPNs);
- a doctor (typically a consultant in old age psychiatry);
- an occupational therapist (OT);
- a psychologist;
- a social worker;
- a support worker;
- a team secretary.

There can be a large degree of overlap in terms of functions. For instance, a CPN would be able to arrange particular care packages (see below) as well as provide therapy. Similarly, a social worker would be able to assess aspects of someone's mental state. Different teams work more or less 'democratically' in this respect. At some point, however, the core skills of the different members of the team are likely to become very important. For instance, if a very complicated package of care is required, where there may be financial irregularities and perhaps the need for legal intervention, it would seem likely that the social worker in the team would take the lead. On the other hand, if the issue were to do with the use of medication and possible drug interactions, it would seem sensible for the doctor in the team to make decisions. All of this requires close and harmonious working. There is evidence that this sort of approach works better when the social worker is embedded in the mental health team so that the integration of health and social care is more likely to be achieved.

In the service in which I work, the multidisciplinary teams meet weekly. The psychologists attend the meetings very regularly to discuss particular cases. Other professionals also come to the meetings if their patients or clients are being discussed. The meetings have four sections: first, new referrals are discussed and allocated for assessment; second, difficult, pressing cases are discussed; third, new assessments are reported and care plans are agreed; and, finally, there are regular reviews until cases are closed.

An OT home assessment is an important part of the process. It allows a firmer grasp of the person's functional abilities. The OT can also make recommendations concerning adaptations to the person's home in order to make it more likely that he or she will be able to function in their own environment.

Assistive technologies

Increasingly, new technologies are being developed with the aim of making independent living, or at least safer living, more possible. There are, for instance, 'smart' homes. These incorporate various devices that can sense when a person is doing various things. They might sense if a tap or cooker is not turned off properly. They can also sense when someone gets out of bed at night and the sensor then switches the lights on.

Telecare is a way of monitoring people from a distance. It may be that a carer is able to monitor simultaneously several people sleeping in different homes, and contact them if necessary if there are problems. There are also various memory aids. If a person with dementia is leaving the house it can be arranged that there is a recorded message to remind him or her to lock the door or take their keys.

The best-known types of assistive technology are probably tagging and tracking devices. These have to be worn by the person with dementia, but they can then sound an alarm if the person moves away from a safe area, or they can allow the person to be found if they have become lost while out walking. Some of these systems allow the person themselves to activate the device in order to seek help, for instance, if they were to become unsure what they should be doing while out. The range and sophistication of such devices are increasing rapidly. Local Alzheimer Societies would be able to give advice concerning what might be available locally. There are debates about the ethics of these technologies, which can be regarded as an invasion of privacy and as a restriction of liberty. Cases need to be judged individually. The Nuffield Council's report, *Dementia: Ethical Issues*, discusses the relevant points. Its ethical framework is discussed in Chapter 14 (the full reference is in Appendix 2).

Types of care

A **care package** may involve different types of **home care** (e.g. prompts to remind the person to take medication, help with shopping and cleaning, bathing and food preparation, or meals-on-wheels); and **day care**, where the person is picked up, perhaps once or twice a week, and taken somewhere to be looked after where there are activities, perhaps including outings, during the course of a day. In a sense, day care is also a form of **respite care**, because it allows the family carer the opportunity to do other things while the person is at the day centre. Respite care can vary greatly. For instance, it might involve a short holiday both for the person with dementia and for his or her family carer. On the other hand, it might more simply involve the person with dementia living for a week in the place where day care is normally provided. Sometimes respite care allows further assessment to take place.

Family carers can be ambivalent about the usefulness of respite care because, although they may benefit from the break in caring, they sometimes find that the person with dementia is more disorientated when they return home so that things again become much more difficult. Similarly, home care sometimes does not work if, for example, carers turn up too soon to help put the person to bed, or too late to help get him or her up. This is where personal budgets might help family carers to make more suitable arrangements.

The move from the community into **long-term care** is often made with great reluctance on the part of family carers. Long-term care is also quite varied. In Australia, a distinction is made between low and high care. In the UK, the distinction is between **residential** and **nursing care**. There is a further distinction to be made between general and **elderly mentally infirm** (EMI) nursing care. Residential care can also be EMI (i.e. specifically for people with cognitive impairment and dementia). Although these distinctions are meaningful, it has to be said:

1. They are confusing for family carers who approach the possibility of long-term care for their loved one for the first time; and

2. The boundaries between the different types of care are not always absolute.

For instance, someone who has lived in residential care for some years may then develop nursing needs, on the grounds of physical health (general nursing needs) or mental health (EMI nursing needs). The residential home may feel they wish to try to manage the person, because the staff know the individual so well. Unfortunately, this sort of goodwill cannot be pushed too far because homes are bound by their registration, which means that they are only allowed to have certain types of resident, and by financial concerns, because they might require extra funding if the person's needs have become more complex. Under these circumstances, a person may have to move from a residential to a nursing home despite the disruption and disorientation this can cause.

Choosing a home for a relative with dementia is stressful and difficult. The advice is always to visit several homes before making a decision. Visiting unannounced, as long as it is not at a time when staff are very busy (such as meal times), is a reasonable strategy to see how the homes are really functioning. The 'feel' of a place is often very important, perhaps more so than how spick and span it might be. This will reflect the relationships in the home: do staff and residents interact naturally? It is very worthwhile to talk to other people with experience of the homes, e.g. through the local Alzheimer's Society. The Alzheimer's Society website (see Appendix 1) contains very useful suggestions about how to choose a home. An obvious source of information is the most recent inspection report, which either the homes can provide or can be accessed via the Care Quality Commission's (CQC) website (also recorded in Appendix 1). However, inspection reports need to be set alongside other information, which includes the experience of visiting and asking questions.

Before moving away from discussion of long-term care, it is important to make the point that there is increasing recognition of and expertise concerning social environments. There needs to be good signage, windows to help orientate the person to the time of day and year, comfortable places to sit, and—while meaningful activity is very important—a peacefully quiet environment (disruptive noise can be very upsetting for people with dementia).

Acute hospital liaison

We should keep in mind that the other social setting for people with dementia is the acute hospital. Estimates for the UK NHS suggest that people of

65 years or more occupy about two-thirds of hospital beds. The prevalence of dementia in hospitals may be as high as 45 percent and about half of these have not previously been given a diagnosis of dementia. This stresses, therefore, the importance of liaison old age psychiatry teams. Such a team may well have an old age psychiatrist, mental health nurses, and perhaps some psychology input. The function is to liaise with the general hospital doctors and nurses, along with the hospital social worker, physiotherapists, and OTs in order to make certain that the person with dementia is treated appropriately in hospital and receives a suitable care package when they are discharged. Appropriate help in hospital should also include attention to, for instance, the person's visuo-perceptual abilities. These may affect the person's ability to communicate and their food and fluid intake. Such perceptual difficulties might mean that the person with dementia will not see the white potato and white fish served on a white plate. For this reason, in our hospital the liaison nurse has arranged for the colour and shape of all the mugs used for patients to be changed and the early indications are that using brightly coloured mugs, which people can more clearly identify, has increased fluid intake. This is of medical importance, but is also a feature of social care. Similarly, a major problem for people with dementia may be to do with communication. This might not be recognized on a busy medical or surgical ward. The input of the speech and language therapist may be of great benefit.

Social care as person-centred care

The sort of issue I have just been discussing emphasizes the importance of person-centred care. This was an approach to dementia pioneered by Tom Kitwood, whose book *Dementia Reconsidered* is listed in Appendix 2. Kitwood taught that the person comes first, not the dementia. He also emphasized the effect of the social environment on the person. He referred to a 'malignant social psychology', which can surround the person with dementia. This can be seen in many different contexts, but is particularly relevant to long-term care. An obvious manifestation of this malignant social psychology is what Kitwood called infantilization. This is where the adult person with dementia is treated, perhaps ignored, as if he or she were a mere child. Professor Steve Sabat has spent much time observing and talking with people with dementia. The results are recorded in his book *The Experience of Alzheimer's Disease* (the details of which are also in Appendix 2). Sabat similarly emphasizes the way in which people can be 'malignantly positioned'. That is, even a well-meaning carer might presume that a particular behaviour is the result of the person's dementia. The person is accordingly treated as if he or she might be more incompetent. But, in fact, it might be that the behaviour was a perfectly reasonable response to the situation in which the person found him or herself. Luckily, it is possible to change the malignant social environment. Sabat, for instance, gives examples of good communication strategies that allow the person with dementia to convey meaning rather than it seeming as if he or she was speaking nonsense. Kitwood developed an observational tool, called 'Dementia Care Mapping' (DCM), which allows institutions to assess the extent to which they are truly person-centred. For instance, any meaningful activity in a care home is likely to be beneficial to residents. DCM in such settings often shows that there is very little meaningful activity. Some things can be put right by a slight change of attitude and by increased self-awareness on the part of carers.

Legal considerations

In the UK, local authorities will have in place safeguarding procedures, which come into effect if there is evidence that any form of abuse (physical, emotional, sexual, or financial) may have taken place. There is a host of other laws that may be relevant to the social care of people with dementia. I shall consider capacity legislation in Chapter 14 when discussing decision-making. But one aspect of this concerns the decision to place someone in long-term care. Under Article 5 of the European Convention on Human Rights, it is illegal to deprive someone of their liberty. Although the law in England and Wales allows a proportionate restriction of a person's liberty, in other words the restriction of liberty must be proportional to the risks associated with the person having complete freedom, the Deprivation of Liberty Safeguards exist to provide protection for the person who lacks capacity but requires to have his or her liberty deprived. The distinction between a restriction and a deprivation of liberty is not clear-cut. But in essence a person is deprived of his or her liberty if someone else has complete and effective control over their living arrangements. It is easy to envisage that this situation might arise in the context of 'placement' into long-term care. For instance, decisions about long-term care are often made relatively swiftly on acute medical wards (where, remember, the diagnosis of dementia may only just have been made) because of pressure on beds. Families may find themselves unprepared in a multidisciplinary meeting in which the decision about long-term care is made. It might be that a slower discharge process would allow more support to be given in the community. It has to be said that the move to long-term care may be something of a relief to worn-out family carers. The important thing, however, is to keep in mind the perspective of the person with dementia.

It will sometimes be the case that a person with dementia refuses hospital admission or medical treatment. In England and Wales, if the treatment is for a physical illness, this situation would be covered by the Mental Capacity Act (see Chapter 14). If, alternatively, the assessment or treatment is for a mental disorder, then it may be necessary to use the Mental Health Act. Mental health legislation varies in different countries. The principles, however, are usually similar. First, compulsory admission for assessment or treatment, or compulsory treatment in the community, or guardianship, will almost always require that several professionals have agreed that the proposed action is necessary. Second, the patient will normally have rights of appeal. Similarly, there will be provision for families to object or appeal on behalf of the person concerned. Third, there have to be good grounds for the suggested plan of action. Not only must the mental disorder be of such severity as to require the admission for assessment or treatment, but it must be established that this cannot be provided in the community. Then, in England and Wales, the proposed assessment or treatment must be required on the grounds that:

- There is a risk to the person's health; or
- The person poses a risk to him or herself; or
- The person poses a risk to others if the compulsory treatment does not go ahead.

Guardianship means different things in different countries. In England and Wales, it allows a guardian to stipulate where someone must live. This can sometimes be useful in dementia, as long as the person can recognize the authority of the guardian.

Conclusion

Social care of the person with dementia must put the person first. But the social context inevitably means that the provision of such care can be extremely complicated. There are numerous different aspects of social care to consider, from financial to legal advice, to issues around activities of daily living, such as cooking, washing, and shopping. Finally, social care has to be provided in a variety of settings. All of this means that there has to be good communication between all those involved. Inevitably there are many bureaucratic and legal procedures that have to be followed. All the more reason, therefore, to remember that at the centre of this social complexity is the person with dementia.

11

Psychological approaches to management of dementia and depression

Key points

- There is a great variety of psychological approaches to the management of behaviour that challenges in dementia.

- The evidence base is thin for many of these individual approaches, but there is good evidence for behavioural management and for particular techniques in specific circumstances, such as aromatherapy hand massages or the use of music for agitation.

- A needs-led approach, regarding behaviour that challenges as a sign of unmet needs, seems to be very promising.

- Depression can occur in a number of situations in dementia. It requires standard treatment: psychological therapies are helpful, especially in mild to moderate depression; antidepressants become more relevant as the depression worsens.

- The notion of 'vascular depression' suggests a more biological link between depression and dementia.

Introduction

Discussion, in the last chapter, of the social context has already brought into view personal psychology. Psychological approaches in dementia are mostly considered in connection with BPSD. In this chapter, I shall briefly consider a broad range of psychological therapies, but I also want to look specifically, albeit briefly, at depression.

Psychological interventions

Box 11.1 summarizes a raft of possible interventions. Of course, we should be thinking of each individual on an individual basis and different therapies will be useful in different situations.

Box 11.1 Psychological interventions

Generic therapies

◆ *Reality orientation:* is one of the most widely used management strategies for dealing with people with dementia. It aims to help people with memory loss and disorientation by reminding them of facts about themselves and their environment.

◆ *Reminiscence therapy:* involves assisting the person with dementia to relive past experiences, especially those that might be positive and personally significant, such as family holidays or weddings. Group sessions tend to use activities such as art or music, and often use artefacts to provide stimulation.

◆ *Cognitive stimulation therapy* (CST)*:* involves an activity with a particular theme in order to engage people. It is a development from reality orientation therapy. It is intended to have cognitive effects, because it requires processing of the information in connection with the activity. But it also has a group social dimension and can have effects on behaviour, mood, or quality of life.

◆ *Validation therapy* attempts to communicate with the person with dementia by empathizing with the feelings and hidden meanings behind their seemingly confused speech and behaviour. It is the emotional content of what is being said that is, therefore, more important than the person's orientation to the present.

◆ *Activity therapy:* is a rather amorphous group of behaviours, such as dance, sport, drama, and so on, all aimed at improving or maintaining general health.

◆ *Multi-sensory approaches*: e.g. use of a *Snoezelen* room with various smells and sounds, lights (flexible fibre optics), and textures.

◆ *Bright light therapy:* probably works through its effects on the sleep–wake cycle.

◆ *Aromatherapy*: the two main essential oils used in aromatherapy for dementia are extracted from lavender and Melissa balm. They have the advantage that there are several routes of administration such as inhalation, bathing or massage, or topical application in a cream.

◆ *Music therapy:* may involve the person engaging in a musical activity, or merely listening to songs or compositions.

◆ *Art therapy:* has been recommended as a treatment for people with dementia as it has the potential to provide meaningful stimulation, improve social interaction, and improve levels of self-esteem.

◆ *Dog therapy:* may also involve other animals, and has been shown to increase social interaction and decrease agitation.

◆ *Doll therapy:* may also involve other toys, the introduction of which can seemingly improve well-being in residents in homes.

◆ *Simulated presence therapy:* this is where a family might record something relating to positive personal memories, which can be played over the phone or on a personal stereo to the person if he or she is upset or agitated.

◆ *Other complementary therapies:* e.g. herbal medicine, massage, reflexology, and therapeutic healing, for which there is generally little empirical evidence.

Targeted psychotherapies

◆ *Behaviour therapy:* at its most basic involves rewarding 'good' behaviour and not 'bad' behaviour; the aim is to reinforce 'good' behaviour. A common approach in dementia care, if there is behaviour that people find challenging, is to use ABC charts, which note the **A**ntecedents of the **B**ehaviour and the **C**onsequences. The aim is to understand the behaviour and to see if there is something that can be changed, which tends to happen either before or after the behaviour, which might alter it.

◆ *Cognitive behaviour therapy* (CBT): uses elements of behaviour therapy, but lays much greater stress on thoughts (also known as cognitions). The underlying theory is that the ways in which we tend to think can affect our mood and how we behave. We do not just have to change behaviour therefore; attempts can be made to change the way people think. This may be more relevant in the early and middle phases of dementia, but even in the later stages the CBT model might be helpful as a way to understand behaviours.

♦ *Interpersonal therapy* (IPT): attempts to understand a person's distress in the context of interpersonal relationships using four domains to give the therapy a structure. They are: interpersonal disputes; interpersonal/ personality difficulties; bereavement; transitions/life events. As with CBT, this approach is more useful in early dementia, but can be used as a way to understand behaviour later on too; and it may also be useful as a way to help close carers of people with dementia (e.g. in connection with bereavement).

Adapted from: James I, Douglas S, and Ballard C (2006) Different forms of psychological interventions in dementia. In: Hughes JC (ed.) *Palliative Care in Severe Dementia*, London: Quay Books; pp. 55–64

It is important to remember the points made in Chapter 3, namely that the term BPSD covers a variety of behaviours that cannot all be lumped together. Individual behaviours may have different causes. The general motivating thought behind psychological therapies should be that any behaviour which in some way is challenging on the part of a person with dementia is almost certainly the result of a need that is not being met. In other words, the behaviour needs to be understood from the perspective of the person with dementia.

To return to Box 11.1, it is split into generic therapies and more targeted therapies. Generic therapies are those which aim to create a general atmosphere which will promote the well-being of, for instance, residents in a care home. Targeted therapies are standard psychotherapies that have a more specific aim in mind for a particular person.

What is the evidence that these therapies work?

Assessing psychological therapies is extremely difficult. This is for a number of technical reasons. As a general point, however, the studies are normally criticized for being of poor quality and, in addition, there are relatively few of them for any individual therapy. It also has to be said that different reviewers of these interventions, looking at more or less the same evidence, sometimes seem to come to dissimilar conclusions! For instance, there are some completely contradictory statements concerning the efficacy of **reality orientation**, some saying it is useful, others that there is no good evidence of significant benefit. Studies of **reminiscence therapy** similarly are said to be of poor quality, even though a systematic review showed good results in terms of cognition, mood, caregiver strain, and functional abilities. **Cognitive stimulation therapy** seems promising, but has so far given equivocal results. The results of studies on **validation therapy** are said to be either inconclusive or show a lack of efficacy. **Activity therapy**, such as exercise, may have some beneficial effects on the sleep–wake cycle, but some types of exercise (e.g. walking up and down in a corridor) might be boring and frustrating, whereas other forms of exercise might have a greater degree of social interaction. **Multi-sensory environments** such as *Snoezelen* rooms, which should encourage relaxation, have not been found to have any prolonged beneficial effects, although there was a hint in smaller studies that agitated behaviour might improve briefly around the time of the therapy. **Bright light therapy** does not have sufficient evidence to recommend it. It could be added, however, that attention to the environment would seem to be sensible so that people are as oriented as possible. The trials of **aromatherapy** can also be criticized, but there is some evidence that aromatherapy can reduce agitation and other neuropsychiatric symptoms. A recent meta-analysis has shown that aromatherapy, hand massage, and thermal baths all led to short-term benefits for agitation. **Music therapy** seems to have good effects in terms of apathy, agitation, or disrupted behaviour, but again these effects seem to be in the short term rather than in the longer term. For **art therapy**, **animal therapy**, and **doll or toy therapy**, there is some indication that these activities may be helpful. Further studies are, however, required. As with reality orientation, so too with **simulated presence therapy**: some reviewers feel it may be helpful, others feel the evidence is too limited.

The evidence in favour of the targeted therapies, namely **behaviour therapy**, **cognitive behaviour therapy**, and **interpersonal therapy**, is much better. Once again, however, it has to be said that these therapies are used in different situations. The important thing is to use the therapies with particular symptoms and individuals in mind.

Depression

With these comments in mind, it seems appropriate to consider depression in more detail. We know, for instance, that cognitive behaviour therapy and interpersonal psychotherapy can both be effective in depression. Guidance from the National Institute of Clinical Health and Excellence in the UK suggests that these sorts of psychotherapies should be the first line of treatment for mild to moderate depressions. Treatment with antidepressant drugs becomes more relevant when the depression is in the moderate to severe stages. However, depression in connection with cognitive impairment or dementia is a complicated subject. Estimates vary, but it has been suggested that the rate of depression in people with dementia ranges from 30 to 50 percent.

There are three possible scenarios. First, it is possible that depression and dementia simply coexist coincidentally as two separate disorders. In the mild to moderate phases of dementia it may well be possible to use a mixture of cognitive behaviour or interpersonal psychotherapy to treat depression in the way that anyone else would be treated. A second scenario is that the depression is a direct result of the dementia, in that it is a psychological reaction to the diagnosis. Depression is, for instance, very common in DLB. A psychological therapist would then need to address the issue of the dementia more overtly, because the work may be to do with coming to terms with the diagnosis. Problem-solving therapies can be useful in dementia as a way to treat depression and anxiety.

A more complex situation is when depressive symptoms seem to be a prodrome to dementia. In other words, a person presents with depressive symptoms, which can sometimes be difficult to treat, and after a year or two a frank dementia emerges. This has led to the suggestion that there is a type of depression that can be called 'vascular depression'. According to this theory, some depressions have vascular causes, which later show themselves in cognitive impairment and dementia. Depression was one of the items on the Hachinski ischaemia score, which was mentioned in Chapter 5: depression seems to be common in vascular dementia. This type of depression can have a more 'biological' feel to it, but nonetheless, psychological therapies should still be considered and used appropriately. It would seem sensible to look for and treat any vascular risk factors, therefore, in anyone presenting with cognitive impairment and depression. It has to be kept in mind that cognitive impairment, e.g. problems with concentration, can also commonly feature in and improve on treatment of depression. Hence, careful assessment is required.

In moderate to severe depressions, antidepressant drugs are usually used. Sometimes this has to be on an empirical basis. For instance, it might be that a change in behaviour in someone with advanced dementia (e.g. loss of interest in an activity that used to be enjoyed, or increased irritability) may indicate a depressive disorder (even if the person cannot describe low mood and other depressive symptoms). The use of an antidepressant on an empirical basis (i.e. as a trial) would under these circumstances seem reasonable, as long as the risks of side effects or interactions did not outweigh the potential benefits. The evidence on which to base the use of antidepressants in dementia is surprisingly thin. A recently completed trial of antidepressants in dementia in the UK should help to clarify the situation. There are other treatments that have been used in research, such as transcranial magnetic stimulation for the sort of 'vascular depression' referred to above. This involves using a high frequency, rapidly changing magnetic field to stimulate particular areas of the brain. Finally, electroconvulsive therapy (ECT) remains an option for people with severe depression: dementia does not in itself prevent its use. ECT has been used safely and with good effect in dementia. Obviously, this needs expert assessment. A recent stroke would be one reason to avoid ECT and the person's physical fitness for an anaesthetic would need to be considered. ECT is a controversial topic and is itself covered by NICE guidance (see Appendix 2).

Needs-led therapies

Using a CBT framework, and given the hypothesis that behaviour that challenges in dementia reflects unmet needs, a model has been developed that tries to understand the needs of the person with advanced dementia. This requires the therapist to seek information from every source possible, that is, from family and friends, as well as from formal carers (presuming that the person is in a home) and from medical records. Once the data has been collected, the therapist would normally aim to meet with all those involved in order to come up with hypotheses about the needs of the person and to explain how the behaviour relates to these needs in order to arrive at a set of interventions that might be helpful. The case below illustrates this process.

 Case study

Miss Clutterbuck was a teacher who had always lived on her own. Things became precarious in the community and her niece arranged for her to be admitted into care. She originally went into a residential home, but she was constantly aggressive towards other residents: initially verbally aggressive, but as time went on she was sometimes physically aggressive. Following assessment it was decided that she should be moved to an EMI nursing home. The behaviour continued in the nursing home and, if anything, worsened. Drugs were given to calm her, but she became oversedated and suffered a fall. At the request of her niece, the drugs were stopped but she continued to be very agitated.

When the challenging behaviour team were brought in to assess the situation, the therapist spent some time talking with the staff about the exact circumstances in which Miss Clutterbuck tended to become most agitated. These seemed to be at mealtimes and also during personal intervention.

She also became agitated when she found she could not get back into her room, or when staff tried to encourage her to go into the lounge. The therapist also talked at length with Miss Clutterbuck's niece in order to gain background information. It was not possible to hold a conversation with Miss Clutterbuck, given her advanced dementia, although what she did say suggested that she wished to be on her own and that she did not like other people around. Indeed, this was the story from her niece as well. She had always been a loner. She did not seek out the company of others. It was known that, when alone, she always preferred (even years ago) to listen to The Third Programme. When the staff met with the therapist and the niece, it was agreed that Miss Clutterbuck's needs were to hear classical music, to enjoy the quiet of her own company, and to retain some sense of control and dignity. Having identified these needs, various interventions were developed. Staff agreed that it would be reasonable to allow Miss Clutterbuck to spend more time alone in her room listening to her music and arrangements were made so that she would have ready access to Radio 3 and to a collection of her favourite music on CDs. Staff also agreed that there was no point in trying to encourage Miss Clutterbuck into communal rooms, unless the rooms were particularly quiet. It was also decided that one or two staff would spend more time with Miss Clutterbuck in the hope that they could establish a quiet rapport with her, which might then make it easier to provide personal intervention and care if full explanations were given prior to and during the interventions.

Although Miss Clutterbuck continued to become agitated during personal interventions, her agitation seemed less and at other times her general well-being seemed to be improved, with fewer episodes of verbal and physical aggression.

Although this type of needs-led therapy seems to make a good deal of sense, as with other psychological therapies, the evidence base remains somewhat thin.

Conclusion

A number of the psychological approaches to the management of behaviour that challenges in dementia seem to make intuitive sense. It does not, however, make much sense to think that one type of therapy will solve every different sort of problem. It seems right to say that individual therapies must be tailored to particular situations for the individuals concerned. I should conclude this chapter with three points.

◆ First, it is well said that a lack of evidence does not mean a lack of efficacy. It may simply mean that it is difficult to carry out trials of enough methodological rigour.

◆ Second, in response to this point, it might be that, with respect to psychological therapies, we have to change the nature of the investigations undertaken. At the moment, the gold standard is a randomized controlled trial in which one group is given the intervention and another group is not. This leads to group statistics. In other words, we can say that on balance group A did better or worse than group B. Within the groups, however, it may be that some individuals did very well and some individuals did very badly. But such studies only really measure averages. It might be, therefore, that we should start to look at the results of individuals, rather than averages, in order to assess the efficacy of particular interventions. This sort of methodology is now being used, but will have to be more widely used for its significance to be appreciated.

◆ Finally, I return to the intuitive appeal of needs-led assessments and therapy, which are so obviously attuned to the character of the individual. The psychologist Graham Stokes has worked in the area of behaviour that challenges for many years, and his collection of clinical stories, recently published as *And Still the Music Plays*, lends support to this whole approach (further details concerning this work are in Appendix 2).

12

Drug treatments

Key points

◆ Most of the research effort is aimed at finding drugs that will modify the underlying processes causing Alzheimer's disease.

◆ Current drug therapies for Alzheimer's disease are purely symptomatic (they are not disease-modifying) and are modestly effective.

◆ The drug treatment of BPSD is mainly based on thin evidence.

◆ The best evidence for the drug treatment of BPSD is probably in relation to the anti-psychotics, but the evidence also shows that they carry significant risks in terms of strokes and death.

◆ New disease-modifying treatments are likely to appear on the market shortly, but there are no indications at present that any particular drug will cure dementia; combinations of drugs may help to improve the situation.

◆ Prevention, particularly of cardiovascular and cerebrovascular risk factors in mid-life, remains better than cure and needs to be pursued.

Introduction

The biological management of dementia in essence means drug treatment. We can approach treatment in terms of cognitive and non-cognitive symptoms and signs. As in the case of depression (covered in the last chapter), the treatment of non-cognitive manifestations of dementia will often be specific to the particular symptom or sign. In this chapter, therefore, I have not said anything about, for instance, the drug treatment of anxiety or panic. On the whole, the treatment of such conditions in dementia would follow standard lines and the reader might wish to look elsewhere (e.g. to the book on panic disorder in this series) for relevant information. There is, however, a caveat: part of the point of BPSD—the name now given to non-cognitive aspects of dementia (see Chapter 3)—is that it is not always clear what drives the behaviour in more advanced dementia. It might be panic, or it might be frustration. So treatment can rarely follow straightforward standard paths, but must often be empirical.

Another distinction to make in connection with drug treatment is between symptomatic treatments and disease-modifying treatments. At present, the available drug treatments are symptomatic, that is, they will alleviate some of the symptoms of the disease, but do not change the underlying disease process. There are occasional claims that the treatments may have disease-modifying properties, but these have never been conclusively proven. Nevertheless, drug companies are working hard now to develop treatments that will target the underlying pathology.

The final caveat is that this chapter will mainly be about Alzheimer's disease. Of course, BPSD can occur in any form of dementia, so treatments are general across the dementias with only slight variations (the most important being the need for awareness of neuroleptic senisitivity in DLB, as described in Chapter 6). There is no specific drug treatment for vascular dementia. The aim of treatment is mostly to decrease the risk factors for cerebrovascular events (see Chapter 5), which may involve drugs to lower blood pressure (i.e. anti-hypertensives) or to decrease the risk of clots forming which might then cause a stroke (e.g. warfarin, aspirin, or clopidogrel). In DLB, as stated in Chapter 6, it may be that the cholinesterase inhibitors are more effective than in Alzheimer's disease. Other aspects of DLB may respond to standard treatments for parkinsonism. Some authorities have suggested that behavioural manifestations of frontotemporal dementia may respond to selective serotonin reuptake inhibitors (SSRIs), which are mentioned below. The variety of possible other symptoms and signs in rarer dementias—often involving movement disorders—have specific treatments, concerning which readers will need to consult other texts, such as the book on Huntington's disease in this series (but support organizations for the different conditions whose websites are listed in Appendix 1 may be able to give further details).

In the remainder of this chapter I shall discuss the current drug treatments for cognitive signs and symptoms in Alzheimer's disease and for BPSD. I shall then look at future developments that might lead to disease modification. I shall finish by considering other agents, including complementary therapies, and the prospects for prevention.

Current symptomatic treatments

Table 12.1 lists the four currently available drugs licensed to treat Alzheimer's disease in the UK, and gives other information, for instance about side effects.

Cholinesterase inhibitors

Donepezil, galantamine, and rivastigmine are all cholinesterase inhibitors. As discussed in Chapter 2, acetylcholine is a major neurotransmitter in the nervous system. It was once thought that the lack of acetylcholine was the main deficit in Alzheimer's disease. The deficit certainly correlates with poor recall ability. So, even though it turns out not to have been the main problem in Alzheimer's disease, it looked likely that any drug which could restore the level of acetylcholine would be able to restore the person's ability to recall events. And, in fact, it turns out to be true that boosting acetylcholine improves memory. After acetylcholine is released into the synapse (the gap between two nerves), it is broken down into smaller parts and taken up again by the nerves so that the parts can be reused. This process of breaking down acetylcholine is encouraged by the enzyme acetylcholinesterase. Neuronal transmission ceases once acetylcholine is broken down by acetylcholinesterase. The cholinesterase inhibitors stop the breakdown of acetylcholine in the synaptic cleft (see Fig. 2.2) by stopping acetylcholinesterase from working. Hence, any acetylcholine that is released by the nerve cell acts for longer. This can only continue, however, for as long as there is acetylcholine to be released. In this sense the drugs are not disease-modifying, because they do not stop the underlying steady loss of acetylcholine. Once there is little acetylcholine to be released, the drugs become less effective.

The big question is: how effective are the drugs? Having stated that they do improve cognitive function—which has been shown in many studies—it has to be said that the effect is only modest. In general, people score one or two extra points on tests of memory and other cognitive functions. There is evidence, however, that the drugs can also help in terms of activities of daily living; and some studies have suggested that they improve behaviours that challenge.

Side effects can be explained by the effects of acetylcholine in other parts of the body. Thus, they can slow the heart rate and increase acid production in the stomach (see Table 12.1), and may cause muscle cramps. But on the whole, the drugs are tolerated quite well and relatively few people suffer significant side effects. However, the fact that they can all cause increased agitation should be noted.

In the UK, the National Institute for Health and Clinical Excellence (NICE) has issued different guidance at various times on the use of cholinesterase

Table 12.1 Current symptomatic treatments for Alzheimer's disease

Name of drug	Trade name	Mechanism of action	Usual dosage	Form of medication	Side effects[1]
Donepezil	Aricept	Acetylcholinesterase inhibitor	5–10 mg once daily	Tablets and orodispersible tablets (which instantly dissolve in the mouth)	Nausea, vomiting, anorexia, diarrhoea, fatigue, insomnia, headache, dizziness, fainting, hallucinations, agitation, gastrointestinal bleeding, rash, slow heart rate, abnormal heart rhythms or problems with conduction of electrical impulses in the heart, seizures, parkinsonism
Galantamine	Reminyl	Acetylcholinesterase inhibitor (also acts on nicotinic receptors)	Starts 4 mg twice daily, but usual dose is 8–12 mg twice daily; once-daily preparation available, starts at 8 mg and goes up to 24 mg once daily	Tablets and once daily (modified release) capsules	Common side effects as recorded for Donepezil
Rivastigmine	Exelon	Acetylcholinesterase inhibitor (and also a butyryl cholinesterase inhibitor)	1.5 mg twice daily, increasing to maximum of 6 mg twice daily; for patches, the 24-hour doses are 4.6 mg or 9.5 mg	Capsules, oral solution, and patches	Common side effects as recorded for Donepezil
Memantine	Ebixa	NMDA-receptor antagonist affecting glutamate transmission	5 mg once daily increasing to 20 mg daily	Tablets and oral drops	Constipation, hypertension, shortness of breath, headache, dizziness, drowsiness

[1] I have only recorded the side effects that are listed in the *British National Formulary* (BNF) (Number 59, March 2010) as being common to all the cholinesterase inhibitors. Individual drugs have different side effects—information leaflets should be consulted and concerns discussed with the prescribing doctor or the pharmacist. For memantine, I have only listed the common side effects shown in the BNF.

inhibitors for dementia (see Appendix 2). At one time it was said that the drugs, though clinically effective, were not cost effective. In early 2011, however, it was declared by NICE that the cholinesterase inhibitors could be used to treat mild to moderate Alzheimer's disease.

Although there are slight differences in the ways that the three cholinesterase inhibitors work (as Table 12.1 shows, they affect slightly different receptors), there is no compelling evidence that one is better than another.

Memantine

The other drug in Table 12.1 is memantine: a NMDA-receptor antagonist, which affects glutamate transmission (see Chapter 2). An antagonist is an agent that binds to a receptor to block it. The effect in this case is that it stops the excessive influx of calcium to the neuron, which is otherwise toxic to the cell. The drug is, however, 'non-competitive' so that it still allows glutamate to carry out its functions in connection with learning and memory. The evidence is that memantine has an effect on cognition, behaviour, and activities of daily living.

But these (still modest) effects are only really significant in the moderate to severe stages of dementia. NICE recommends that the drug might be useful in the moderate to severe stages of Alzheimer's disease. It seems to be a safer drug for some people than the cholinesterase inhibitors in the moderate phase, and there is some evidence that it is effective in people with agitated behaviour.

Drug treatment for BPSD

There are several principles that guide the use of drugs to treat behaviours that challenge, or other non-cognitive symptoms or signs, in dementia. First, the drugs should, as far as possible, be targeted. In other words, if agitation seems to be caused by hallucinations, it would be sensible to consider using an anti-psychotic drug (but see below). If agitation seems to be caused by pain, analgesia would be better (see Chapter 13). Second, it is always important that there is nothing else, such as an infection, which might be making a person's behaviour worse. In other words, it is important that delirium has been considered. In a similar way, poor hearing or vision might be the factors that are aggravating the person. In general, then, it is sensible to consider whether some form of non-pharmacological approach (see Chapter 11), even just reassurance, might be more appropriate before drugs are tried.

Table 12.2 lists the numerous classes of drug, with examples, that might be used, often on an empirical basis, for BPSD. As a broad generalization, it can be said that there has been some evidence in favour of using these drugs at

Table 12.2 Types of drugs that might be used for behavioural and psychological symptoms of dementia (BPSD)[1]

Class of drug	Examples	Possible reasons for using	Possible bad effects[2]
Anti-psychotics	*Conventional:* haloperidol; *Atypical drugs:* e.g. amisulpride, aripiprazole, clozapine, olanzapine, quetiapine, risperidone	To achieve relatively quick control of agitated and aggressive behaviour; or where there are indications of distressing hallucinations or delusions	A range of side effects, including the risk of death or severe stroke, worsening cognitive function, parkinsonism, drowsiness, and convulsions
Anti-anxiety or sedating drugs	*Benzodiazepines:* lorazepam, temazepam, diazepam; *Others:* zolpidem, buspirone	To calm anxious, or agitated, behaviour; to induce sleep at night	Over-sedation, unsteadiness, slurred speech, falls, and confusion
Antidepressants	Mostly *SSRIs:* citalopram, sertraline, fluoxetine; *Non-SSRI:* trazodone; lofepramine (an older antidepressant); moclobemide	To treat depression, but also to treat anxiety and agitation	Gastrointestinal upsets (nausea, diarrhoea), occasionally sedating may lower sodium (hyponatraemia), can increase risk of bleeding (especially if on drugs such as warfarin or NSAIDs)[3]
Anticonvulsants	Carbamazepine, sodium valproate, lamotrigine	To treat agitated or aggressive behaviour; also as mood stabilizing agents	Unsteadiness, sedation, gastrointestinal upsets, blood and liver disorders
Beta-blockers	Propranolol	For anxiety, but also for disruptive behaviour	Slowing of the heart, hypotension (and therefore the risk of falls), sedation, worsening heart failure, asthma, depression, and confusion
Others	Seleligine	Main use is in Parkinson's disease, but also found to be useful in treating disturbed behaviour in dementia (evidence is limited)	Nausea, constipation, diarrhoea, hypotension, confusion, and hallucinations

[1] Many of the drugs mentioned in this table do not have a licence in the UK for use for behavioural disturbances in dementia. Nevertheless, many of them are used 'off-licence'; this is not bad practice, but the prescriber should be able to justify his or her decision to use a particular medication. Prescriptions should, in any case, be discussed with the patient and/or his or her carers.

[2] The actual side effects and interactions for specific drugs should be checked on the information leaflet provided with the medication, or in an authoritative source such as the BNF.

[3] NSAIDs = non-steroidal anti-inflammatory drugs such as ibuprofen or even aspirin.

some time, but the evidence is mostly poor. Hence, the scientific foundations for practice are thin. But experience and knowledge mean that decisions should not be random! One key, however, is that possible side effects should always be kept in mind. Some drugs, for instance anticonvulsants, require monitoring of the blood from time to time, e.g. to check the effects on the liver, and there may be interactions with other drugs.

Although many of the studies can be criticized for their poor methodology, gradually some useful evidence is emerging. Table 12.3 summarizes data on the use of drugs (apart from anti-psychotics) for the neuropsychiatric symptoms and signs that can appear in dementia.

It should be kept in mind that estimates are that more than 90 percent of people with dementia will experience BPSD at some point in the course of their condition. Aggression and non-aggressive agitation are said to occur in about 20 percent of people with Alzheimer's disease, but in as many as 60 percent in long-term care. In addition to agitation, the other groupings of BPSD are psychotic disturbances (e.g. hallucinations) and mood disorders (e.g. depression).

Table 12.3 Evidence concerning non-anti-psychotic drug treatments used in Alzheimer's disease for behavioural and psychological symptoms of dementia (BPSD)[1]

Drug	Indication	Comment
Sodium valproate	Agitation and/or aggression	Low doses are ineffective; higher doses are not tolerated well because of side effects
Carbamazepine	Agitation and/or aggression	Two good small studies with positive outcomes, but need further evidence and analysis
Trazodone	Agitation	Insufficient evidence
Citalopram	Agitation	Promising good studies, but need further evidence and analysis
Memantine	Agitation and psychosis	Evidence of significant benefits in terms of behaviour. May also be of benefit in vascular dementia, but need further evidence
Cholinesterase inhibitors	Agitation	Ineffective over 12 weeks, but benefits over 6 months in terms of neuropsychiatric symptoms and mood
Sertraline	Depression	Some studies seemed to favour for treatment of depression in Alzheimer's disease, but this has recently been called into doubt

[1] This table is adapted from Clive Ballard and Dag Aarsland's chapter 'Pharmacological management of neuropsychiatric symptoms in people with dementia', pages 105–15 in *Supportive Care for the Person with Dementia*, edited by Hughes, Lloyd-Williams, and Sachs (2010) (see Appendix 2 for further details).

Anti-psychotics

There has been much controversy over the use of anti-psychotics in dementia. Two things can be said, which can seem to pull in different directions: first, the use of anti-psychotics is too widespread; second, they are sometimes useful and necessary. Anti-psychotic drugs are used to treat psychoses, that is, conditions where the person has lost touch with reality (e.g. involving hallucinations or delusions). Anti-psychotics are also called neuroleptics. There are two reasons why they may be used in dementia. First, it may be suspected that the person is suffering from hallucinations or delusions and, therefore, an anti-psychotic seems like the best treatment. Second, the drugs have been found to be useful at calming people with dementia who are agitated or aggressive.

In response to the first point, there are several reasons to be cautious. Sometimes what seems like a delusion in dementia may actually be a confabulation (something made up to cover a gap in memory), in which case an anti-psychotic is not indicated, because this will not correct the underlying memory problem. We can also infer that there may be other states of agitation in dementia that do not reflect true psychosis, but more simply cognitive impairment, so again the rationale for using anti-psychotics is removed. Furthermore, it may not be true, even if it is a real hallucination, that an anti-psychotic is the best treatment. It would not be the best treatment in DLB (because of the risk of neuroleptic sensitivity). We know that visual hallucinations, which can occur in DLB, respond well to cholinesterase inhibitors.

In response to the second point, we shall see it is true that anti-psychotics can be useful in dementia in some cases of agitated or aggressive behaviour. But I shall shortly mention the reasons for being cautious about this. An immediate point is that the drugs sometimes work just because they are sedating. In which case, they are not treating the underlying problem—compare this to the sort of needs-led psychotherapeutic approach outlined in Chapter 11—but are seemingly being used in the way that their opponents suggest, as a chemical cosh.

These drugs are often split into 'typical' (older or 'conventional') and 'atypical' (newer) anti-psychotics (see Table 12.2 for examples). By and large, it is the newer, atypical, drugs that are used for older people (although haloperidol is still used as a short-term treatment for delirium). This is mostly because they tend not to give the troublesome parkinsonian symptoms that are associated with the older drugs. However, the reality is that they are not significantly more effective and they do still produce side effects, such as accelerated cognitive decline (i.e. worsening dementia), ankle oedema (i.e. swelling from fluid retention), sedation, postural hypotension (i.e. falls in blood pressure on standing, leading to dizziness and the possibility of actual falls), chest infections, and indeed parkinsonism (even if this is not as bad as it was with some older anti-psychotics). The biggest worry, however, has been to do with the risk of stroke.

Such has been the concern about these drugs that the UK government asked an expert to provide an independent report. Professor Banerjee's report, *Time for Action*, which only related to England, appeared in 2009 (see Appendix 2). Here are some of the main estimates:

* 180 000 people with dementia are being treated each year with anti-psychotic medication (there are about 560 000 people with dementia in England);
* Up to 36 000 will derive some benefit from the treatment;
* There will be an additional 1 620 cerebrovascular adverse events (i.e. strokes or stroke-like episodes) each year, of which around half may be severe;
* There will be an additional 1 800 deaths per year;
* Looking at various studies, it appears that a clinically significant improvement in one additional behaviourally disturbed patient would result from treating between 5 and 11 patients (this is known as the number needed to treat or NNT);
* The number needed to harm (NNH) is about 100, meaning that this number of people with dementia would need to be treated to result in one additional death in the first six to twelve weeks;
* Thus, if 1 000 people with BPSD were treated with an anti-psychotic for three months, there would be:
  * an additional 91–200 patients with behavioural disturbance who would show a clinically significant improvement **or**
  * an additional 72 patients with psychosis who would show a clinically significant improvement;
  * an additional 10 deaths;
  * an additional 18 cerebrovascular adverse events, of which about 9 would be severe;
  * an additional 58–94 patients with gait disturbances;
  * no additional falls or fractures.

These estimates do not, however, tell us what will happen if the treatment is continued beyond three months. The response to this report has been to encourage education about BPSD and the Department of Health has indicated a firm commitment to reduce the use of anti-psychotics by two-thirds by November 2011.

It should be said that the NNT of between 5 and 11 is good. The worry is that the NNH is high. A higher rate of stroke had already been identified in olanzapine and risperidone, so that neither drug was recommended for treatment in dementia. But the effects look as if they are more general, i.e. the whole class of anti-psychotics seems to cause problems. So the upshot is that anti-psychotics may be useful for BPSD, but they need to be used appropriately and cautiously. Best practice guidelines now suggest that, if anti-psychotics are going to be used in Alzheimer's disease, they should:

◆ be restricted to people suffering from severe symptoms (causing risk to others or suffering extreme distress);

◆ be targeted at particular symptoms, which should be quantified and documented if possible;

◆ be given with an awareness of other conditions that might be contributing to the behaviours (including, e.g., depression);

◆ be discussed fully with the person with dementia and/or his or her carers, with attention being paid to risks, especially cardiovascular and cerebrovascular risks;

◆ only be used where other measures (i.e. in the first place, non-pharmacological measures) have failed or cannot be put into practice because of urgency;

◆ initially be given at a low dose and the dose raised only gradually;

◆ be reviewed regularly;

◆ only be continued beyond 12 weeks under exceptional circumstances.

Future developments[*]

Given the increasing understanding of the brain and of the pathology of the dementias, we might expect that advances in pharmacological treatment should be just around the corner. Indeed, we are expecting to see novel treatments very soon. They will be novel partly because they will aim to be disease-modifying and not simply symptomatic treatments. Having said this, however, we then have to concede that—despite the advances—there is still much that we do not know. Consequently, we must also expect there to be disappointments.

There are a number of potential targets for new therapies, where the focus is mainly on Alzheimer's disease. The central target is amyloid (see Chapter 4). But the other targets are tau, neural regeneration (e.g. using stem cells), inflammation, mitochondria, neurotransmitters, and so on. In the examples that follow I have chosen some of the key possible developments to highlight. I have not tried to mention every possibility, because many promising avenues will turn out to be a dead end.

---

[*] This section is based on the excellent chapter by Michael Woodward in *Dementia*, edited by David Ames, Alistair Burns, and John O'Brien (see Appendix 2), which should be consulted for further details.

Active immunization against amyloid

This is where $A\beta$ is injected into subjects so that they form antibodies to amyloid. This was tried in mice with great success: amyloid was either prevented from being deposited or it was reduced. It seemed to improve memory. In humans, however, first it did not lead to any clinical benefit, even when it could be shown that it had helped to clear amyloid and, second, it caused meningoencephalitis (a serious brain inflammation) in 6 percent of those studied. The fact that removing amyloid plaques turned out to be insufficient to stop the Alzheimer's from progressing is important and is already altering the research effort to find a cure.

Passive immunization against amyloid

This involves injecting antibodies themselves, rather than $A\beta$. The antibodies can be aimed at particular parts of $A\beta$. The most promising agent is bapineuzumab, which showed some success in those who were ApoE ε4 non-carriers. Carriers of ApoE ε4, however, were more prone to side effects, which included evidence of small bleeds in the brain. Other antibodies aimed at different portions of the $A\beta$ are also being tested, with variable results.

γ-Secretase inhibition or modulation

Recall that it is γ-secretase that cleaves the APP to release the toxic $A\beta_{40}$ or $A\beta_{42}$ (see Chapter 4). Hence, if it were possible to inhibit this action, it might be possible to stop the deposition of amyloid. A drug called semagacestat is being tested, again with results that are promising, but the studies have not yet shown any significant clinical improvement. Trials of β-secretase inhibitors are also in progress.

Inhibition of amyloid aggregation

As an example of this approach, the spice turmeric (*Curcuma longa*) contains curcumin, which is both an anti-oxidant (i.e. it stops the damaging effects of oxidation) and anti-inflammatory (i.e. it decreases the inflammatory reaction that occurs in response to amyloid). It also has properties that stop the aggregation of amyloid. It reduces $A\beta$ in mice and is now undergoing further studies.

Inhibition of tau aggregation

Methylthioninium chloride (also called 'Rember') comes from a dye that stains neurofibrillary tangles. It turns out that it also inhibits the aggregation of tau (see Chapter 4). Studies have shown significant differences in terms of cognition, with promising results on brain scanning. If larger trials are positive this could be a useful treatment for all patients with tauopathies, including those who have FTLD.

Promoting nerve growth

A small protein mixture, called cerebrolysin, which comes from pig brains, has been shown to reduce Aβ deposition and to promote nerve growth in animals. It appears to improve general function and cognitive function in humans.

Neurotransmitter modulation or receptor antagonism

There are several neuroreceptors (e.g. histamine-3, 5-HT$_6$) which can enhance neurotransmission of acetylcholine and glutamate. Several compounds are being tested. Like the current treatments, these would only be symptomatic treatments, rather than disease-modifying. But they might be useful as part of a broader armamentarium to combat Alzheimer's disease and other dementias.

Anti-inflammatory treatments

As already commented, there is inflammation around Alzheimer's pathology (both amyloid plaques and NFTs). It was observed that people on non-steroidal anti-inflammatory drugs (NSAIDs), such as ibuprofen, had a lower prevalence of Alzheimer's disease. But trials of NSAIDs have been disappointing. However, another anti-inflammatory agent, etanercept, has been found to improve cognitive function in a small number of cases.

Mitochondrial agents

The drug latrepirdine has effects on acetylcholine and glutamate, but also enhances mitochondrial function (see Chapter 8). In clinical trials involving people with Alzheimer's disease there have been promising results.

Antioxidants

Oxidative stress (a manifestation of the cell's inability to control the process of oxygen metabolism effectively, which can lead to the production of damaging free radicals) is connected to ageing and the death of cells, as well as to a host of degenerative diseases. Antioxidants, such as vitamin E, were thought to be potentially protective. But studies have been very disappointing.

Statins

People taking cholesterol-lowering drugs were noted to have a reduced risk of Alzheimer's disease. The drugs also have an effect on Aβ production. Studies to date have been variable, but statins may have a role in treating either Alzheimer's disease or vascular dementia.

Homocysteine lowering treatments

Raised homocysteine levels in the brain are thought to have an excitatory toxic effect via the NMDA receptor (see Chapter 2) and may also damage blood vessel walls. Because folate and vitamins B6 and B12 are known to lower homocysteine, it was thought they might be therapeutic in Alzheimer's disease. Sadly, studies have mostly been negative. However, a recent study in Oxford showed that taking B vitamin tablets halved the rate of brain atrophy in older people with MCI. But the effect mostly related to those with high homocysteine levels. The study did not attempt to show clinically therapeutic effects, so more work needs to be done. It remains true that a good diet is probably protective. The B vitamins are mostly found in bananas, beans, whole grains, and some meats.

Other complementary therapies

For some while there were high hopes that *Gingko biloba* might be beneficial in Alzheimer's disease, but the most recent systematic review shows that the evidence is unconvincing. Apart from curcumin, mentioned above, other herbs have shown no better results. The exception is tea, and especially green tea, where there is evidence from several sources that it may protect the brain against the effects of ageing. There are reasons to think that fish oils might be useful, partly because of the effects on the cardiovascular system generally, but studies to date have been equivocal.

Prevention

The *NICE-SCIE Guideline* (see Appendix 2) splits prevention into modifiable and non-modifiable risk factors. (In passing, it is worth commenting that aluminium is not thought to be a risk factor, although there was a worry about this at one time.)

The non-modifiable risk factors are:

◆ age (see Chapter 1);

◆ learning disabilities (see Chapter 8);

◆ gender—there are higher rates in women;

◆ genotype—in particular, apoE and possession of the ε4 allele (see Chapter 4).

Potentially modifiable risk factors for dementia are the following:

◆ alcohol consumption (see Chapter 8);

◆ smoking—which increases the risk of dementia in general, as well as for Alzheimer's and vascular dementia in particular;

- obesity—raised body mass index (BMI) in mid-life also increases the risks of dementia in general, as well as Alzheimer's and vascular dementia in particular;

- hypertension (see Chapter 5)—this is a risk for vascular dementia and studies suggest that antihypertensives may be beneficial for Alzheimer's disease too, but further research is required;

- hypercholesterolaemia—is a risk factor for vascular dementia and lowering cholesterol may help in Alzheimer's disease, but (as mentioned above) using statins has had mixed results;

- head injury (see Chapter 8);

- low folate and high homocysteine levels (see above);

- hormone replacement therapy (HRT) has not shown efficacy;

- depression may be a risk factor (see Chapter 11), but there are no studies to show that reducing depression reduces later dementia;

- NSAIDs (see above);

- Antioxidants (see above);

- exercise—the evidence is insufficient to recommend exercise as a specific preventive measure, but there is some evidence that 20–30 minutes exercise twice a week in mid-life decreases the risk of dementia generally and of Alzheimer's disease in particular;

- education and mental stimulation—lower educational attainment is associated with an increased risk of dementia; whether mental stimulation can help to prevent dementia is difficult to prove, but there have been a number of studies indicating that this might be so; intuitively, mental stimulation seems like a good idea.

Conclusion

Our current ability to treat the dementias successfully with drugs is very limited. The prospect of real progress seems close with the advent of disease-modifying drugs. But even then, the holes in our understanding—for instance, the lack of clinical improvement despite decreased amyloid in the brain—suggest that we are still some way off anything that could look like a complete cure. It might be that, as in cancer chemotherapy, greater improvements will be achieved when there are mixtures of agents that can be used in different combinations at different times. This is certainly not a time to give up! But it may be that we should endeavour to make sure that enough attention is still given to the non-pharmacological approaches so that drugs and psychosocial interventions can be used as adjuncts to each other. This hints at the notion of supportive care, which aims to do away with the conceptual gaps between aiming at cure and aiming at care. I shall say more about this approach in the next chapter.

13

Spiritual, palliative, and supportive care

➲ Key points

◆ The supportive care model emphasizes the need for dementia, at every stage, to be thought of in broad terms so that no aspect of any potential therapy is ever ruled out.

◆ Prognosis, in terms of survival, is very variable in dementia.

◆ Palliative care is a part of supportive care and the palliative care approach will often be applicable to specific situations, especially in the advanced stages of dementia.

◆ An important element in palliative care is attention to the spiritual needs of the person with dementia and his or her carer.

◆ Advance care planning, which can take various forms, seems sensible in the context of a condition that will increasingly make decision-making difficult.

Introduction

Earlier I wrote of the biopsychosocial approach to care. However, this leaves out the notion of spiritual care. Palliative care is always presented in terms of a biological, psychological, social, *and* spiritual approach. To palliate suggests decreasing suffering without curing. The palliative care movement started in hospices, which were mainly aimed at providing care at the end of life for people with cancer. Gradually, however, the notion of palliative care has become broader. Nowadays, the palliative care approach would be seen as applicable to any chronic disease that cannot be cured. There are many reasons, therefore, to think that the palliative care approach is the right approach for people with dementia.

This can sound either odd or worrying because people associate palliative care with the end of life. There is no need for this association. With any sort of chronic condition that cannot be cured, there will be times when suffering needs to be alleviated, which is what palliative care is about. A key feature of palliative care is that it is holistic, both in the sense that it pays attention to all of the person's concerns—from physical ailments to existential worries—and in the sense that it considers the person in his or her social context. Palliative care is interested in overall quality of life, but it is recognized that this will often depend upon the person's family relationships. The appropriateness of palliative care is emphasized in the *NICE-SCIE Guideline on Dementia* (see Appendix 2).

In the remainder of this chapter I shall discuss spirituality a little further before moving on to talk of particular issues in palliative care and, finally, in conclusion, I shall mention the notion of supportive care.

Prognosis

Having raised the issue of dying, however, it is worth considering prognosis in dementia. It is very difficult to be precise about survival. For instance, an individual with vascular dementia might live for some while with only gradual deterioration, or might die suddenly from either a large stroke or a heart attack. There is similar variability in other types of dementia. Some things, however, can be said more specifically. For instance, in prion disease the prognosis for sporadic cases is only a few months. In some inherited cases of prion disease the illness can last for twenty years. Studies of Alzheimer's disease have shown survival of somewhere between four and six years. It is well known, however, that some people live fifteen years or more from the time of diagnosis. The main predictors of mortality in Alzheimer's disease are the severity of the dementia, the person's age, and gender. These are not surprising findings. If a person is diagnosed early they are likely to live longer because the disease will have longer to run its course. If a person is older, he or she is more likely to die in any case. And we know that mortality generally is higher for men than for women.

Spirituality

Spirituality is notoriously difficult to define. In discussing the issue, Stephen Sapp says that spirituality is usually associated with finding 'meaning' and 'purpose' in human life. This becomes especially important towards the end of life, or when a person is under threat. With this broad understanding of spirituality, which brings into play thoughts about our connectedness, not only to other people, but also to the world and indeed to the universe, it is possible to see particular religions as ways in which we make sense of our standing and connectedness. As Sapp says in his chapter 'Spiritual care of people with dementia and their carers', which appears in *Supportive Care for the Person with Dementia* (see Appendix 2):

'Serious illness and impending death focus one's attention on ultimate concerns, and these are precisely the issues that religion has always addressed.' (page 200)

Facing serious illness and the possibility of death, therefore, can cause the sort of existential concerns that I alluded to above. In other words, we start to wonder about the meaning of our existence.

This helps to establish the importance of spirituality and religious observances for people with dementia. At a more mundane level, therefore, it may well be that religious practices, which are often deeply ingrained, will provide solace and comfort for a person with dementia even in the severer stages. This is another way in which cultural and ethnic differences will need to be respected even in the midst of dementia. Families may well have a role to play in educating the professionals providing care, who will not always be aware of particular religious practices. Even if families no longer share the religious beliefs of their elders, ensuring that the practice of the person's faith is supported can be considered a way to maintain the person's dignity and selfhood.

As dementia becomes more advanced, religious practices may have to accommodate the person's deterioration. It is quite likely that the person will not be able to concentrate and, at a later stage, swallowing may be compromised, which may affect some religious observances. Many people have recorded stories concerning how people with poor memory and speech difficulties can, nonetheless, join in with hymns or prayers that they have known for many years. Recognizing a person's spirituality is a way of recognizing the person's true individuality in a manner that can be sustaining and supportive. Robert Davis, a minister of religion in America, has recorded his own experiences of dementia in his book entitled *My Journey into Alzheimer's Disease* (see Appendix 2). The sense of the spiritual is well recorded by Barbara Pointon, who looked after her husband, Malcolm. He was at home when he died with Alzheimer's disease after sixteen years. Barbara reflected in her chapter 'Who am I?–The search for spirituality in dementia. A family carer's perspective' (see Appendix 2) a little while prior to Malcolm's death, as follows:

> 'Malcolm is surrounded by love. We reach out to communicate with him at a profound level—often through eye contact and gentle whispering and touch—and from him there flows a deep child-like trust, luminosity and reciprocating love—as though it were his very self, the self he was born with, that we are privileged to glimpse... does it matter what we call it—spirit, soul, inner-self, essence, identity—so long as we have experienced it?
>
> '... so the search for spirituality and the real Malcolm ends here—in the revelation of his essential self because of the loving care he receives and the trust that it engenders.'

Issues in palliative care

The palliative care approach, as I said above, is relevant from the time of diagnosis until death and it involves a holistic approach with attention to the person's broadly conceived quality of life. There are, however, particular problems that start to arise towards the end of life which lead to specific palliative concerns.

In general, physical health starts to deteriorate. For instance, there may be weight loss despite a reasonable diet. In the more severe stages people can develop contractures, where they hold their limbs in a stiff and bent posture. There can also be concerns about pressure sores to the skin and problems to do with incontinence. All of these problems need assessment and expert advice. It should not be presumed that nothing can be done. It is certainly sensible for clinical staff to consider whether there might be something that is treatable. An example would be constipation, which can lead to increased agitation and confusion, but can be very easily treated.

Other specific issues are the following.

Pain

The worry is that people with severe dementia may be in pain but may not be able to communicate this. Pain can lead to agitated behaviour. It should always be considered, particularly if there is a previous history of a condition that might now be giving the person pain. Often the remedy is fairly simple. Someone who has arthritis may experience pain if they have to be moved, for instance hoisted in and out of the bath. A fairly ordinary analgesic, such as paracetamol, given regularly might be helpful. There are also various check-lists or instruments that can be used to try to assess whether someone is in pain. Typically, these look at things such as facial grimacing, or whether the person is making noises, or showing other signs of distress. These checklists can be very helpful in alerting carers to the possibility of pain. However, it has to be remembered that distress may be caused by something else. None of these signs is specific for pain. A person may pull an odd face not because they are in pain, but perhaps because they are frustrated or embarrassed. Hence, there is a need for careful assessment. Stronger analgesia may, however, be required on occasions. Details of treatment can be found in standard texts (see Appendix 2). Expert advice from a palliative physician may sometimes be required.

Infections and fevers

Infections can become an increasing problem in advanced dementia. Pneumonia remains the most common cause of death. The use of antibiotics to treat bacte-rial infections is an area that can sometimes be difficult. On the whole, most clinicians will use antibiotics when a person with severe dementia has an infec-tion. This is because many infections will be painful and it seems wrong not to treat them appropriately. It is sometimes said, however, that it seems cruel to treat someone with an antibiotic rather than allowing him to slip away. People have in mind the notion that pneumonia is the 'old man's friend'.

There are a number of things to be said in response. First, there is evidence that pneumonia causes suffering and is not, in this sense, as friendly as people imagine. Second, many infections, including pneumonias, will not actually kill the person, but will simply lead to prolonged discomfort. The use of antibiot-ics under such circumstances simply decreases the length of suffering and this is a perfectly proper aim of palliative care. Third, if the infection is severe, it is quite likely that the antibiotics given by mouth might not be sufficient. In this case, it can still be argued that the antibiotics provide some palliation in that, for instance, they may help to decrease the stickiness of secretions. This does raise the issue of when there should be an upper limit to the level of treatment that is given. So, while it might be perfectly reasonable to give antibiotics by mouth, it might be that a decision is made *not* to give antibiotics intravenously (i.e. directly into a vein), which would otherwise be the treatment of choice if the infection is in the blood (which is called septicaemia). In particular, it might seem wrong to move a patient from their familiar surroundings in order to admit them to an acute hospital ward where they are likely to be more con-fused. There is also the danger that they will pick up further infections in the hospital.

Therefore, it may be decided that only ordinary means will be pursued to treat the infection, rather than extraordinary means, especially given that the evidence that transfer to hospital in advanced dementia is beneficial is lacking. A recent study in London showed that many people with advanced dementia admitted to an acute hospital ward died within a few days. A question arises about the point of the admission when the person could have been kept comfortable in their normal place of residence. There is, indeed, some evidence that using conservative means, such as tepid sponging and paracetamol to keep the temperature down, is as effective as antibiotics in terms of preventing distress.

Artificial nutrition and hydration

People with advanced dementia have increasing problems with swallowing. This can affect both food and fluids. Much can be done to make things more manageable. Carers may need advice from the speech and language therapists who are experts at dealing with swallowing problems. It is important that the person is in an upright position and food will often have to be pureed and thickener added to fluids. Sometimes, however, a question arises about whether the person should be fed artificially. This can be done via a tube passed through the nose and into the stomach (a nasogastric tube) or by a tube that is inserted under general anaesthesia directly through the abdominal wall into the stomach. This is called a percutaneous endoscopic gastrostomy (PEG) tube. The consensus recorded, for instance in the *NICE-SCIE Guideline on Dementia* (see Appendix 2), is that artificial feeding is usually not warranted in advanced dementia. There may be specific circumstances under which a PEG tube is required. For instance, a stroke may compromise the swallowing ability of a person for a short while during which a PEG tube might be appropriate.

But there are dangers associated with artificial feeding. At the very least, many people try to pull out nasogastric tubes. The evidence is, however, that artificial feeding does not tend to achieve the very things that we think it should achieve. One worry is that, if the person's swallow is bad, he or she may aspirate when fed. This means that the food goes into the lungs and sets off an infection. It might be thought that PEG feeding gets around this problem. But in fact there is no good evidence that it does, because infected secretions can still get into the lungs. It might be thought that artificial feeding prevents malnutrition, but when a person is in the most severe stages of dementia, nutrients seem simply not to help—at least not in terms of putting on weight. In short, the evidence that artificial feeding is helpful is simply lacking.

The use of intravenous lines to provide hydration may sometimes be required, but might also seem an unnecessary intervention. People can be kept hydrated by using subcutaneous drips. This is where a small needle is inserted just under the skin, rather than directly into a vein. This is easier to do, on the whole causes less discomfort, and can be positioned (e.g. between the shoulder blades) so that it is less likely the person will pull it out. When it is clear that the person is actually dying, the necessity for continuing hydration should be reassessed. It is at this point that the Liverpool Care Pathway may be considered (see the *End of Life Care Strategy*, detailed in Appendix 2).

Resuscitation

Families often feel put on the spot when the issue of resuscitation is raised. Strictly speaking, however, this is a medical decision. Guidance and laws will be different in different countries. In England and Wales, covered by the Mental Capacity Act, where the person lacks capacity (see Chapter 14) a decision has to be made by the decision-maker in the person's best interest. Where the decision concerns a medical treatment, which is what resuscitation is, the decision-maker will be the physician. So the decision is not made by the family, and any understandable feelings of guilt they may have should be lessened by this knowledge. However, the decision-maker has the responsibility of speaking (if practicable) to everyone who has a rightful interest in the person's welfare. Therefore, the views of the family carers must be given considerable weight. In particular, any light they can shed on what the person's own wishes would have been must be considered very carefully. But the doctor making the decision about resuscitation should also be thinking about whether or not resuscitation is likely to be effective. In a situation where the treatment is unlikely to work and it may be burdensome to the person concerned (in this case because resuscitation can lead to injury of the ribs) there is no moral obligation to pursue the treatment. In the case of resuscitation for people with advanced dementia, the evidence is that it is unlikely to be successful and it is burdensome, so the general tendency would be not to provide cardiopulmonary resuscitation for someone with advanced dementia. This does not mean, however, that other treatments should be stopped. It simply means that this particular type of treatment is, on clinical grounds, thought to be inappropriate.

Advance care planning

The issues that I have just been discussing suggest the possible importance of advance care planning. In the UK, advance care planning is now a recommended feature of the national *End of Life Care Strategy* (see Appendix 2). Box 13.1 outlines the different types of advance care planning that are possible in England and Wales. Similar provisions apply in most other countries.

Although in the UK advance care planning is now enshrined in public policy, it is not entirely clear how this should be undertaken in the context of dementia.

Box 13.1 Types of advance care planning

Advance refusal of treatment: This is where a person specifies a particular treatment that they do not wish to receive if they were to be unable to make a decision at the time through lack of capacity. Although this is a way of expressing deeply held beliefs, it can be problematic. The advance refusal of treatment must be both valid and applicable. It is *valid* if it is recorded in an appropriate fashion. If the advance refusal of treatment is to do with life-saving treatment, in addition to being a written statement, it must also be signed, dated, and witnessed. Such a refusal of treatment is only *applicable* if the circumstances are exactly those that were considered when the advance refusal of treatment was made. The difficulty here is that all sorts of circumstances may have changed since the advance refusal of treatment was drawn up. Perhaps, for instance, new treatments have become available which were not previously known about. Or, perhaps, whereas the person had dreaded having dementia, it might turn out that they seem to be leading a reasonable life in circumstances that maintain general well-being. If these were not the circumstances envisaged when the advance refusal of treatment was prepared, then it cannot be said that the refusal of treatment is applicable.

Advance statement (or *Living Will*): This is a much broader document. It may be written down, but it could be recorded orally. It is a way for the person to record their wishes and preferences. Whereas the advance refusal of treatment, if it is valid and applicable, is legally binding, an advance statement of wishes and preferences is not legally binding. Nonetheless, it does have a legal standing in that it would have to be considered by anyone making a judgement about the person's best interests. It would be a way, therefore, for a person to influence future decisions when they are not capable of participating in the decision-making.

Lasting Power of Attorney: Under the Mental Capacity Act it is possible to appoint someone to act on your behalf. This could be to do with financial issues and decisions about where you live, or it might be to do with health issues. The same person or persons might be appointed both to make decisions about property and finances and to make welfare decisions, e.g. about healthcare and place of residence. In this way, it is possible for people to make sure that someone they trust makes decisions for them. The extent of the decision-making can be limited if the person wishes. In particular, if healthcare decisions are going to extend to decisions about life-sustaining treatment, then this must be stipulated explicitly.

Whereas in cancer, detailed planning about the end of life may in some cases be entirely feasible and realistic, this may not be the case in dementia. Nonetheless, it does seem sensible for people to think about future decision-making in a situation where this is likely to become more difficult. This would tend to suggest, at the very least, that a person might wish to consider whom they would want to make decisions for them when they are no longer capable themselves. The current situation is that we do not yet know whether advance care planning will have a significant impact on practice. At the moment, there is some evidence that professionals ignore specific elements of advance care planning. It may be that the culture will change, but even then we do not know whether advance care planning will improve matters for the individuals concerned. This is not an argument against advance care planning. It is simply to state the fact that there is as yet no good evidence concerning the full effectiveness of advance care planning. There is, however, some evidence that advance care planning can decrease the possibility of unnecessary admissions to hospital from nursing and residential homes. This in itself would seem to be a benefit of advance care planning, given that there is evidence that such admissions to acute medical wards often achieve very little and do not seem to serve the person's overall welfare.

Conclusion: supportive care

In this chapter I have encouraged the thought that palliative care provides the appropriate model for looking after people with dementia. However, there are some issues attached to the notion of palliative care. Perhaps the main issue to highlight is that palliative care emerged in a climate where there was a clear distinction between care and cure. When it was no longer possible to cure a person's cancer, they were passed over to the palliative care team. In parallel to the split between care and cure, there is also a split between the thought that treatments should be potentially 'high tech' and invasive (which, again, it is possible to imagine as appropriate when you are trying to cure cancer) and, on the other hand, 'low tech' and non-invasive measures (which seem more applicable to palliative care). But one might wish to get rid of both types of split. Hence, some people have started to talk about supportive care.

Palliative care is a part of supportive care. But in supportive care the idea is that there should be no dichotomies. Thus, even if we cannot cure dementia itself, there may be particular elements of the condition that we should aim to cure. And, indeed, there are some types of dementia where talking of cure makes more sense. For instance, in Chapter 8, I discussed the possibility that a shunt might help to cure some aspects of normal pressure hydrocephalus. Furthermore, as discussed in Chapter 12, it may be that it becomes plausible to think in terms of curing particular types of dementia. Even now, for instance, the treatment for HIV-associated dementia can be thought of in curative terms.

It may be, in a similar way, that whether we are thinking of care or cure, 'high tech' invasive procedures start to seem more reasonable. Perhaps in the future it will seem apt to undertake brain biopsies in order to be certain about the exact diagnosis. I have already discussed the possibility of biomarkers, for instance in the CSF, obtained by lumbar puncture, being used for diagnosis. We are already using high-tech neuroimaging to try to improve diagnostic accuracy. To call all of these things palliative care does not strike the right note. Hence, it can be argued that we should think in terms of supportive care. Here is how we have summed this up in *Supportive Care for the Person with Dementia* (see Appendix 2):

'Supportive care represents a broad view; it is a broad view of the person with dementia…, who must be seen in all of his or her biological, psychological, social, and spiritual complexity, where care is aimed broadly, holistically, impeccably, and with enthusiasm, but also with clinical judgement.'

14

Challenges in caring

→ Key points

- Informal, usually family, carers often have to shoulder huge burdens—which can be physical, emotional, social, and financial—to look after the person with dementia.

- The difficulties carers face are frequently ethical in nature: the decisions that have to be made are to do with right and wrong.

- An ethical framework to assist thinking through these difficult decisions can be useful.

- Decisions are also made in the context of a legal framework.

- Despite the difficulties, caring can also have some rewards: carers occasionally describe a sense that they have grown through the experience.

Introduction

In this chapter I shall highlight some of the issues for informal carers. By this I mean non-paid carers who are usually family members, but may be close friends or neighbours. I shall then consider some of the issues that arose from a study undertaken with the help of the Alzheimer's Society in the UK, which looked at the difficulties around making decisions. The study showed that many of these difficulties were ethical in nature. In other words, they were difficult because they were to do with right and wrong. This will lead me then to present a framework for making ethical decisions. Although this will be a conceptual, philosophical framework, it incorporates awareness of the legal framework for decision-making, and in the final part of the chapter I shall discuss capacity legislation.

The experience of caring

Becoming an informal carer is by no means straightforward. It will often become inevitable that a particular member of the family should provide the care for someone with dementia. But the carer does not always choose this role. Most carers are spouses and if not spouses they are often daughters, although many are sons. The amount of time spent caring can be considerable and it increases as the person's dementia worsens.

The effects of caring for someone with dementia have been discussed under a number of headings. These are outlined in Box 14.1.

For all of the reasons contained in Box 14.1, it is important that carers receive appropriate, timely, and helpful support. In order for this to be the case, they must be assessed in their own right (see Chapter 10). The aim of respite care is to try to alleviate some of the difficulties for family carers. Eventually, however, many family carers have to give in to the stresses and strains and accept that the person they are caring for must move into long-term care. At this point there is an understandable, and very real, sense of guilt and often of failure.

Making difficult decisions

Because of the awareness of the difficulties for carers, about ten years ago a team based at the Ethox Centre in the University of Oxford, funded by the Alzheimer's Society, undertook a study in which carers throughout England were interviewed and were asked what the difficulties were for them. This led to the publication *Making Difficult Decisions: The Experience of Caring for Someone with Dementia* (see Appendix 2 for details; all the quotes from carers that appear below come from this work). Although the opening question was simply to do with difficulties, the problems that were then discussed were almost entirely ethical. In other words, carers were concerned to make the right decision rather than the wrong one. They wanted to do what was good rather than something that was bad.

Table 14.1 contains a list of the different areas in which family carers experienced ethical dilemmas. The obviously striking feature is the range of ethical issues that arise for family carers.

It is not possible to consider all of these issues in detail. But there was often a strong sense of conflict. For instance, some people felt very strongly that they would never wish to deceive the person with dementia. So, for instance, they would not wish to hide medication in food or drink. Other people, on the other hand, felt that if this were the only way to help the person to settle, then

Box 14.1 The effects of caring

Objective burden: There is no doubt that the person with dementia, especially as the condition worsens, places a burden on the family carer as he or she has to take over more and more roles within the home.

Subjective strain: Different people cope in different ways with the burden, but some carers can feel the subjective strain more than others. There is no doubt, however, that carers do feel strains in connection with the considerable work that they must do, which can be both physically and emotionally draining.

Psychological ill health: There have now been many studies that have shown increased depression and anxiety among carers. Depression has been shown in up to 85 percent of carers in some studies. Along with these high rates of morbidity go considerable stress, which can affect the person's ability to care, so a vicious circle of increasing emotional morbidity (i.e. illness) develops.

Physical illness: A number of studies have shown that the carers of people with dementia suffer higher than expected rates of physical health problems. One explanation is that the person's immune system is affected, for instance by the chronic stress. It is also true that carers simply have less time to look after their own health by doing things such as taking regular exercise. Their sleep can be radically disturbed too.

Social isolation: It is a common experience that, when someone has dementia, many friends stop visiting. It becomes more difficult, in any case, for the person with dementia and his or her carer to find the time to socialize in the way that they once did. They might also become embarrassed by different behaviours. All of this both adds to and results from the stigma associated with dementia, but the immediate effect is that the person with dementia and the carer lose their social supports.

Financial burden: Informal carers save their economies huge amounts of money. In Chapter 1 we saw that a large part of the cost of dementia relates to the costs associated with informal caring by families. The report by the National Audit Office in 2007 recorded that there were about 476 000 informal carers in England who were providing a service valued at the time at £5.4 billion (see Appendix 2 for details).

it was fine. Carers were also concerned about taking over the functions of the person they were caring for. Part of the concern here was that this would undermine the person's standing as a person. A particularly difficult issue is often to do with driving. For many people, driving has been a way of life, or

Table 14.1 Typical ethical dilemmas

Informed consent	Planning issues	Competing demands
Communication	Resource allocation	Information
Residential care	Inappropriate behaviour	Changing relationships
Professional ethics	Advance directives	Financial issues
Assessment	Friends	Quality of life
Care and control	Genetics	Research
Safety	Confidentiality	Legal issues
Denial	Self and personhood	Loss
Diagnosis	Medication	Services
Treatment	Negative feelings	Driving
Feeding issues	Patient's rights	Drug treatments
Telling the truth	Wandering	Family issues
Pets and belongings		

even a career. To be told that you can no longer drive when you are completely unaware of any problems is immensely upsetting. One daughter said:

> 'She was outraged when she got the letter from the Driving and Vehicle Licensing Agency. She was ranting and raving. I was there because I had planned it to be like that. Of course, I got the blame for it—it was all my fault.'

A wife said:

> 'My husband and I were at each other's throats. We were destroying each other with this awful driving issue.'

Families deal with these issues in different ways. Some find that being honest and straightforward works. But others find it easier to use a degree of subterfuge by, for instance, hiding the car keys and then getting rid of the car. Stories then have to be made up concerning its whereabouts.

Some behaviours can be challenging for family carers. One wife said:

> 'You need to let go of your accepted standards and things like dress code, table manners and social behaviour. If you mind too much about messy eating, you would never go out.'

Nevertheless, messy eating can cause other people to react badly, which increases the stigma attached to dementia. Furthermore, there are some behaviours that would simply not be tolerated, which puts family carers into a very difficult situation. One wife said:

> 'With my husband's particular type of dementia, and the way it manifested itself, particularly with younger children and people in the community, I didn't know how much to tell people, how much to warn them, or how much I could let happen before I intervened. I didn't want to go round painting this picture of some sort of sexual pervert, but I felt it was important that people were aware of the situation.'

An ethical framework

Faced with these difficult decisions, and given that people can have conflicting intuitions about what is right or wrong, it would be useful to have a framework within which to think about the particular issues. In 2009, the Nuffield Council on Bioethics produced its report *Dementia: Ethical Issues* (see Appendix 2 for details). It is well worth reading the report, which involved a large public consultation as well as a review of current evidence and expert opinion. The report presents an ethical framework, which is summarized in Box 14.2.

The report emphasizes that moral judgements must be sound. This does not mean that there is only one defensible answer in any given situation, but it does mean that judgements should be made within a framework that helps to focus attention on relevant facts, values, and principles. There will inevitably sometimes be tensions between the wish to promote the person's autonomy and the wish to promote their well-being. A person may wish, for instance, to leave the house to go for a walk, but others may feel that this would put the person in danger. The interest in autonomy and the interest in well-being will have to be weighed up (component 4). But this will have to be done in the light of the relevant facts (e.g. concerning how safe the roads are and whether the person has ever acted unsafely when out walking). Looking at the facts and comparing this case to other similar cases reflects component 1 of the ethical framework. But then there is the belief, in component 3, that it is possible for the person to enjoy a good quality of life despite having dementia. So, although dementia and its consequences can be harmful (component 2), the need to recognize the individual's personhood and values (component 6) means that we should encourage the feeling that we are with them, showing solidarity (component 5). In other words, although the issue of safety tends to make us think that the person should not be allowed to go out and walk on his or her own, the ethical framework encourages the opposing thought: we should do all that we can to allow

---

Box 14.2 Dementia: an ethical framework

Component 1: A 'case-based' approach to ethical decisions: Ethical decisions can be approached in a three-stage process: identifying the relevant facts; interpreting and applying appropriate ethical values to those facts; and comparing the situation with other similar situations to find ethically relevant similarities or differences.

Component 2: A belief about the nature of dementia: Dementia arises as a result of a brain disorder, and is harmful to the individual.

Component 3: A belief about quality of life with dementia: With good care and support, people with dementia can expect to have a good quality of life throughout the course of their illness.

Component 4: The importance of promoting the interests both of the person with dementia and of those who care for them: People with dementia have interests, both in their autonomy and their well-being. Promoting autonomy involves enabling and fostering relationships that are important to the person, and supporting them in maintaining their sense of self and expressing their values. Autonomy is not simply to be equated with the ability to make rational decisions. A person's well-being includes both their moment-to-moment experiences of contentment or pleasure, and more objective factors such as their level of cognitive functioning. The separate interests of carers must be recognized and promoted.

Component 5: The requirement to act in accordance with solidarity: The need to recognize the citizenship of people with dementia, and to acknowledge our mutual interdependence and responsibility to support people with dementia, both within families and in society as a whole.

Component 6: Recognizing personhood, identity and value: The person with dementia remains the same, equally valued, person throughout the course of their illness, regardless of the extent of the changes in their cognitive and other functions.

Source: The Nuffield Council's report, *Dementia: Ethical Issues*, page 21; Box 2.1

---

the person to continue to live the life that they choose in an independent way in order to allow them to flourish humanly—to do the sort of things that we all do that allow us to feel fully human. There will, of course, be a point at which the issues of safety become overwhelming, but the ethical framework places the issue of safety in its proper context. In simple terms, this amounts to weighing up the pros and cons, but it also involves putting the person at the centre of these deliberations. And it involves a broader framework or background, provided by thinking ethically. This is seen in the following quote where the partner of the person with dementia gave permission to the staff at a home to allow him to be let out.

> 'I had to make a conscious decision about allowing my partner to go out. I know that, at first, the staff at the home were very concerned that they weren't able to contain him. But I used to say to them, "Look, he has road sense, he knows where I live—he's enjoying this." And although I hated the fact that he was on the streets, and it did worry me, I felt that he looked so healthy. That was the point—in some way, the walking and all of that was doing him a huge amount of good.'

Legal frameworks: capacity legislation

I have already made reference to the Mental Capacity Act, which covers England and Wales. Different countries have different ways of dealing with decision-making for people who are unable to make decisions themselves. I discussed in Chapter 13 the different forms of advance care planning. This is covered by the Mental Capacity Act. But the legal framework is broader still. It is not just about healthcare decisions. In fact, it relates to all decisions that might have to be made on behalf of someone who is unable to make decisions. The guiding principles for the different Acts that cover the United Kingdom are shown in Box 14.3.

These principles, taken separately or together, show that the key issue concerns basic human rights. There is a very strong moral underpinning to these legal frameworks and principles, which emphasizes not only the autonomy but also the dignity of the individual.

Judging capacity

In order to decide whether or not a person lacks capacity, the Mental Capacity Act, which covers England and Wales, sets out a two-stage test.

- First, it has to be established that the person has an impairment or disturbance of the mind or brain. If this is not the case, then it cannot be said that the person lacks capacity. It might be said, for instance, that the person is simply doing something foolish.
- If there is a disturbance of the mind or brain, then the second stage of the test is to consider whether the person can:
  - understand the information;
  - retain the relevant information;

Box 14.3 Guiding principles for capacity legislation in the UK

For England and Wales

Mental Capacity Act 2005, from Section 1:

A person must be assumed to have capacity.

All practicable steps should be taken to help the person to make a decision.

A person should be free to make unwise decisions.

If a person lacks capacity, decisions must be made in his or her best interests.

Whatever decision is made or whatever act is taken, it should be the least restrictive of the person's rights and freedom of action.

For Scotland

Adults with Incapacity (Scotland) Act, from Section 1:

Benefit: any intervention must benefit the person and it must be the case that the benefit cannot reasonably be achieved without the intervention.

Minimum intervention: the intervention must be the least restrictive option.

Taking account of the person's wishes and feelings: account must be taken of the person's present and past wishes and feelings.

Consult others: the views of other relevant people must be taken into account.

Encourage exercise of residual capacity: The person must be encouraged to exercise whatever skills he or she has and to develop new skills.

For Northern Ireland

Proposed principles:

Autonomy: This recognizes the right of the individual to decide and act on his or her decisions.

Justice: The law must be applied fairly and equally.

Benefit: The health, welfare, and safety of the person must be promoted while having regard to the safety of others.

Least harm: Actions should minimize the likelihood of harm to the person.

Adapted from Box 5.1 of the Nuffield Council's report, *Dementia: Ethical Issues*, page 76 (see Appendix 2 for further details)

* weigh up the information in order to come to a decision; and
* communicate the decision.

A person must be able to satisfy all of these criteria in order to have the requisite capacity to make a particular decision. But the capacity is decision-specific. In other words, although a person lacks one capacity, this does not mean that they lack capacity to make other decisions. A person may lack the capacity to manage their finances, but have the capacity to state who they would wish to manage their finances on their behalf. In other words, the person may have the capacity to make a Lasting Power of Attorney to cover financial issues; but it may be that the Lasting Power of Attorney has to come into effect almost immediately because the person is no longer able to manage financial matters.

The Mental Capacity Act in England and Wales does not cover every type of decision. There are sometimes other specific tests. The obvious example is the capacity to make a Will. This is called *testamentary capacity*. The criteria for testamentary capacity date back to 1870 and to a famous case called *Banks* v *Goodfellow*. The criteria are as follows:

1. The person making the Will must understand the nature of the act and its effects;
2. The person making the Will must be aware of the extent of the property being disposed of;
3. The person making the Will must be able to understand the nature and extent of the claims upon him or her both of those being included in the Will and those being excluded.

If a Will is being made by someone who has cognitive impairment, it is important that the lawyer involved is aware of this. If they have any doubt, they should involve an expert who can assess testamentary capacity. If a Will is made when a person lacks capacity, or if a Will is changed, it may later be contested. The other ground on which to contest a Will is if there has been any undue influence brought to bear. A person with dementia might well be vulnerable to the influence of others.

Summary

In this chapter I have discussed some of the difficulties that face informal (family) carers of people with dementia. They carry all sorts of burdens, but often the burden is largely an ethical one because the issue that increasingly faces the family carer is to do with making decisions on behalf of the person they care for. This is a matter of great moral importance and it reflects basic human rights.

We should end, perhaps, on a more positive note. Despite the stresses, strains, and burdens, many carers express the view that they have in some sense grown and benefited from the role that has been forced upon them. Despite everything, many carers report a sense of fulfilment. Here is what one husband said (as recorded in *Ethical Issues in Dementia Care*—see Appendix 2 (pages 89–90):

'In a strange sort of way I feel I am a better person now than I was say ten years ago. I think I am more tolerant by and large. I am more patient... so I am more socially outgoing. I think I am better now with people that I notice in the community or in groups that we belong to who clearly are suffering, who are in need, I think I am more willing to make the first move and to try to support them or say something which is helpful or comforting. So I think in those sorts of ways perhaps I am a rather better person than I was ten years ago: certainly less self-satisfied and self-preoccupied than I was then.'

Another carer, when asked what made a good carer, said the following (as recorded in *Ethical Issues in Dementia Care*, page 90):

'I think it is terribly important that they show love and compassion. I used these words many times but they have got to be that sort of a person, to be a caring person you must show love and compassion otherwise you can't care. To be a carer you have got to be proficient in many avenues and one of them, as I say, is love and compassion.'

15

Facts and values

⊃ Key points

♦ Dementia involves a broad range of facts, but these also bring into view value judgements.

♦ The profound issues raised by dementia include issues around the nature of the self and the meaning and purpose of our lives.

♦ These issues highlight the importance of other people and of our standing with others in the world.

♦ The facts of dementia show the breadth of our concerns, from the importance of biological processes to the meaning of our human engagements.

Introduction

This book is full of facts about Alzheimer's disease and other dementias. The breadth of issues that arise in connection with dementia is staggering. It is worth reflecting on this point. In a sense dementia is no different from any other disease. Every disease has biological, psychological, and social aspects; and many (especially if life-threatening) will raise spiritual concerns. I want to suggest that, perhaps, dementia raises these issues to a greater extent. Consider the nature of the biological basis of dementia: it is usually a progressive disease of the brain, which leads to global impairments in function. The complexity of the brain in itself makes this a more challenging condition than many others. Many illnesses will raise psychological issues in that there is always an inevitable emotional adjustment to the realization that you or someone you love has a significant disease. Dementia does this too, but it is also a mental illness in the sense that it affects our mental well-being directly: the disease itself affects the way we think and feel. It can change our personalities. The social impact of many diseases is overlooked. But consider the profound nature of the social changes that will follow from a diagnosis of dementia. Not only is there still a stigma attached to the condition, but it may well affect where you live, and it might strip you of your recognition of those who are close to you. Finally, not only is dementia life-threatening, but it also raises spiritual concerns because of the threats it poses to the way we think about ourselves.

Now, it would be unhelpful to use these points to try to argue that dementia is a worse condition or a more interesting one than any other. But there is something striking about the gap between, on the one hand, the breadth and profundity of the points I have just made and, on the other hand, the lack of importance society tends to place on all aspects of care for people with dementia and their carers.

Let me just remind you of the breadth of which I speak. To understand dementia adequately we have to grasp highly scientific facts about the ways in which receptors in the brain work and the ways in which cells are controlled by genetic factors, which affect why and how they die. And this sort of understanding is aided by techniques of tremendous sophistication, which can look at water transport in individual nerve tracts or the transport and transmission of specific neurochemicals. This level of technical knowledge stands alongside the spouse's knowledge that her husband will be much more difficult to manage if he has to be admitted to hospital and much easier to manage if he can be encouraged to open his bowels. There are the complicated conceptual conversations to be had about what constitutes normal ageing, which stand alongside the discussions about how to get the mother to go to the day centre to allow the family a day to shop and clean. There is considerable breadth associated with the facts that surround dementia, but in this final chapter I shall gesture (as I inevitably already have done) at the depth beyond the facts: values, the self, and the meaning of our lives.

Values

The point is often made that facts are not *just* facts. At the very least they suggest theories; and theories reflect values. To make the point in another way, the world we live in—the human world—is not simply full of facts, it is full of human values too. We decide to emphasize or pick out certain facts, but this is because (in some sense) we value them. We might say that some things just are facts: it is a fact that there is only a modest statistical difference between the effects of cholinesterase inhibitors and a placebo (i.e. a non-active substance). But, first, the decision as to what will count as statistically significant reflects a value judgement; and, second, even if it is only a modest difference, I might argue that the fact that my wife can again help in the kitchen is of tremendous value and significance to both of us. We can easily overlook values, partly because they are everywhere. So when we are presented with facts about dementia, we need to look for the values that are implied or presumed by the facts. In the UK, at one time NICE recommended that we only treat people with cholinesterase inhibitors if they were in the moderate phase of dementia and that this was mainly to be judged by the Mini-Mental State Examination (MMSE, see Chapter 9). But such decisions reflect value judgements—even the facts that the MMSE presents us with need to be understood as reflecting certain values. We need to see the whole picture, which is one of values as well as of facts.

The self

In a very obvious way dementia threatens our sense of self. In Chapter 10, I mentioned the work of Steve Sabat (see Appendix 2). One of the things Sabat has done is to draw out different ways that we might understand what it is to be a self. Self 1 is the self that I pick out when I use words such as 'I' or 'me'; and I can do this by gestures too. This ability to pick myself out lasts even into the later stages of dementia. Self 2 is made up of all my physical and mental attributes. Many of my mental attributes will persist into late dementia, but even when they diminish and disappear I am partly still the same self because of my body. It is this body that, in part at least, links my present to my past. It also links me to others and to a whole history. Finally, there is Self 3, which is the self that exists through others. To my patients I exist as a doctor, to my children as a father, and so on. But in large measure my standing as a doctor or a father depends on my patients and children. If they refuse to see or acknowledge me in these ways, my standing diminishes. So, too, with my standing as a person with dementia: we are back to Kitwood's idea of 'malignant social psychology' and Sabat's 'malignant positioning' (see Chapter 10).

In a variety of ways, therefore, we can argue that our selfhood persists in dementia, even if our personalities change; often this is a function of those around us.

Meaning

Both the topic of values and the topic of selfhood point to a broader context. Dementia, in fact, in its breadth and depth, stands in the world and has to be understood in the world in all its complexity. It ought to raise for us broad and profound questions, which (I suggest) are questions about meaning and purpose. Confronted by dementia, whether as scientists, as clinicians, as spouses, as children, or as the person with dementia, it is only reasonable to ask about the meaning of our lives. What should we make of dementia? How is it to be properly understood? How is it to be lived with?

These are not questions to be answered here. I would simply say that dementia poses for us all a human challenge. It is a challenge at the level of values, meaning, and purpose. It has to be faced humanly, that is with all the resources open to us as human beings in the complex world. This will potentially involve all of our scientific and technological know-how; at a fundamental level it will involve our abilities to engage with one another as caring and compassionate human beings.

Conclusion

Considering the facts that surround Alzheimer's disease and other dementias inevitably raises broader and more profound issues to do with our lives and how we live them. As the world's populations age and dementia becomes more prevalent, whether or not cures are found, the imperative is that we, as individuals and as societies, should keep in view the nature of our interdependent and interconnected lives. Dementia not only focuses our attention on the extent to which our lives are determined by our genetic make-up, it also points to the fundamental sense in which we live in a mutually engaged fashion. Our lives are structured, therefore, both by molecules and by the meaning of our concern for others.

Appendix 1

Useful websites

Alzheimer associations or societies

I have not provided specific addresses for the organizations listed below. It makes more sense to look at the main websites on the internet, because many of them contain huge amounts of useful information. However, for those without internet access, or for those who require more immediate help, it is probably better to make contact with the local branch of the organization. Contact details and addresses for local branches can be found in local directories. Even if information is required about some other form of dementia, the local Alzheimer's Society (at least in the UK) is able to give information, including information about other societies that might be helpful.

The web addresses are as follows:

Australia Alzheimer's Australia: http://www.alzheimers.org.au

Canada Alzheimer Society of Canada: http://www.alzheimer.ca

Ireland The Alzheimer Society of Ireland: http://www.alzheimer.ie

New Zealand Alzheimers New Zealand: http://www.alzheimers.org.nz

Scotland Alzheimer Scotland: http://www.alzscot.org

United Kingdom (other than Scotland) Alzheimer's Society UK: http://alzheimers.org.uk

United States Alzheimer's Association: http://www.alz.org

The following two websites provide much useful information and routes to other national organizations. They also contain information about the important awareness-raising campaigns throughout the world and the political achievements and policies that are being pursued to increase awareness, support, and research for those with dementia and their carers.

For European countries, go to the Home Page of Alzheimer Europe, press the tab button 'Alzheimer Europe', then the tab 'Who we are', and then 'Our members' to reveal the full list of European Alzheimer associations or societies. Alzheimer Europe: http://www.alzheimer-europe.org

For countries in other parts of the world, the ADI address will serve as a useful portal. Its Home Page contains a link entitled 'Find association' which connects you to the Alzheimer's association in the required country. Alzheimer's Disease International: http://www.alz.co.uk

Other (non-Alzheimer) support organizations

With the exception of the Association for Frontotemporal Dementias, the list below records organizations based in the UK. Their websites are, of course, open to anyone in the world, but there will be national organizations in different countries. These can be searched for on the internet using the name of the condition and the home country. Otherwise, help can be sought from the national Alzheimer's association or society.

Dementia with Lewy bodies The Lewy Body Society: http://www.lewybody.co.uk

Frontotemporal dementia The Association for Frontotemporal Dementias: http://www.ftd-picks.org

Huntington's disease Huntington's Disease Association: http://www.hda.org.uk

Multiple sclerosis Multiple Sclerosis Society: http://www.mssociety.org.uk

Parkinson's disease Parkinson's UK: http://www.parkinsons.org.uk

Progressive supranuclear palsy The PSP Association: http://www.pspeur.org

Other useful addresses for national organizations in the UK

◆ Age UK—the organization which resulted from the amalgamation of Age Concern and Help the Aged; it is a useful source of information and help for general issues connected with older age, from pensions and other state benefits to practical advice about living at home or choosing a care home: http://www.ageuk.org.uk

◆ Care Quality Commission (CQC)—the independent regulator of health and adult social care in England. Its reports on care homes can be a useful source of reference when considering a home for long-term care: http://www.cqc.org.uk/findareport.cfm

◆ Carers UK—the voice of carers and a useful source of information for carers: http://www.carersuk.org

- Dementia UK—runs Admiral Nurses, who provide specialized dementia nursing and advice to many parts of the UK, and can provide advice and information for anyone with dementia or for their carers: http://www.dementiauk.org

- Department of Health (UK)—gives access to a variety of reports and policies: http://www.dh.gov.uk/en/index.htm

- The National Institute for Health and Clinical Excellence—provides information on the latest guidelines and technical appraisals of drugs: http://www.nice.org.uk

- UK National Prion Clinic—based at the National Hospital for Neurology and Neurosurgery; will visit patients anywhere in the UK to provide assessment and support: http://www.nationalprionclinic.org

Appendix 2

Useful sources of reference and further reading

This appendix lists a number of the publications that I have used as sources for this book. I have, in addition, included some extra books that help to flesh out our understanding of the broader issues that arise in connection with dementia.

National reports or publications

- *Advance Care Planning: A Guide for Health and Social Care Staff.* Published by the Department of Health End of Life Care Programme, Leicester, in August 2008. Available at: http://www.endoflifecareforadults.nhs.org.

- *Dementia: Ethical Issues.* London: Nuffield Council on Bioethics. Published in 2009. Available at: http://www.nuffieldbioethics.org/dementia.

- *Dementia UK* by Martin Knapp and Martin Prince. A report into the prevalence and cost of dementia prepared by the Personal Social Services Research Unit (PSSRU) at the London School of Economics and the Institute of Psychiatry at King's College London, for the Alzheimer's Society. Published by the Alzheimer's Society, London, in 2007. Available online.

- *End of Life Care Strategy: Promoting High Quality Care for all Adults at the End of Life.* Published by the Department of Health, London, in 2008. Available online.

- *Improving Services and Support for People with Dementia* by the National Audit Office. Published by The Stationery Office, London, in 2007. Available online.

◆ *Living Well with Dementia: A National Dementia Strategy* published by the Department of Health, London, in 2009. Available online.

◆ *Optimizing Treatment and Care for People with Behavioural and Psychological Symptoms of Dementia: A Best Practice Guide for Health and Social Care Professionals* published by the Alzheimer's Society, London, in 2011. Available online.

◆ *The Use of Antipsychotic Medication for People with Dementia: Time for Action.* A report for the Minister of State for Care Services by Professor Sube Banerjee. Published by the Department of Health, London, in 2009. Available online.

Publications from the National Institute for Health and Clinical Excellence

◆ *Depression: The Treatment and Management of Depression in Adults.* This is a partial update of NICE clinical guideline 23. Published by the National Institute for Health and Clinical Excellence (NICE), London, in 2009. Available online.

◆ *Donepezil, Galantamine, Rivastigmine (Review) and Memantine for the Treatment of Alzheimer's Disease (Amended). NICE Technology Appraisal Guidance 111 (Amended).* Published by the National Institute for Health and Clinical Excellence (NICE), London, in August 2009. Available online.

◆ *Guidance on the Use of Electroconvulsive Therapy.* Update on Technology Appraisal Number 59 (April 2003). Published by the National Institute for Health and Clinical Excellence (NICE), London in May 2010. Available online.

◆ *A NICE-SCIE Guideline on Supporting People with Dementia and their Carers in Health and Social Care. National Clinical Practice Guideline Number 42.* Produced for the National Institute for Health and Clinical Excellence (NICE) and the Social Care Institute for Excellence (SCIE). Published by the British Psychological Society and Gaskill (the Royal College of Psychiatrists), Leicester and London, in 2007. Available online.

Technical or professional books

◆ *Cognitive Assessment for Clinicians* (2nd edition) by John R. Hodges. Published by Oxford University Press, Oxford, in 2007.

◆ *Dementia* (4th edition) edited by David Ames, Alistair Burns, and John O'Brien. Published by Hodder Arnold, London, in 2010.

◆ *Excellence in Dementia Care: Research into Practice* edited by Murna Downs and Barbara Bowers. Published by McGraw Hill, Maidenhead, Berkshire, in 2008.

- *Oxford Textbook of Old Age Psychiatry* edited by Robin Jacoby, Catherine Oppenheimer, Tom Dening, and Alan Thomas. Published by Oxford University Press, Oxford, in 2008.
- *Supportive Care for the Person with Dementia* edited by Julian C. Hughes, Mari Lloyd-Williams, and Greg A. Sachs. Published by Oxford University Press, Oxford, in 2010.
- *The American Psychiatric Publishing Textbook of Alzheimer Disease and Other Dementias* edited by Myron F. Weiner and Anne M. Lipton. Published by the American Psychiatric Publishing, Washington DC and London, England, in 2009.

Broader reading on dementia

- *And Still the Music Plays* by Graham Stokes. Published by Hawker Publications, London, in 2008.
- *Alive with Alzheimer's* by Cathy S. Greenblat. Published by University of Chicago Press, Chicago and London, in 2004.
- *Dementia: Mind, Meaning, and the Person* edited by Julian C. Hughes, Stephen J. Louw, and Steven R. Sabat. Published by Oxford University Press, Oxford, in 2006.
- *Dementia Reconsidered: The Person Comes First* by Tom Kitwood. Published by Open University Press, Buckingham, in 1997.
- *Ethical Issues in Dementia Care: Making Difficult Decisions* by Julian C. Hughes and Clive Baldwin. Published by Jessica Kingsley, London and Philadelphia, in 2006.
- *Living and Dying with Dementia: Dialogues about Palliative Care* by Neil Small, Katherine Froggatt, and Murna Downs. Published by Oxford University Press, Oxford, in 2008.
- *The Myth of Alzheimer's: What You Aren't Being Told About Today's Most Dreaded Diagnosis* by Peter J. Whitehouse and Daniel George. Published by St Martin's Press, New York, in 2008.
- *The Experience of Alzheimer's Disease: Life Through a Tangled Veil* by Steven R. Sabat. Published by Blackwell, Oxford, in 2001.
- *Thinking Through Dementia* by Julian C. Hughes. Published by Oxford University Press, Oxford, in 2011.
- 'Who am I?–The search for spirituality in dementia. A family carer's perspective'. Chapter by Barbara Pointon in: Coyte, M.E., Gilbert, P. and Nichols, V. (eds) *Spirituality, Values and Mental Health: Jewels for the Journey*. London and Philadelphia: Jessica Kingsley; 2007: pp. 114–20.

Further books for carers or people with dementia

- *Dementia: Alzheimer's and Other Dementias* (2nd edition) by Harry Cayton, Nori Graham, and James Warner. Published by Class Publishing, London, in 2002.

- *Making Difficult Decisions: The Experience of Caring for Someone with Dementia* by Clive Baldwin, Tony Hope, Julian Hughes, Robin Jacoby, and Sue Ziebland. Published by the Alzheimer's Society, London, in 2005.

- *Understanding Alzheimer's Disease & Other Dementias* by Nori Graham and James Warner. Published by Family Doctor Publications (Poole, Dorset) in association with the British Medical Association, in 2009.

Index

Page numbers in *italic* indicate tables.